A LIFE EXAMINED

A memoir

by

Henry J Baron

Chapbook Press

Schuler Books
2660 28th Street SE
Grand Rapids, MI 49512
(616) 942-7330
www.schulerbooks.com

A Life Examined

ISBN 13: 9781957169040

Library of Congress Control Number: 2022904965

Printed in the United States by Chapbook Press.

"The unexamined life is not worth living."

—Socrates

Contents

Part One: Beginnings 1

Introduction 2

The Early Years 4

Parents and Place 6

Home & Family 10

Grandparents 12

The Baron Uncles and Aunts 14

The Hoekstra Uncles and Aunts 16

Colorful Characters 20

Childhood Memories 21

Education and More 24

Sports 34

Siblings 36

Sex Education 42

Music 43

Church 44

Family Life and Traditions 48

War 51

Post War 65

Part Two: Emigration and New Beginnings 67

Departure and Arrival 68

America – The First Summer 73

School and Farm 76

Wedding Bells and Winter Woes 80

Part Three: The Teenage Years 83

Social Life 88
Church..92

Part Four: Pursuing the Dream 95

Army and Nightmare 100
Recovery and Death in the Family.............107
Last Words 111

Part Five: Continuing the Dream 115

WWCE...116
Faith Crisis 118
The Woman in My Life 120
Teaching...124
A Birth 127
Calvin College...129
Another Birth 134

Part Six: Practicing the Dream 137

The South Christian Years 138
The Europe Trip 146
The U of I Year...147
A Calvin Beginning: 1968-70.....................150
The PhD Years: 1970-72 151
The Summer of '71.....................................152

Part Seven: The Calvin Years – 1972-1997 158

Teaching... 160
Colleagues... 163
Moonlighting... 165
Consulting... 166
Academics... 169
CEJ... 171
Department Work.. 174
1980 Sabbatical... 175
Festival of Faith and Writing (FFW)........................... 179
Frisia.. 182
Simmer 2000.. 194
China.. 203
    Summer '85.. 205
    The Preparation.. 205
    The Team... 208
    The Travel.. 209
    Chengdu.. 209
    The Students.. 212
    The Teachers.. 218
    Reflections... 220
    Public Response.. 221
Music & Drama... 222
Church.. 227
Family... 230
    Weddings – Beginnings and Endings.................. 247

Part Eight: The Retirement Years...................251

Travel... 253

    Nederland 253

    United Kingdom 256

    New Zealand 257

    Hawaii 260

    Cruises Plus 261

Writing 268

C.A.L.L. 272

Church 275

Social 277

Medical 280

Family 287

Friends 300

End Reflections 302

Memoir Supplement 305

Mom's Song in the Night 308

Sinterklaas 311

WWII 313

    Details 314

    Memories 318

    Aerial fights 318

    Plight of the Jews 319

The Crossing 321

Family Letter Excerpts 333

Judy's Birth 335

English Department Writeup 337

Frisian Sermon Translation 342

The Immigrant Adventure: The Quest to Belong 348

The Accident 351

Wedding Talks 356

Prayer for a Parent 363

Sid Eulogy 365

A Family Talk 369

Closing Quotes 376

Part One: Beginnings

Introduction

Each life begins in mystery – the mystery of creation, conception, gestation, and birth.

Each life becomes a story, remarkable and unique.

At its beginning, there are just a few characters – parents likely, siblings maybe.

But soon the story grows to include friends, sometimes enemies, teachers.

And more family – grandparents, uncles, aunts, cousins.

Only a few become important characters in the story.

Each story has a plot, though it often seems to go into hiding or meanders into sideroads, and conflict is not always at the heart of it.

Each has one or more narrators, a point of view, development, personae, tension, and conflict.

Each main story has many substories, some of them more or less important to the main.

Some stories, like lifetimes, are short, and others long and longer.

Some stories end happily, but not all.

Some stories live long in memory, some do not.

This is *my* story.

But is also *our* story, as Richard Rohr pointed out – the human story of "finding one's belonging, attaching, trusting, and loving."

And as Frederick Buechner put it in *Telling Secrets,* "My story is important not because it is mine, God knows, but because if I tell it anything like right, the chances are you will recognize that in many ways it is also yours.

"Maybe nothing is more important than that we keep track, you and I, of these stories of who we are and where we have come from and the people we have met along the way because it is precisely through these stories in all the particularity … that God makes himself known to each of us most powerfully and personally. If this is true, it means that to lose track of our stories is to be profoundly impoverished not only humanly but also spiritually."

So, I begin, encouraged by Madeleine L'Engle's reminder that "the great thing about getting older is that you don't lose all the other ages you've been."

I want to try to get back into the other ages again.

And spurred on, too, by Kierkegaard's observation that though life must be lived forwards, it "can only be understood backwards." I hope to make that discovery.

I will be writing this for family first of all, but maybe some friends too, some of whom have known me well, others not so much. This allows them to look "in my direction as they slowly walk into my past." (A. Van Jordan, "The Flash Reverses Time" from *Quantum Lyrics.*)

Readers will bump into sections that have no interest for them, in which case they should feel free to go on to another part that holds more interest. And those whose interest lies in more detail can pursue their curiosity in the Supplement.

And there are pictures interspersed throughout, most of which lack the quality and clarity I'd like, and yes, color too. But I'll blame it on poor quality cameras and skills and cost.

Undoubtedly, despite diligent effort, some memory and proofreading lapses are likely to have occurred and which I implore the alert reader to forgive and mentally correct.

The Early Years

We all start somewhere.

Because they're still children, offspring don't wonder much where and how life "happened" for parents; it's their own life that tends to require their full concentration. Too often the wondering may begin and the unasked questions surface when parents are no more.

Then, as I know from experience, we may begin to try to put together some details we've tucked away for too long as not applicable to our lives.

Then we may begin to realize how wrong we were, for one life grows out of another, never identical but always related.

Thus, two roads converged, long ago, in a small corner of the world known as Friesland. Two people met, one Jeen Baron and one Aafke Hoekstra.

They shared the same language, Frisian, the same church affiliation, Gereformeerd, and the same work experience, farming.

There were differences too, as there always are between two individuals, even more so perhaps when both are strong-willed. But in time they found themselves in love with each other, and after a five-year long courtship, they became husband and wife on 27 May 1927.

Two roads converged, two people met, two lives were joined, and for their descendants that made all the difference.

Parents and Place

There was no honeymoon, and the trip from Kortwoude to Groninger Opende was hardly more than a mile. Now Aafke Hoekstra, the youngest child of Hendrik and Elisabeth Fokkinga Hoekstra, along with Jeen Baron, the second oldest son of Sietse and Grietje Landman Baron, established a new home on what had been his parents' place, a small farm on a sandpath (the Ketting) on the border of Groningen and Friesland.

This little piece of ground marked our home till 1948. This is where we were born: first Elizabeth (Lies) in 1928, named after her maternal grandmother according to custom; then Sietze in 1930, named after his paternal grandfather; then Hendrik in 1934 (Henk), named after his maternal grandfather; then Griet in 1938, named after her paternal grandmother; and lastly Marijke Janke in 1946, named after her mother's two sisters.

Sometimes one's name grows out of another's too.

This is where they were born, at D219 De Ketting in Opende West, and this is where they grew up, during the years of a world-wide depression and the years of a world war.

This is where the memories linger, not just for the first ten years but for the rest of one's life.

Memories of a small farm with fewer than a dozen cows, some heifers, a bunch of chickens, a few pigs, a goat, two or three rabbits, some beehives, and a horse of course to help with the work.

And then there were the meadows with grazing cattle, but also the fields with beets and potatoes and corn and turnips and rye and even a garden not only with a variety of vegetables but even tobacco plants, and the orchard with apple and pear trees. None of the fields was large, but the crops fed the animals and family.

Their modest home was attached to the milking parlor and the hay and storage barn. Food was cooked in the kitchen on a kerosene burner and in wintertime on the woodstove top. The home was largely unheated in wintertime, except for the kitchen where a woodstove kept it warm. The stove in the front room would be used only in case of company. The bedroom was totally unheated. Frost designs would thickly cover the windows in the morning when the temperature took a serious dip and the night's breathing from four or five pairs of lungs had moistened the glass. wintertime the family would wear their long woolen underwear to bed, with a hot water bottle to keep the feet warm.

There was no running water and no electricity till the early forties. A wash shed or pump house had been built as an attachment to the house and featured a hand pump and a cistern for catching the rainwater.

For sleeping, the front room had two cupboard or closet beds and in the bedroom that had been built as an addition there was one cupboard bed and space for a crib and a double bed.

The family was never rich and never poor.

It was just an ordinary family (if such there be) that lived in a certain place at a certain time with memories that many years later could still make them laugh, or grow quiet – sometimes in pain, or wonder, or gratitude.

The father had no more than five or six years of formal schooling, not untypical of anyone born in 1896, in Friesland's Rottevalle, to ordinary small-farmer parents.

But he remained an avid student all his life.

He took courses in bookkeeping so he could more effectively manage the financial affairs of a farm and of the forage business he developed on the side. He took a course in First Aid. And he read voraciously, not only in agriculture and business but especially in theology.

He developed into an excellent writer with beautiful penmanship, a skill he used frequently as clerk of the church council or secretary of the Christian School Board, and he would carry on considerable correspondence with well-known theologians in the land during the time of doctrinal disputes.

But theology wasn't his only avocation; perhaps as important to him was music.

His specialty was the trumpet, the instrument he played as a WWI soldier in the military band.

Later, in 1922, he helped start a band in Opende, "Crescendo," and for the first ten years served as its conductor.

He also loved to sing and started a small church choir in the middle '40s.

One of the favorite memories goes back to WWII when the family would gather around the pump organ in the living room, sister Lies playing, and sing hymns, psalms, folk and patriotic songs with the mother's clear soprano on top, the father's tenor somewhat lower, and the children blending, or not, with gusto.

The mother too had to leave school early, going to work for her older sister's household when she was only 11. As the youngest of the Hoekstras, she became accustomed to hard work at a young age, helping her dad with farm chores, often doing the lion share of the work herself, but not without resentment.

She always retained fond memories of her elementary school days, short as they were, and had loving memories of her teachers; and throughout her life she displayed a remarkable memory of the songs she had loved and learned in the classroom (see Supplement p. 308).

She too loved music and greatly enjoyed joining a Christian choir when she was still in her teens.

She was not a reader like the man she married, but always an extremely hard worker and a very caring mother. The children often thought that she would've made an excellent nurse, for she was at her best in giving them tender loving care when they suffered the various childhood ailments like croup and measles and diphtheria and whooping cough.

Home & Family

The Jeen and Aafke Baron children were all born in the house on the sand path, about 200 yards off the main road that runs through the little town of Opende and connects the two provinces of Groningen and Friesland. This was the time when home deliveries of babies were the rule rather than the exception. No sterile hospital room for the newborns; instead, they were introduced at once to the sounds and smells of farm life, for the birthing room was less than forty feet from the nearest cow, since the home was built with the barn attached. That's why the sons, whose first love was never farm smells and sounds, chose to be born in May when the cows were sent to pasture for the season. It was not unusual, of course, to have the cow stall, the barn with storage for hay and straw and feed and equipment, and the house itself all under one roof, and the kids never gave that a thought. They would go to sleep with the sounds of cows yanking their stanchions, going number 1 and number 2 as familiar as the ticking of the wall clock in the living room. Even the fact that the gutter was only about ten feet from the kitchen where the family ate three times a day never seemed to be a problem: the smells mixed most aromatically. Of course, a hallway and two sets of doors separated the cows from the kitchen, partly blocking the sounds and smells.

Self-consciousness went up a notch or two, though, when there were guests, like a visiting preacher for Sunday dinner, which actually happened quite often since Dad was on the council. Invariably, the preacher would feel some lower body pressures after a good, solid Sunday farm meal, and then one of the children would have to escort the dignified man of the cloth through the cow barn, hoping that in the process no cow would seek relief from similar pressures, lest the clergy's striped pants and long tails would get decorated with the unholy splotches of "stront" (manure). Before such a post-meal journey, father Baron would usually have made sure that the path behind the cows was clean and strewn with white sand. At the end of the journey, a thin wall removed from the cows, was the family inhouse (vs. an outhouse). The WC was built right above the holding tank into which the gutter would be emptied regularly, and to this throne the stately guests would be led, usually by Henk. At such times the children, and maybe even the parents, may have wondered a bit whether their accommodations were all that a human being had a right to expect, but of course they were not used to anything else.

As mentioned earlier, there was no running water in the house and until the early forties no electricity. For the most part, kerosene would light the lamps and cook the food. All would wash their hands and face in the adjoining wash shed. There was also a hut, called a stook (stoke) hut, close to the house in which Mom Baron could do some cooking and boil a large container of water for such purposes as the weekly bath. Although there was no private place to take a sponge bath or any other kind, no one recalls ever catching big brother or sister or parents in such a cleansing ceremony.

The house was built of brick (originally before 1900 but with later additions), had a narrow hallway running between kitchen and barn, had a fairly large sitting or front room used only on special occasions when there was company, but featured two cupboard beds, one of which was used regularly and the other only occasionally when needed for overnight guests.

Then there was a large bedroom with one cupboard bed, one bedstead, and one children's-size bed. Normally five Barons would be sleeping in this room, plus the parents.

And then there was one other small room next to the large one that had served as Beppe Baron's private quarters before she passed on and that would later serve as a hiding place during the war.

Home, school, and church were not heated, and one of the teacher's very important jobs in cold weather was tending the fire. Even then, pupils' cold fingers often had trouble unbending enough to do a neat job of ciphering or penmanship. And the church custodian was busy on Sundays putting hot coals in the foot warmers for the older ladies who had paid for such a service. There was no stove in the sanctuary to warm it up. There were no mice either; they froze to death.

But none of this struck the family as a hardship then. In fact, they never considered themselves poor. And they weren't, really. They had a farm of about 25 acres or so, with fewer than ten cows to supply their milk, a few pigs for meat, chickens for eggs and meat, and lots of apple and pear trees and veggies in the garden to keep them munching. There were many people in the area who could claim far less. For many, jobs were hard to come by in the post-depression era, two or three decades before the age of affluence would arrive and drastically transform lifestyles.

Grandparents

Only the older children remembered Grandma (Beppe) Baron. Grandpa (Pake) Baron's death preceded their birth in 1922. But Beppe was still around, in fact living in with the newly-weds, when Lies and Sietze were born; her death came in 1933 when she collapsed under the pear tree in the orchard from a heart attack.

According to reports, Pake Sietze was a good-natured and God-fearing man, with a heart as good as gold.

Some say that Beppe Grietje, on the other hand, was weaned on a pickle, which made her a bit formal and stiff with family and strangers, combined with a mania for cleanliness.

The grandchildren all think, of course, that they have inherited Pake Sietze's golden heart, but their sister Grietje also honors the Beppe she never knew by keeping a very neat house. And their mother Aafke always spoke appreciatively of her mother-in-law, and that must mean something, for mother was not easily given to praise.

All the children, however, remember Pake and Beppe Hoekstra well – all except Marijke Janke, that is. Pake Hendrik had been a small farmer who had done quite a bit of cattle dealing on the side, a trade he liked apparently rather better than farming, often leaving many of the farm chores to his youngest daughter, while he walked everywhere to do his dealing. He had tried biking, but after he had swung into a deep roadway ditch one unfortunate day (after imbibing a tad too much at his favorite "watering hole"), he swore off the bike as a trustworthy mode of transportation.

The children would go over to Pake and Beppe's place quite often, sometimes with their parents but often without, just to stop in and sit with them awhile. In the wintertime, Pake would sit nearly on top of the stove, bundled up in an old coat shiny from much wear and never dry-cleaned, chewing tobacco, its juice streaking his white goatee whenever he'd have to unload a mouthful into the spittoon nearby.

None remembers ever sitting on his lap, though he never used his walking stick on them.

Beppe Lies (Lees) struck them as the kinder sort, the kind who looks for a cookie and puts a smile in her touch when a grandchild pops in.

They remember too that on Sundays and special occasions like birthdays and anniversaries Beppe would wear her gold headpiece, and then, in their eyes, she would glitter like the Queen of Sheba. When all gold and jewelry had to be turned in to the occupying Germans during the war, Beppe's golden skullcap was melted down and transformed into smaller brooches for her daughters in order to keep the gold out of Nazi hands. For the grandchildren, Beppe lost some of her glitter then, but she was always a dear part of the family clan.

Maybe the family felt closer to the Pake and Beppe Hoekstra side than to the Baron side because they were still living. The children knew the uncles and aunts on the Baron side, of course.

The Baron Uncles and Aunts

Father's oldest brother, Hindrik-om, was a widower who lived only a mile or so away, at the end of the sand path that ran past the family home. He would visit sometimes and help his brother with farm work now and again. He was less complex than his brother, a friendly man with a quick laugh and a hearty appetite that hated to see anything go to waste, like the moldy slices of bacon we saw him retrieve one day from the bucket of pig slob and consumed with satisfaction. And how he loved to sing, especially the old Genevan Psalm tunes. But because he was a widower who had lost his wife to a peritoneal infection in 1928, there was no visiting as families. It wasn't until years later that the children of the two brothers became acquainted as the cousins they were, like Sietze and Jeen and Ali and Barbara.

But there was yet another brother, younger and handsome. Hâns-om was also Jeen's best friend and a favorite uncle to his children. They loved to visit the Hans Baron place in Lutjegast, about six miles away, where they lived in what impressed the children as a stately farmstead with a house larger and more imposing than their own in Opende. The get-togethers with the cousins in Lutjegast were always a highlight with a lot of fun. There was Grietje, close in age to Lies, with the sharp tongue that said it like it was; Rennie, a bit younger and with seizure spells that were a source of fascination to me; Albert, somewhat older than Sietze, with a mole on one cheek and a mouth that seemed to be shaped especially for the Groninger dialect; and Sietske who was about the same age as me and nice and pretty and therefore the object of my early attraction to the opposite sex. When she died of polio at 17, I was deeply grieved; she had been my favorite cousin, and I had been half in love with her.

But all were stunned with grief that day in 1941 when a neighbor delivered a telephone message with the news that Hâns-om had suffered a fatal farm accident. He died when he was 43, in the prime of his life, and the loss was heartbreaking for all, especially for Tante Anke and her family, and for brother Jeen, for he had lost the dearest sibling of his family.

Father Jeen had sisters too, but the family knew them less well than his brothers.

One of them, Fintsje-muoi, was a neighbor until they moved to another town. Fintsje-muoi and Liekel-om (Boersma) had a rather difficult marriage, for Liekel-om was a man with a flair for far-out ideas but a weakness for work and a likely bipolar disorder, and hence provided little economic or family stability in that home. But Fintsje had inherited her father's good heart and solid faith, and suffered through these years with an heroic spirit while serving as an exemplary mother to her seven children.

One of those children, their youngest, was my first friend and playmate. As pre-schoolers, Martsje and I would often set out for the Komize Bosk, a nearby woods that for us held all the wonder and adventure of Robin Hood's Sherwood Forest.

One of her older brothers was Riekel, who had a glass eye that made him rather self-conscious and withdrawn. Later in life, Riekel would sadly cut himself off from all contact with his family and became somewhat of a recluse.

Another sister of father Jeen, the oldest, was a widow, Metsje-muoi (van Dellen), whom her nieces and nephews didn't get to know very well. She apparently took more after her mother. A daughter, Martsje, did often come to our home on the sand path. She was probably born with spina bifida and needed a wheelchair, but she was a good seamstress who helped mother Aafke with many a sewing chore.

The Hoekstra Uncles and Aunts

And then there was the Hoekstra side of the clan, nearly all of whom would be seen when Pake or Beppe had a birthday. Then uncles and aunts and cousins and great-uncles and aunts would fill the little house along the cobble-stoned street that ran through Kortwoude, though once the men lit their pipes and cigars and cigarettes, they could see each other but dimly, and as the party wore on and the wine flowed freely, there would be so much laughing and talking that it became almost impossible to tell what anybody was saying, especially for Beppe's sister, Tante Aaf, who was quite deaf and tried to compensate by holding an ear trumpet or horn-like device to her ear that I found utterly fascinating. Too young to participate anyway, the kids would often cut out and gather in the barn of the grandparents' old homestead next door where Omme-Roel and Tante Luts and their children now lived. The cousins would play with each other and try to play the brass instruments which seemed to be everywhere, for the whole family played in the village brass band. In fact, cousin Tollie, a bit older than me, would eventually become a brass instrument instructor.

Those birthday celebrations were something special. Everyone would take most of the day off, and for the children that included school. Sometimes the festivities included a ride on the soft seats of an automobile, for Omme-Marten had a taxi business and Omme Hidde was a milk truck driver and would often rent his boss's car for the occasion in which he would pick us up. It was a tremendous thrill for little kids whose riding was usually limited to the hard backseat of a bike. But an equal source of pleasure were the special treats for them on such occasions: cookies, sumptuous pastries (gebakjes), citroentjes (a sweet lemonade) – such delectable sweetness and intoxicating liquids that one savors long before and long after and that still give feelings of nostalgia for those special celebrations that marked one's early years.

But apart from such celebrations, the Baron family would see Mem (Mom) Aafke Hoekstra Baron's side of the family rather frequently.

I spent vacation time staying with all of mem's kin, except Omme-Roel, and that was likely because they lived too close to us. Omme Marten was her oldest brother and had a taxi and charter business in Veenwouden. Omme Marten and Tante Trien had only one child, Lies, who was rather sickly in her early adult years. But I enjoyed my stay there, for going out with Omme Marten riding all over the countryside was exactly the kind of thing I thought I was born for. In fact, with some encouraging hints from my uncle, I already saw myself as his worthy successor to all the cars and busses parked in my uncle's garage.

Because Tante Trien wasn't exactly the hospitable kind, the two families seldom visited each other.

Omme Roel and Tante Luts lived much closer. The Hoekstra cousins, Hendrik, Aaf, Sjoerd, and Tollie were fairly close to the Baron kids in age, though they only spent time together on those special occasions at Pake and Beppe's home. Omme Roel would sometimes come to the Opende place with his horse and mower to help when the grass was ready for making hay. He too was a small farmer, though it seemed that his first love was hunting with gun and Nimrod, his hunting dog; and his second was love of brass band music.

Father Baron was never into hunting; maybe that's why his sons haven't been either. But he did share the Hoekstra love for brass bands. And no doubt his children would've joined him in that had it not been for their dad's falling out with the brass band Crescendo he'd started in 1922. He lost his treasured position as conductor ten years later and never touched a brass instrument again until many years later in America. And during those years of bad feelings, the children were not expected to touch trumpet or drum either, though many of their school mates were playing in a community band.

But the Baron family was closer to mother's sisters than to her brothers. They probably spent the most time with the Prinses. Tante Janke was mother's older sister, married to Om-Anders (Prins), and lived in Oudwoude. They too, like Marten Hoekstra, had only one child, Reinder.

OUDWOUDE

I spent parts of more than one summer vacation there, riding along on the milk wagon to De Wielen, getting spoiled a little by Tante Janke, and eventually learning to smoke under the expert tutelage of my big cousin Reinder. That's also where I had my first taste of homesickness (a surprising and painful experience), and my first encounter with folk medicine when Tante Janke put a raw slab of bacon on a toe that looked like it was in the first stage of gangrene. By the time Tante eventually took me to the doctor, the miserable toe looked like it was in the last stage.

But Oudwoude was always a good place to stay because Tante Janke was a good-spirited and hearty soul, blessed with a disposition that was above moodiness. Her easy-going friendliness effectively made her guests feel at home and happy to be there.

And Om-Anders, that bent little man gave the impression that he had been caught in a twister, for like a puppy dog he couldn't walk in a straight line, always veering to the right, while his long nose was bent perversely in the opposite direction. He was much more of a "stewer" than his wife, but the Baron kids enjoyed all three of these Prinses and could still hear years later the peculiar voices and phrases that became so familiar.

The oldest sister was Tante Marijke in Oosterwolde, a lady whose life had been far from easy through a painful divorce when all her children (Lies, Tine, Henk, Rein) were still quite young, and whose second marriage to Omme-Hidde had been more a marriage of convenience than of love after the loss of her first husband, Omme-Anders's brother Sieds, when his alcoholism ruined the business and their marriage. This Tante was much more complex than her sister Janke, a curious mixture of tenderness and hardness, of honesty and conniving, of affection and spite. It wasn't hard to have a good time and feel love with Tante Janke; but in later years I came to appreciate the depth of thought and emotion that inhabited Tante Marijke far below the surface.

In the summertime especially, I would bike to Oudwoude or Oosterwolde, an adventure in itself for a young kid like me whose traveling was mostly limited to the neighboring village of Surhuisterveen for groceries on Saturdays. When Sietze and I both stayed at Tante Marij en Omme-Hidde one summer week, the adventure also included seeking out girls for the older brother, and close but surreptitious observation for the younger one. Tante Marij was not easily deceived and only slightly amused when the adventure caused a delay in being home for dinner.

But family times were the highlights of their childhood, and not of their childhood only, but as they so often discovered later, a very meaningful and appreciated part of their older years as well.

We didn't get to know all our cousins well; some of them not till many years later, and some of them not at all.

Colorful Characters

Looking back now, I think it was a pretty good age to grow up in, a good age to grow slow and to dream of possibilities (except for the sounds of alarm coming out of Germany).

And it was a pretty good place, small enough to get to know nearly everyone, including the eccentric and colorful. Some of those we didn't want to get to know too well. There were some characters in our area we tried to keep our distance from.

One of them was Aaf Lippe, for example, who lived on the same sand path. Especially in those days, characters were often nicknamed for an obvious physical feature or handicap. As kids we would know these characters only by their given nickname. Thus Aaf had a very fat lower lip, gravity pulling it down and baring an uneven set of yellow teeth; so she became Aaf Lippe. This hefty chunk of a non-lady would tend to heed the call of nature when she was in sight of observers who were either peeking from behind kitchen window curtains or happening to bike along the way. Aaf Lippe would descend from her bike, head for a gully or ditch, unceremoniously hoist her multi-color layers of dress, pull down a long woolen underpants, and spread. Obviously, the Baron clan has retained a fairly vivid mental picture of her. When I attended the academic middle school (ULO), I would have to pass her house on the way and was particularly spooked by this demonstrative specimen. I began to think of her house as haunted, and one day almost turned into a pillar of salt right on the bike saddle when Aaf Lippe appeared in front of the window and began to undress her ample bosom.

There were other town eccentrics too, like Haaie, called Lange Haaie, a skinny tall beanpole of a man with a monkey riding his back (and "decorating" his jacket) whose tricks would earn Lange Haaie a dime here and there. Eccentric or not, many acquired nicknames, like Eabe, known as Eabe Hasse (hare) with the hare-lip whom Sietze "honored" in later years with many a hilarious story told in Eabe Hasse fashion. And Fokke (a perfectly normal Frisian name) Mol (mole) because he was the mole-catcher in the area. And meester Pukje (shorty/shrimp), the super short prancing principal of the public school. And Siebe Fodde (rag), the dog-cart riding tobacco-chewing ragman.

It seems to me now, thinking back on those years, that we learnedand practiced some disrespect for fringe members of society that needed unlearning later.

Childhood Memories

This is where we lived, in the Frisian-speaking part of Opende (De Peen) where there were more poor than rich and where farming (and farm labor) was the main industry.

This is where we went to school, De School met de Bijbel or Christian school.

And this is the story of one of them, Henk, the second boy in the family that lived on the border of Groningen and Friesland.

Memories are somewhat of a mystery. Why do we remember some things so vividly throughout our lives and have only dim recollections, if any, of most other happenings?

Why, for example, would this boy (who was me, and still is part of me?) always remember the day when he needed his dad to help him pee? He must've been very young when he couldn't unbutton his fly. His dad was close by, working on the yard next to the water-filled ditch that ran along the driveway. He remembers that his dad paused his work and stooped to fumble with the buttons. But what made him remember this incident was the peculiar look on his dad's face and especially the self-conscious expression in his light-blue eyes as he dug inside his young son's clothes to help him go.

He remembers seeing that same expression twice more. Once when his dad asked him to come along to a nearby neighbor with a cow that needed breeding. When the bull mounted the cow and made its thrusts, he saw that same expression but this time his dad's eyes widened, his mouth pulled into a half smile, and a kind of embarrassed wonder crossed his face.

He still has a vivid image of his dad's look and has always wondered about the nature of its source, intuiting even then that it had something to do with the mystery of sex.

Though that was likely the earliest one, there are other pre-school memories that remain vivid in their detail.

Strangely, he remembers when riding on the back of Klaas Pos's bike when he and cousin Lies (oldest daughter of tante Marij) rode through the countryside on a sweet summer vacation day. Young though he was, he enjoyed listening closely to adult conversation. Klaas and Lies had not been married long, and they were talking about having children. Then he heard his cousin say, "Wouldn't it be wonderful to have a nice little boy like him?" Did it register permanently because receiving another's approval is a lifelong needed gift?

There was no pre-school or kindergarten education in those years. Children ready for school but too young for grade one would have to devise their own ways to filling those long days when older siblings were at school and no potential playmates lived close.

I didn't start school till I was seven, so there were a lot of days and hours to develop an imagination.

I would often imagine a church service in which I would sometimes occupy the pulpit, but my favorite role was that of deacon who would handle the collection pouch attached to long poles that were just long enough to reach everyone seated on the church bench. My pole would be a long broom handle, my imaginary congregation would be seated on imaginary benches on the front lawn, and I would slowly move from bench to bench, swinging the pole expertly from the aisle where I stood over the heads of the bench sitters to the next bench, slowly moving the imaginary pouch from one person to another. I loved watching that drama every Sunday in church and eagerly anticipated the long black pole and the black silk pouch moving down their family bench till I could drop my nickel in the coin-filled collection pouch.

Many years later, when I saw these collection pouches hanging in a church, I couldn't resist grabbing one and indulging my lifelong fascination born in my childhood years in our little Opende church.

But I also often switched roles from deacon to teacher.

The church would transform into a school, and the green wooden partition that partially hid the stookhut became the classroom chalkboard. Not yet having learned to write or do arithmetic posed no problem to the wielding of the chalk and filling the board. For such occasions I would don an old moth-eaten dress jacket of unknown origin that had inside and outside pockets and fit this little boy more or less.

When the Liekele Boersma family became neighbors, I also found a playmate in cousin Martsje. She was a year older, but before she could start school, she would often join her young cousin in adventures of the imagination. She would come over, and we would play pretend games or walk to the woods together that lay way in the back of the farm.

That became a favorite adventure – an excursion to the Komize Bosk. To us it became a kind of daring adventure as we walked through the fields, climbed over the gates that divided the fields, and crossed a small bridge across a stream toward those spooky woods we imagined to be haunted by wild ghosts if not real persons in unseen hiding places waiting to capture innocent little children. On a narrow path we would enter the woods. Inside the woods the sun did not shine. The deeper the path would lead us into the woods, the more cautiously we walked. "Sssh," we would whisper, "don't let the boogey man hear us!" Sometimes we would spot a rabbit caught in a wire trap and then we knew there were dangerous poachers around. Then scaring ourselves, we would soon turn around and hurry back to the sunshine and a view of our home in the distance, and then we would feel safe again. Sometimes on the way back we would pick a bouquet of buttercups from the field next to the woods and take it to Mem. That made Mem so happy that she would treat the little playmates to a cookie or candy.

To this little boy and his cousin, the woods were scary and exciting. Back at home, we would play school or church, until Martsje had to go home. We liked to play with each other. Life was simple, and it was sweet.

But that did not last long. My cousin started school a year before I did. Now I had to play by myself. I missed my cousin who had also been my best friend.

Education and More

My mind goes back now to that little boy on his first day of school.

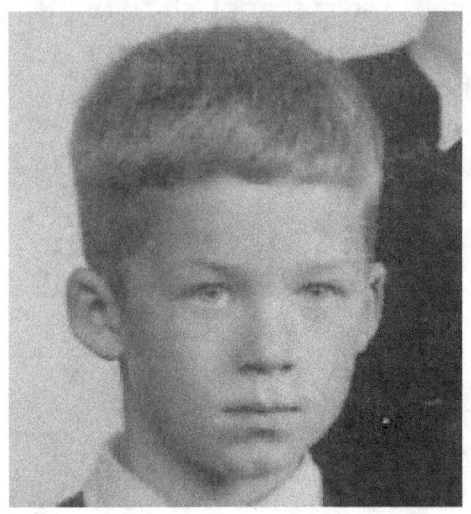

Maybe the first day of school is always a bit scary – being benched in a classroom with others, mostly still strangers, new rules to obey, and a teacher who's the boss and speaks Dutch instead of the Frisian you're used to.

All of which maybe induced bowel pressure.

At the end of the school day the pressure had reached the need for relief, but the boy did not like the looks of the school's outhouse that did not offer the privacy his shyness demanded, so he decided to try to make it home. But the bowel kept moving; his silent but urgent messages of "hold" went unheeded, and the most embarrassing accident in his young life made him want to turn instantly invisible. He could not possibly walk now with others on the normal public path homeward. Instead, he opted for the open fields, prompted by a vague notion of how to head in the right direction.

He climbed over gates, crawled under fences, stumbled through ditches, every second aware of the odious presence of the accident, and kept hoping he would soon spy the place called home in the distance.

At last he reached his destination, sweaty and disheveled. But he didn't dare to go inside.

What he always remembered with a grateful heart was that Mem came outside, heard his story, calmed him down, dried his tears, cleaned him up, never said a blaming word, and never mentioned the incident to the rest of the family.

And he doesn't remember ever having used the school's uninviting WC. But he never had another accident.

I mostly liked the elementary school experience.

All three of us siblings were there.

In first grade I liked my gracious but strict teacher, Juffrouw Schipper, and had a special fondness for story time.

I could not know then that someday, many years later and many miles away in a distant land, I would enjoy exchanging letters with this special teacher.

And what I also liked especially about this first-grade classroom was the "library." The school had only four rooms and this was the only room that had one grade, so there was room for a few bookshelves. In my six years there I read nearly every book on those shelves, the beginning of a lifelong love for books, for stories that would turn on my imagination, that would make me think sometimes long and hard about people and stuff I was trying to understand.

In second and third grade I had Meester Posthumus. I remember that this teacher had two suits. If on Monday he would wear the brown one, matching his big brown eyes, on Tuesday it would be the charcoal one, and I saw that each one had a shine to it from too many years of use. Teachers were not paid well in those war years.

Again, I could not know then that many years later, and coming from a distant land, I would meet this teacher again, now an old man already in his 90s. But that story has to wait.

In fourth and fifth grade, the teacher was Meester Meester. He was not tall like Meester Posthumus, but lively and full of energy. This teacher would at times take his class outside for some physical exercise, which meant they would then go on a march like soldiers into the countryside. It was wartime after all, and the marching was to the liking of all, especially the teacher who would put his students in formation and give the marching orders. I would find out later that my teacher was really a man of military training and active in the underground Resistance. But that too is another story.

I liked this teacher and especially the times when the worn-out reading books would be passed out for reading time. He loved the feel of those books and its stories. One afternoon my teacher returned a paper I had written. It was about a story I had read. I always remembered the special smiling look of approval the teacher gave me when he handed the paper back. Sometimes even a look of encouragement from a teacher can last a lifetime.

That teacher is on the far left of this fifth-grade class.

And I'm in the back third from left.

The class atmosphere changed for me in sixth grade.

It was taught by the principal of the school, Meester Talstra. He was not well liked. The students called him "tolhout," a made-up word meant to make fun of their principal.

In this second-grade class picture our principal is on the far left. And cousin Martsje is on the far right, second row from the top. In the front row from the left are cousin Berend Boersma, brother Sietze, and next to me buddy Henk.

Because I did not have learning problems and my dad was often on the school board, I was one of this teacher's favorites. But I never developed a liking for this man with the short gray crew cut, cold pale-blue eyes, praying with his eyes open to spot a pupil who dared to open an eye during a prayer. Punishment would follow.

This teacher could be cruel. I would never forget about the time my best friend Henk was late for class, knocked on the closed door, and when Meester Talstra opened the door received a hard slap to the face without asking the boy for the reason of his tardiness.

There came a day of revenge.

It was a Friday afternoon when a group of older students gathered after school and in chorus started to chant the principal's offensive nickname.

The furious principal in pursuit. The taunting throng would run and stop when Talstra stopped, and then take up the chant again. The principal back in pursuit but eventually gave up when he realized to his teeth-gnashing frustration that he would never catch up to them.

I took it in from a safe distance and wondered if my older brother was somewhere in that daring group of rebels.

Toward the end of sixth grade, the principal decides which of his students should be recommended for ongoing study to a choice of various kinds of middle schools, from academic to industrial arts to domestic educational institutions. Some girls, like my older sister, would go to a domestic or housekeeping school where they would learn to sew and cook, etc. Other students would go on to an agricultural school or a trade school. I, like my brother before me, was tagged to go on to an academic school, the ULO. This meant that the principal during the last weeks of school would sit down with his academic students and give them some supplemental enrichment lessons as extra preparation for the upcoming transition.

Those pupils who would not go on would stay for their seventh and eighth grade years in elementary.

Those elementary school years were really not very memorable for me.

I liked these lines from "The School Where I Studied" by Yehuda Amichai (tr. by Chana Bloc) when I came across them:

> "I passed by the school where I studied as a boy and said in my heart: here I learned certain things and didn't learn others. I think I will go on studying those other things till the day I die, like the beginning and ending of 'things,' the sources and impact of good and evil, the failure and power of love."

I do remember the season that I served my brother as a kind of courier. Sietze had become fond of a local store owner's daughter, Miene Folkerts. When she became sick with tuberculosis and needed to stay home for lots of bed rest, a note exchange began. Sietze would give his "love notes" to his little brother who in turn would give them to Miene's sister in his class, who would then bring them to their intended destination, and in due time hand a note back to him from Miene, which would then be eagerly received by his older brother. All of this had to be done as a strictly secret operation. It gave me as a "secret agent" a feeling of importance.

But there were some other memories that stuck with me. One was the bully who threatened to beat me up and was sometimes waiting for me to pass the public school the bully attended. I discovered that I was not very brave when physical danger threatened. When I suspected that the bully lay in waiting for me, I would choose another way home that would take me safely way around the danger point but delay my home arrival.

A happier memory was the time when some of the older girls seemed to have a dare contest during a recess time, and shy me was the lucky one who was kissed by what I thought to be the cutest girl in the whole school. I would never forget that girl, the sister of a schoolmate, but when I saw her again many years later, I was sorry to observe that nature in the intervening decades had not been kind to her.

The daily walk from home to school and back again twice a day accumulated its own memories too:

The snoep winkels (candy stores) along the way where a few pennies could get you some "zwart en wit," a mix of salty and menthol flavored powder; the old lady who in her dementia now and then managed to escape her home and had to be pursued by her aged husband who was no longer steady on his feet; the self-appointed wandering minstrel Jan de Roos who would make his way to towns throughout the northern provinces, pick his spot, place his collection box in a conspicuous place,

adjust his coat bedecked with buttons and medals of all sorts and commence to "enthrall" whoever gathered with his made-up "opera classics" in a high pitched trilling voice while swinging his cane and bending backward on the extended lower notes as far as his back would take him, becoming vertical again when reaching for the climax. The name Jan de Roos was known by folks throughout the region and beyond, and most indulged him with some amusement. But I remember school children would sometimes arouse his anger by making fun of him and tossing stones in his collection "plate." I did a Jan de Roos imitation at The Pyramid in Opende when we had a big family gathering there in 2012.

After sixth grade came ULO, a three-year academic type of middle school for those capable of and interested in more advanced studies than the elementary 7th and 8th grades would provide.

Attending the ULO meant the need for a bike, for the ULO was located several miles out into the Frisian countryside down back-road sand paths most of the way and a stretch of a brick road. It was the opening year for a still-to-be built Christian ULO in the area, and a small evangelism chapel would have to do to receive its first class of students. (I'm in front row left.)

The early postwar years were economically hard. The new ULO student's parents had to give me the use of an old, dilapidated bike with wartime solid strips of rubber for tires, making it hard to plow through loose sand and making an awful noise on hard surface, especially on a brick road. I was the only pupil there who had to bear the stigma of such apparent poverty. The kids from the Frisian side of the border and from a higher social class rode on soft air-filled tires, speeding past the noisy slowpoke from De Peen in a flash.

One afternoon when all were heading home from school, that superiority assumed an ugly expression of disdain. Years later I would describe that scarring experience this way:

"Right after the war in 1946 or '47 was a rough time. That's why, when I needed a bike for attending the ULO, I got mom's old bike, a bike from the war years with thick strips of airless rubber.

It was an afternoon after school when everybody was heading home. I pedaled as hard as I could to stay ahead of the others. But it was slow going and the old bike rattling over the brick-cobbled road made a lot of noise. I felt deeply embarrassed when a group of girls from my class rode past me, trying not to notice this boy on the ramshackle bike.

Then I heard them come up behind me. A group of loud-talking boys with new bikes with air tires and a swagger that kids sometimes develop when they get at home whatever their heart desires.

They were right beside me in no time. At full speed, one of them gave me a hard sidekick so that I plunged right smack into a deep ditch. I can still hear the mocking laughter of my classmates. I was badly hurt, in more than one way.

When I got home, my parents took me to the doctor; he ordered a week in bed.

The pain and the bruises of the body fade after a while, but the scars deep inside one's being stay around longer. That's the way it is with cruelty."

But the new ULO student enjoyed the academic challenge. Every late afternoon and into the evening I would sit at the table in the living room to do the homework on a demanding array of new subjects that included English, French, German, as well as Dutch, but also mathematics, algebra, geometry, history, plant and animal science.

And I discovered that I liked sitting in the very back of the "classroom" next to a cute girl from Eastermar, Ali Talma. I didn't mind that she needed a little help with her schoolwork now and then.

I couldn't know then that more than fifty years later we would hug each other as long-lost friends from that first year in the small weathered old chapel on a rural sand road.

Also, more than fifty years later I would reflect on the years of my early education in a speech prepared for a meeting in Friesland of educators and administrators.

Here's a part of that talk:

> "I'm really thrilled to be here today and I thank the GCO for the invitation.
>
> I've spent all of my professional life in teaching, at various levels, from elementary to graduate school. I spent many years teaching teachers, encouraging them to discover ways of more effectively helping students develop their interests and abilities.
>
> So I feel at home here among teachers and educators.
>
> I wish I could say that my childhood education had a terrific impact on my ambitions to become an academic. I wish I could say that my teachers observed that I loved books and enjoyed learning and did everything they could to encourage my reading. That they introduced me to new books, they supplemented the regular curriculum with enrichment materials that whetted my appetite for more; in short, that they opened up the exciting world of the mind and the imagination to me.
>
> But that wouldn't be true. In fact, I doubt that during the years of WWII that kind of teaching was done.
>
> I will say that I never hated school; I liked to learn, and because I liked most of my teachers, it was easy to like learning too. Even those

students who are not really interested in learning are likely to go through the paces at least if they know that the teacher likes them and accepts them. More often than not, it's the teacher who either stands in the way of the student's learning or who helps to make learning a joy. In my case, the teachers never stood in the way of my interest in learning.

In fact, I remember a couple of small incidents that actually gave me a kind of thrill.

One was simply a teacher's smile and encouraging nod when he noticed my zest for literature. Another time he made an appreciative remark when he gave back a paper I had written about a visit to my uncle's place. Small gestures of encouragement, but large in their impact on a young student not used to be noticed by adults very much.

And one more thing.

The headmaster would in grade six assess his students as to who should be encouraged to go on to more study, rather than terminate his/her education in the 7th or 8th grade. I will always be grateful that he recommended the ULO for me and met with a small group of us for a period of time to prepare us academically for that greater challenge.

It was the ULO that incited my interest in languages and that also gave me the discipline for lots of home study.

Most frequently, the key to a person's academic or any other kind of success is that inner motivation that is personal, individual, and mysterious. The best thing teachers can do is to help students discover it, and then nurture it in ways that may often deviate considerably from the standard curriculum.

Sports

I liked sports. But I was shy and didn't easily mix with the other kids. And because I lived on the edge of town, away from the main road and not close to neighbors with kids the same age, there was little chance for pick-up games or small group adventures.

The school had a small playground and there would be the recess games, but I was not an initiating leader type then and would more likely hang back on the sidelines. And because I would go home at noon for the day's hot meal, about a mile's walk, I missed the noon hour time for play that others who ate their lunch at school had.

I loved soccer as nearly all the boys did but had few chances to play it. Some boys joined a soccer club, but dad, who never played sports in his life, made no allowances for that.

Many kids would go to a nearby swim hole on warm summer days, but mother Aafke ironically would not allow her children to come near water since as a child she lost her older brother to drowning when he had one of his epileptic fits. The older Baron children never learned to swim. I would always regret that, for I loved the water and had wanted to learn how to swim like a fish.

But in those winters when water would freeze, there was ice skating. I learned how when very young behind a chair at first on a flooded frozen field or on the mini-river The Lauwers behind our house. Eventually I joined others of all ages skating on the Opende's Kaats Poel, large enough to accommodate group skating or races or sprint contests for prizes. Hot chocolate and koek (a kind of breakfast or snack bread) never tasted as good as from the vendor's tent on a winter's ice-skating day.

There came a day when I was old enough to have my parents' permission to go on a cross-country skating excursion with my best friend. We followed The Lauwers all the way northward, crossing a wide shipping canal and other streams, to where it empties into the Wadden Sea. At the end of that ambitious and exhilarating day I felt like I had almost become a grownup.

The best friend who joined me on that cross-country adventure was Henk Boersma. We had become friends from almost the first day of school. We were both on the shy side but different in interests and academic performance. But we clicked, spent much leisure time together, celebrated each other's birthday with little gifts and treats (during wartime when bakery sweets were not available, Henk's mom improvised by putting a sweet pudding filling between two Dutch rusks with fruit on top, a treat enjoyed as much as any birthday cake), and when we got older spent holidays biking together to various musical or dramatic performances. My friend lived in a simple small farmhouse attached to a barn with enough space for maybe a cow or two and a couple goats and some chickens; and homing pigeons, which became my friend's lifelong love – to raise them, selectively breed them, and race them in competition.

Siblings

I was a middle child. Oldest sibling Lies was close to me only when we slept in the same bed, as we did for a while. That was also the time when she would scare me with the threat of a large living fingernail hiding in the corner cupboard of the bedroom, threatening (and she would scratch her fingernails across the wood siding

of the bed) to come out in the night and leave deep bloody gashes on my skin. I'm not sure I ever forgave her for that.

Younger sister Griet kept a close eye on her brothers and would sometimes alarm the parents with colorful reports on their mischief. The brothers made up an equally colorful name for her: Lytse Kieke

Proemedante Barbarossa Klikspaan Woarst (it rolled off the tongue more charmingly in Frisian than it would in English: Little Kieke [a nickname for Grietje] Prune Face Barbarossa Tattletale Sausage).

But brother Sietze figured large in his younger brother's life.

Though four years separated the two, I never felt that I wasn't part of my big brother's life. I never felt teased, belittled, or ignored. Sietze was my big buddy I looked up to as daring, smart, mischievous, and inventive.

Daring, yes.

One afternoon he invited his brother and older sister to climb into the car parked on the yard. It was the car of a salesman for the national supplier of Dad's fertilizer and feed business. Sietze, too young to ever have driven a car, was going to treat his two siblings to a ride. Somehow, he discovered how to start the car and even put it in gear! The car was moving, bucking like a wild horse that for the first time feels a rider on his back. Lies screamed from the back seat when Sietze steered too close to her pet goat Emmy, and his little brother next to him hung on for dear life when the car slalomed too fast around the apple trees, while their old neighbors across The Lauwers watched in open-mouthed alarm from the windows overlooking our backyard orchard. Somehow Sietze managed to miss the objects that loomed in his way, except the manure wagon that had the gall to scrape the car's side. When the car was parked again, its occupants knew it had been the ride of a lifetime.

But Dad was not amused when he was told by the angry company rep that his car had been driven and damaged. It meant the loss of Dad's valuable dealership for that prestigious company.

Still, my brother's daring failed when it came to helping Dad neuter the new-born male piglets. One would have to hold the baby piggies tightly in the right position while Dad would lift the scalpel (really a razorblade on a long handle) out of its box and proceed to cut the skin on the scrotum, and after the incision extricate the testes. Sietze would have nothing to do with it! So little Henk was pressed into service, much against his will. Dad put him in a chair behind the house, told him to hold the squirming piglet's body between his legs and pull its little hind legs apart and hold them tight as the scalpel went in. I can still remember the squealing and the flicking of the tiny testes onto the grass at my feet while my big brother watched from a safe distance. As those memories flit through my mind now, how I would like to give him a call and chat and laugh about that long-ago event. Alas, he is no more with us, and writing this story of our early years together rouses again the sadness of his absence.

Smart, yes.

Sietze was known to his teachers as one of the smartest students they had had.

He didn't have to study much to get good grades. But he was more interested in business than in academics. He was quick to figure out ways to have a little money-making business, like going from house to house selling garden seeds, selling black market cigarette paper for rolling your own cigarettes during wartime, selling used radio parts a couple years after the war. His brain was constantly exploring new possibilities of doing and being.

Mischievous, yes.

The time he and his followers had switched the town drunk's plug of tobacco he had left on his bicycle saddle when going into the bar for another drink with a dry piece of horse dropping; when the inebriated old fellow eventually discovered that his precious tobacco had turned into a horse fig, he came swearing and swinging and weaving after the rascals who had been hiding behind a tree. But there was no catching us.

(The story is vividly told in *The Way It Was* by Sietze himself.)

The time he pushed a buddy into Meester Pukje, the short prancing principal of the public school, sending the hapless little Napoleon sprawled on the pavement. But Meester Pukje didn't take this insult lying down. He reported to Berga, the goliath policeman in the area. Berga came to have a talk with father Baron, and he in turn had more than a little talk with Sietze.

The time he poured some kerosene over the plums in neighbor Little Pieter's basket with which he went from one neighborhood to another to peddle plums and other fruits. Sietze's brother was often his invited audience, and he would watch, both entertained and a bit bewildered, wondering what his big buddy would think of next. In retrospect, none of these was an example of admirable virtue; in those days and at that age one's sensitivities were not yet highly developed. Only later would I begin to think about the impact on the recipients of my brother's mischief.

There was the time when mischief turned bloody.

This is how I described it years later:

(Sietze also described this scary incident in his book *The Way It Was*.)

Every Saturday afternoon the two were given the chore of peeling the potatoes for the family's Sunday meal. They would sit across from each other, the basket of potatoes between them.

It was a tedious and boring task, and Sietze did not take kindly to boredom. He would usually invent a way of lessening the tedium, a way of amusing himself.

On this particular late afternoon, Sietze took a piece of potato peel and reached across the basket to "paint" a swastika on his little brother's forehead. It felt clammy and dirty. "Quit that!" protested the victim.

The peel hadn't made enough of a mark to satisfy Sietze. He took another peel, this one a little thicker and dirtier to do a better job. Again he reached across to put the mark of the hated enemy on his brother.

But this time the younger boy was ready to retaliate. He had his own dirty peel ready on his paring knife and now leaned toward his good-natured tormentor to pay back in kind.

But that's not how it turned out. It wasn't only the peel that reached Sietze's forehead; it was the blade of the sharp little paring knife as well.

The blade went in smoothly and deep, and blood came out—lots of it.

Screams.

The mother rushing. Gasping. Grabbing a towel, pressing it to Sietze's bloody forehead, yelling for somebody to get the doctor, quick!

More blood.

The mother finally pressing the two lips of the gaping wound firmly together with thumb and forefinger of each hand, stemming the bleeding till the doctor arrived at long last.

The doctor sewed Sietze up right then and there, without anesthetic.

But the young boy, though unintentionally, had spilled his brother's blood, and the shock and fear of it drove him into hiding. He lurked nearby until the doctor came and it was clear his beloved older brother would live. Then he sought a hiding place where he felt safe. He could not face anyone. The shame of his careless mistake weighed on him like the curse of Cain. He simply had to hide because he was afraid of himself, of his parents, even of life itself that so quickly could turn teasing into near tragedy.

So, he hid inside a large open wooden box that functioned as a liquid manure tank in all seasons except summer when the cows were in pasture as roving manure spreaders. With the box resting on a wagon and a spreading device behind it, the farm horse would pull it across the fields. The home-produced fertilizer was potent both in smell and in effectiveness. But in late spring, when the cattle were released in pasture, the manure box would be thoroughly cleaned and disinfected and treated with pungent-smelling creosote. It was then ready for use as a playhouse; sometimes it even functioned as a huge kind of crib for children and friends to sleep in.

This is where the young fugitive hid, cowering at first under the awful knowledge of what his hand had done. Visions of his mother, her face tight with tension and a terrible exertion of will power to keep the gate shut tight against her son's lifeblood. His brother's blood stained his conscience, though he knew it had been an accident.

The late afternoon turned into evening. When voices began to call for him to come to supper, he did not respond. He heard them searching, but they looked in the wrong places. After a while it grew quiet, and he knew they were eating without him.

He hoped they worried a little about him. If they worried enough, maybe their anger at his misdeed would subside.

Even when it grew dark, he stayed in his hiding place. Only when he felt some confidence at last that his parents might regard his self-exile as sufficient punishment, did he emerge.

He went to sleep that night, not filled with food, but filled with a kind of grace that came from his brother beside him that said, "It's all right now."

The trauma ended, but a two-inch scar would always remind the brothers that once blood flowed between them because of a mischievous potato peel.

Inventive, yes.

Sietze's fertile mind thought of a way to generate electricity so that the cows could be milked by lamplight at night instead of the kerosene lanterns. He somehow secured the parts necessary, and one night the lights turned on when a large propeller attached to the roof and connected to a generator began to turn in the wind.

(That story, too, is found in Sietze's book.)

In his inventive mind he had envisioned an x-ray kind of device that could look through clothes one was wearing, and he told his brother that he had actually used this device to look through Gerkje Lubberts' dress, the young lady who later married cousin Albert Baron. The young brother never looked the same way at Gerkje again.

And then there was the time when he figured out how to hook up a speaker hidden in the kitchen to a microphone in his attic den and from there send messages to the startled family and sometimes visitors sitting around the kitchen table.

Later he hooked up with Joop Hanekamp in Apeldoorn and became an active radio ham using Morse code, one time sending me a telegram from Apeldoorn to alert me to tune in that evening for a personal message.

Yes, at the beginning there were Sietze and Henk. They would eventually move into different directions, but the brother bond forged in their young years would never be broken.

Sex Education

Farm life has a built-in curriculum of sex education.

There were cows and bulls, sows and boars, goats and billies, horses and stallions, chickens and roosters, cats and toms.

Each was bred, often under close observation of curious young eyes. Then there would be calves and a litter of piglets and foals and a brood of baby chicks and too many baby kittens.

But there was also the time when this curious young boy watched through the living room window a young couple on a sunny Sunday afternoon doing their amorous coupling behind one of the haystacks in the nearby field.

By sleeping with his older sister for a short time and for a much longer time with his older brother, he became an insider to the surging hormones that marked their pubescence.

When he walked to the field one Saturday afternoon where Kees van Dekken, a strapping big youth of about sixteen, was working, he was a bit bewildered when Kees treated him to showing off his recently acquired potent erection. The young boy said nothing, walked home, thoughts and wonderings about this mystery called sex coursing through his mind; he confided the encounter to his brother, but never to another.

And then there was the night when he woke up and heard sounds coming from his parents' bed close by. Those sounds and whispers became a permanent memory, especially when about nine months later his youngest sister was born.

Schools offered no sex education classes in the 1940s. But what this boy learned about sex in his young years probably exceeded any sex curriculum that might have been offered in the classroom. Still, what he felt more deeply than anything was the privacy, the intimacy, the mystery of it all.

Music

Music was a part of the family home. Father, as mentioned earlier, had been a trumpet player in the Dutch army during WWI. He also co-founded a community Christian band and was its director for the first ten years.

Sometimes he played an accordion.

Mother used to sing in a choir in her younger years and had a clear soprano voice.

But music became a family affair when on many a Sunday evening it would gather around the pump organ, with Lies playing, and sing the familiar hymns from the Johannes de Heer hymnal. That led me to enjoy singing and wanting to learn to play the organ.

I took some two or three years of lessons from different teachers. Of the three I remember best, this one's face had a continuing eruption of pussy pimples, and the hapless man tended to fall asleep while his pupil played the assigned pieces. I didn't stay long with that teacher. The other teacher's mark of distinction was that he had webbed fingers which remained a source of fascination for me. But I learned most from that teacher and was heading for advanced lessons had the family remained in the land of their birth.

Church

The Opende Gereformeerde Kerk was important to the Baron family *(there's some detailed information on earlier generations of Barons and their church life in a separate document)*. I would get dressed in my Sunday clothes (the only day that I would wear shoes rather than the daily klompen [wooden shoes]) and sit with the rest of the family in the hard bench about halfway to the front on the right side of the sanctuary. In one pocket I would keep my collection money, in the other the peppermint. Sometimes I would cut the peppermint in several pieces to treat myself more than once during the long service, especially when it was a communion service.

The family attended twice Sundays, extra Christmas services, New Year's Eve service, New Year's Day service, Ascension Day service, Pentecost service, Prayer Day service, Thanksgiving service. No one questioned the why of all these services. Attendance was as normal as attending school.

In those years there was no children's service or Sunday school, no children "sermon," no children participation. Church services seemed to be for adults only. Children simply had to endure.

At one's adolescent stage, the church offered boys and girls Bible study and catechism, and even outings on holidays.

But questions began when a crisis occurred that I would remember most vividly and sadly; it happened in 1944 when a theological controversy resulted in a nasty denominational church split, a split occasioned when many pastors and members refused to go along with the General Synod's demand to hold to "presumed regeneration" at infant baptism.

The protesters were kicked out. Families split. Engaged couples split. Customers were lost.

Christians went to court to sue each other for possession of the church building or parsonage or both. This happened when the WWII experience – that human conflict for power and possession – was at its worst. The Church conflict mirrored the political one.

Ever since I have felt an aversion to conflict, especially theological conflict.

Many years later I would write about that painful experience this way:

Betrayed.

I was ten when I discovered that grownups don't necessarily mean what they say in church.

It was a Sunday morning.

I was staring through the window at the people passing by. I knew those people. Some were out neighbors. One was my best friend. All were heading for our church, which now was not our church anymore.

Instead, our family and some others were gathered in the town's tavern for worship.

As I watched the people through the window, I felt deep shame. I heard some boys chant, "Har, har, har—they go from church to bar."

I also felt a deep sense of loss. Sundays would never be the same again. I felt cut off from the people we belonged to. Why couldn't we be together anymore? How could people who had worshiped together all their lives split apart like this! All I knew was that something terrible had happened.

I remembered the visits of church members, some of them family friends, and the arguments about baptism and covenant and about big words like regeneration.

I cringed as I remembered the times voices became strident and the words became angry and friends would leave as enemies.

I remembered Dad's elder meetings that lasted until midnight.

I remembered him writing letters late into the night to theologians like Klaas Schilder.

I had noticed the deepening lines on his forehead and the weary look in his eyes.

But I hadn't understood his preoccupation and deep anxiety.

It was 1944. The Nazis had our country, and life wasn't safe.

I was scared that more planes would be shot down over our town, that more soldier bodies would have to be buried in our churchyard.

I was scared that someday the Germans would discover our hiding place, shoot the family we were hiding, and then shoot my dad as well.

I was scared that patrols would stop my mom on one of her courier excursions and find the incriminating material.

I was scared of guns and bombs and enemies.

I was scared of fighting.

I wanted Holland to be free again; I needed a world where people got along, where no one needed to be afraid anymore.

That's why I had liked my church. It was a good place to be, especially in wartime.

In a hostile world, we felt closer to each other there.

We were united, and we were protected by God against a common enemy.

With one voice we would sing Psalm 68: "God shall arise and by His might/put all his enemies to flight," and that gave us hope.

We would pray for God's care, and that gave us trust.

But then some of the people in the church started fighting each other.

They didn't use guns.

They used the Bible for words to shout at each other, to prove right and wrong, to condemn, to call each other nasty names.

They used the Bible as a gun.

And now we couldn't go to the same church anymore; we didn't belong together anymore.

My dad said it happened because synod forced everybody to accept a belief about baptism that wasn't biblical. But I didn't understand it.

And I didn't understand why Christian people threatened by a terrible war were now threatening each other and taking each other to court.

I didn't understand why as kids we couldn't spend time with our friends anymore, why my dad's business lost so many customers, why a lot of people didn't talk to us anymore.

I didn't understand how any of this was possible among people who believed in God, who listened to the Ten Commandments every Sunday, who sang the Psalms together, who prayed together for a new heart, who were supposed to love God and each other.

The world became more confusing, more frightening to a ten-year old in the pub on that Sunday when the war and hate that had entered the church tore it apart and splintered it to pieces.

He felt betrayed, and for a long time he found it hard to pray.

For a long time church was not God's house anymore.

Family Life and Traditions

Home was a safe place and family life had its own rhythm.

I gathered memories, unaware of how they might shape my future self or if indeed they might.

Memories of:

- Mealtimes – parents and children seated around the kitchen table, Dad beginning and ending each meal with prayer after which the children would say their ritualistic "Lord, bless this food" and "Lord, thank you for this food, Amen." And Bible reading at each mealtime, the young boy listening especially closely to the Old Testament stories of Noah and Jacob and Joseph and David and Samson and battles and bloodshed; maybe the birth of a lifelong interest in biblical writings and meaning?

- Game times – when card and board games would come out on leisurely evenings, games like checkers, the Dutch version of Aggravation, Strategy, Monopoly, and a Quartet card game. I discovered my competitiveness in those games.

- Sales rep times – when I would observe a visiting sales rep for Dad's business sit in our kitchen, sharing a cup of coffee, and I'd feel a wistful longing when I looked at his classy dress socks and leather shoes, a clear message that I had no aspiration for future farming.

- Sick times – when the mother's care was at its finest, bestowing TLC when it was measles, whooping cough, chicken pox, diphtheria or something else. But not only children, parents could get sick too.

- Mother needing a long period of bed rest, and I not quite understanding why; father needing hernia surgery and hospitalization in Groningen. I, still pre-school, accompanied him to the surgeon's office in the provincial capital for a diagnosis; in the waiting room I pleaded with God that Father would be all right, that nothing serious would happen to him. I would remember this as my first cry to God for help.

- Harvest times – when new potatoes tasted so unforgettably good, when apples would be stored in the attic and filling the space with a scent that rivaled even the best of colognes, when tobacco leaves would be hung there too, mixing its scent with the apples.

· Holiday times – when the family would head for a park with a playground for kids, a kind of amusement park; or sometimes to a lake where they would rent a fishing boat; or to an outdoor performance of music or drama; or, when a sjees, a two-wheeled carriage, entered the family, taking us for rides into the countryside; holidays included New Year's Day, Good Friday, the day after Easter Sunday and the day after, King's Day, Ascension Day, Whitsun's Weekend, Pentecost Sunday, Christmas Day, St. Stephen's Day.

· Celebration times – when all the uncles and aunts and cousins would gather for a good part of the day at Pake and Beppe's place for birthdays or anniversaries, everybody simply taking the day off and even grandchildren enjoying an early release from school for such special occasions, filling the little house in Kortwoude with warm bodies and clouds of smoke, feasting on taart (fancy pastry, specialty cake), koek (cookies) and strong and soft drinks.

· Sinterklaas – maybe the most popular tradition for kids. They learned Sinterklaas songs in school, got really excited about what Sinterklaas would surprise them with, and celebrated as a family with special treats.

They didn't care to know much about the history of Saint Nicholas, the 4th century bishop from Myra whose generosity made him a patron saint, and who has been celebrated in the Netherlands for more than 700 years. The tradition of a Zwarte Piet and a steamboat from Spain was added in the 1800s.

I would always remember with great pleasure and nostalgia the wintry evening of December 4 when my clothes were neatly folded by the bed and I would have a hard time falling asleep from the excitement of anticipation.

Years later I would tell a story of Sinterklaas to my grandchildren on December 5, maybe with some augmentation to raise the tension for his young listeners. (The story is included in the Supplement p. 311)

- Vacation times – when aunts and uncles expect the nephew to spend some vacation time with them, a tradition in which young nephews or nieces are "farmed out" to an aunt and uncle for a week or more; the young boy biked to Oudwoude to stay on the farm with tante-Janke and omme-Anders and cousin Reinder where early in the morning I would wake up to the sweet sounds of the rhythmic clip-clopping on the cobbled street of horses pulling the milk wagons on the way to the cow pastures outside the town; where I would be spoiled by my favorite tante who'd buy the bakery goodies from across the street she knew I liked; where I'd be taken fishing sometimes by an older neighborhood boy; where I would ride on the wagon with om-Anders to haul a load of feed for the cattle, while above them there were fierce wartime dogfights and planes falling from the sky; and where, as mentioned earlier, I also experienced my first bout of intense homesickness when I spent an idle day wandering outside not having anything to do and missing home; but also the stay with om-Marten en tante-Trien and cousin Lies in Veenwouden and having the joy of riding in a car with my taxi-service owning uncle across the province and having some grownup conversations; and riding with om-Hidde on his milk truck route, enjoying the crazy stories this uncle loved to share; later, sometime after the war, there was also the very special experience of a train trip with my dad to Schiedam where we stayed for a long weekend with the Van Steens, whose son Jakob had stayed with the Baron family right after the war for a time to recover from the malnourishment suffered in the last hunger winter year of the war.

War

No one forgets war when it comes close enough to touch. No adult, and certainly not a child.

For me, just a week into my sixth year, WWII was my life-changing experience.

Many, many years later I would tell audiences about what I never forgot.

Childhood Memories of WWII

My story begins with a little boy who lived in a farmhouse. There were cows in the barn attached to the house, chickens in the chicken coop, pigs in the pigsty, a horse in the horse barn, and bees in the beehives. I was happy, for all was well.

But shortly after I had my 6th birthday, something very frightening happened.

My birthday had been wonderful. The early day in May had been warm, like a summer day. All growing things were rushing to show off their colors and smells and beauty. I loved this time of year, when the cattle were back in the fields, farmers were plowing, and all the children were playing outside.

But one morning in this beautiful springtime, I woke with a start. I heard voices outside the window of my bedroom, many voices, talking loud and fast, as people do when they are excited or afraid.

And then I heard something else: the droning of an engine, a great big engine not far away. Maybe that's why there were people outside talking so much, even though it was only breakfast time.

I was curious and for some reason felt fear flutter inside. I quickly got dressed.

Nobody was in the kitchen. When I came outside, I saw Dad and Mom, and my brother and older sister gathered in front of the house, busy talking to a group of neighbors. And the noise of the engine was much louder now. But I didn't see an engine. Everybody was looking up at the sky.

When I looked up too, I saw where the awful rumble came from: hundreds and hundreds of airplanes darkened the sky, like a huge swarm of locusts I had heard Dad read about from the Bible.

I ran to my Mom. I could tell by her face that something very serious was happening.

"What's wrong, Mom? Why are all those airplanes in the sky?"

Mom took my hand and pulled me closer. Her voice trembled when she said simply, "It's war."

I was too young to understand fully what that meant, but I knew it was something that was very bad. I heard people talking about the dirty Germans who had invaded our country and were bombing cities in the south.

It was the first time I began to understand that there were enemies in the land, in my land, enemies that would make life dangerous.

From that day my self-conscious life began, and I would never again feel completely safe in the world into which I had been born. For the next five years, fear would be my constant companion. I'm talking about a profound fear one has for the possibility that a loved one would lose his/her life, fear felt by and for those in hiding and those in resistance, a fear so deeply engraved in one's memory that it always stays with you. That morning, later than usual, we gathered as a family around the table for breakfast. Everyone waited quietly for father to pray the morning prayer. We listened to every word as Dad prayed earnestly for God's protection.

On that day, May 10, 1940, a dark cloud of an enemy air force had appeared in the sky, and even I as a young boy had an ominous feeling that the cloud would only grow bigger and darker.

On the 50th anniversary of Liberation Day I wrote it this way:

> I woke up that May-day morning
> from intimations of immortality
> to the sounds and sin of World War II.
> Behind me were five years of hazy bliss
> of much innocence and memories few,
> before me lay five years of fear
> and much darkness of experience
> whose recollections have the power
> to haunt me still this year.

And when I looked at our 6-yr old grandchild now, I shake my head in wonder at the thought that one so young, so small, was forced to absorb a reality that threatened the fragile sense of security that is such an essential part of childhood.

***

Small children are not so much participants in adult life as they are observers.

And they have keen observation powers, especially when there's tension in the air, and life feels vulnerable.

And there would be plenty tension all around, like invading enemy troops marching through our small town; blackouts to keep bullets or bombs from coming inside; turning in the family's heirloom jewelry, and radios, and bikes, and weapons, and later on horses and trees; no venturing out after curfew; no display of anything orange; no butchering on the farm; no strikes on penalty of death; sudden disappearance of neighborhood young men.

I remember on my way home from school, I would often see people stop to read notices the enemy occupier would attach to a post, a worried expression on their face. Once I saw a lady from our town stop. She stared at the piece of paper for quite a while. When she turned to leave, she was crying.

I wondered what she had read that made her so upset. But I was too short to read the paper nailed high on the pole. When I came home, I heard my parents talking about a new rule that required all young men, 19 and above, to report for duty. The lady I'd seen crying had three sons now wanted by the enemy.

Such things are not forgotten, especially not by the young.

***

Often the sounds of roaring planes and angry guns awakened me during the night. Then, scared, I tried to hide more deeply under the blankets, at the same time crawling closer to my older brother.

One night Dad came through the darkness in the room and quietly told all the children to get dressed and come to the kitchen.

We groped for our clothes in the dark.

It was wartime in Holland, and any show of light was strictly forbidden. We dressed hastily and gathered in the kitchen then, a single candle playing grotesquely with our shadows against the walls and ceiling, while in the air above us others fought against the shadow of death.

Parents and children huddled together, silent and scared.

Then came the moment that for me hallowed that place and time forever in my memory.

Dad asked us to kneel.

We had never knelt in prayer before as a family.

But we knelt that night in the flickering shadows, and Dad prayed for us, his voice pleading above the din of war for protection, for peace, for faith and trust.

We went outside after that and watched planes fighting and falling, parachutes drifting in the light of the firebombs exploding all around. It was a fearful spectacle, and yet to me, then and now, not nearly as impressive or memorable as that sacred moment when knees touched the cold linoleum of the kitchen floor in prayer that reached out to the mystery and power of God.

***

As I've intimated, a child experiences the world differently than an adult does.

That's certainly true in a world at war too.

Wartime fear is common to all.

But for a child that fear is more selective and more constant, if not more intense, I think.

That fear intensified considerably when we took in a fugitive, an onderduiker (one who dives under).

It started when my first-grade teacher came to the house one night to talk to Dad and Mom. They talked long into the night, softly and seriously, and though I couldn't hear what they were saying, I knew somehow that danger would come closer now.

One night later, long after dark, a stranger came to join the family. Dad explained that Mr. Visser was wanted by the Germans and that the family was giving him a hiding place till the war was over. Under no circumstance should anyone tell anybody about him.

When Mr. Visser (not his real name I discovered one day when I saw the real name on a prescription bottle) moved in to hide with us, and when later his wife and baby joined too, a secret moved in that weighed a ton, a deep, dark secret for a young boy to bury inside himself, and fear kept it there.

Many years later, when you become a parent yourself, you reflect on what saying "yes" to hiding people from the enemy entailed.

The man we took in was wanted dead or alive by the Gestapo for directing the Allied weapon drops in our region, and that as a police officer no less who had presumably pledged loyalty to the occupiers.

It was more dangerous to hide such a resistance leader than a Jew. Discovery by the Germans of involvement in the resistance often meant an immediate execution.

We all knew of victims in our surroundings who had been summarily executed even for the most inconsequential acts of resistance.

In our case, they were hunting for the man who had been involved in the worst kind of resistance – organizing weapon drops and hiding those weapons to be used against the enemy. Had they found him at our place, it would've meant death to our dad, likely to mom too, and likely the burning down of our property.

When my parents said "yes," they put their own lives on the line too.

How can you do that, I've often wondered, when doing so places their own future and especially the future of their children in severe jeopardy. Could I have done that? Could you?

That haunts me, and I wonder if it ever haunted my parents.

And how could they possibly expect that none of their children would leak the big scary secret to anyone, not even to their friends and playmates.

(When one time I was back in my birth town, I asked one of my schoolmates from those years: "Did you have any idea that we were hiding someone in our home?" He said he didn't; and I doubt that anybody did in town, except the carpenter who had to do some remodeling to create a hiding place for our man, and some others who were also involved in resistance. I still find that astonishing.)

The fact was, of course, that many needed a hiding place, and many found them in our area; about 700-750 onderduikers were aided in our area; many among them were Jews, especially Jewish children who had to be represented as non-Jews in school.

***

Many memories still have the power to make the heart skip a beat.

There was the most feared and hated German collaborator in our area, Pier Nobach (more about him in the Supplement p. 314).

I knew, as everyone did, that this fiercely pro-Nazi was hell-bent on catching any of

55

his fellow-Dutchmen in any act of resistance to the occupying forces. Pier Nobach was renowned for his ferocious dedication to helping Germany to victory and for his extreme cruelty to his victims. I knew also that the man farming a piece of land next to our own was Pier's brother, who kept a close eye on what was going on nearby.

And I remembered that Dad had recently been accosted by Pier Nobach and threatened with a pistol when Dad as an elder in the local church had told Pier that he would not be admitted to the Lord's Table on Sunday.

And I worried – when would Pier send his henchmen to search our place, and what would happen when they found what they came to look for?

***

And then the memory of the night when I felt the presence of disaster that could doom my family.

I knew that sometimes police would come to search a house for "onderduikers."

And I was afraid that the hiding place would easily be discovered.

I slept with my brother in a cupboard bed, a bed like a cupboard built into the wall, behind doors. Underneath the bed we slept in was a crawl space, used for storage. But since Mr. Visser came in hiding with our family, the crawl space could also serve as an entrance to the secret hiding place, a very narrow room behind a false wall that had once been my widowed grandma's apartment. In my fearful imagination I would see a German or a policeman crawl under the bed, knock against the false wall, and discover the hiding place.

One night, after midnight, I and everyone else woke to a pounding on the bedroom window. My heart stopped. My worst fear was about to come true.

Someone outside the window spoke, but I couldn't hear what. I heard Dad get up and go to the front door. I hardly dared to breathe as I grabbed on to my older brother. Then I heard voices in the front room, but they were quiet voices. After a few minutes Dad came back into the bedroom to tell us it was the family doctor who had knocked on the window; the Germans were after him, and he needed a place to hide for the night.

It took some time that night for my pounding heart to slow and the eyelids to close, and to fall into a fitful sleep.

***

The day came when everything was on the line and the doom of disaster moved in from all sides.

One afternoon, the word came that German soldiers were in the town next to ours, going from house to house looking for people in hiding—a razzia. They were coming our way, and I knew we would be next.

I was standing next to my hero, my friend, the police officer, the commander in the underground—the person wanted dead or alive.

We were standing inside by the front room window, watching the Germans making their way across the fields, toward our little farm.

I didn't want him to be there. I wanted him to hide where he could never be found. But I was also sure the hiding place might not be good enough.

I looked at my friend. And then I saw the gun halfway out of his pocket, his hand on it.

And I wondered: to shoot himself, or the enemy?

Meanwhile the Germans were closing in.

In the tension of this moment, I felt as if time was suspended, and I was in a freeze-frame.

Only later, when I began to feel again, did I remember everything, and then the nightmares came.

But now we stood there and watched the soldiers run across our field, and then we heard shouts and shots, and we saw the hired man try to run away from his pursuers, and then we saw that he was wounded and being led away by the Germans.

The Germans would not be interested in the hired man, of course, an older man known as a bit of a simpleton, but they didn't know that then. Maybe that simple hired man unintentionally saved my hero and my family that day.

For we watched the soldiers retreat from the place and move on to the next one, and we knew: no German was coming inside, not this day. Yes, the soldiers skipped our door, thank God, but I had been terrified.

***

One day I saw planes falling out of the sky. And bodies falling out of the plane. Because there was war in the sky too.

Large formations of Allied planes would fly over our town on the way to bombing missions in Germany. German attack planes would be on the lookout for them.

One day I watched dozens of bombers fly high overhead, escort planes circling around them constantly like sheepdogs.

Then I saw the German fighter planes suddenly appear out of nowhere and racing fast to get to the bombers before they'd be spotted. Three got tangled up into dogfights with Allied planes before they could penetrate.

I stood there, hardly breathing, as I watched the planes chasing each other, like a dog chasing a rabbit, shooting at each other, and then one got hit and there was smoke and the plane came tumbling out of the sky and I saw a parachute come floating down too.

But then I watched in great fear as two enemy fighter planes got to a straggling bomber. The Flying Fortress crew didn't have a chance.

I saw puffs of smoke and the bomber exploded in the air and went out of control and I saw no parachutes come out and the plane looked like it was going to come down right on top of me and two other bombers now were hit too and hurtling down, and I stood frozen to the spot as the first plane plunged into the ground about a half mile from our house.

Nine Allied Air Force soldiers were buried in the churchyard of our town.

And for a long time I kept the belt buckle I found in the burned-out wreckage of the airplane that I and my friends sneaked into when the German guards weren't looking. I remember the smell of death in its burned-out fuselage, and I'll never forget it. That's what war is all about—death.

***

Death and the fear of death:

I remember now my mother on her bicycle, side bags bulging with papers from the underground she would deliver on her special paper route while I feared constantly that she'd be caught and we would never see her face again.

I remember now the power of the flying bomb, the German V-2s sent to London as a hoped-for coup d'état. One fell not far from us and left a crater deep and wide enough to drop a house in.

I remember now the protest day when farmers spilled their milk upon the ground instead of shipping to the factory. And Germans eager to retaliate grabbed some townsfolk here and there, and lined them up; they were shot and killed, all sixteen of them, execution-style, then thrown into a mass grave, as of no account. One was a boy only a few years older than I was.

***

The longer the war went on and the more desperate the German situation became, the more cruel and extreme their reign of terror, especially in response to resistance.

Some examples, and there are so many:

I remember now the awful day when the underground resistance in our own area decided that Pier Nobach's reign of terror had to end—he had to be eliminated.'

Two young men (one of whom later became an immigrant CRC minister in Ontario) waited in the half-darkness of an early morning for Pier to milk his few cows in the pasture. Then they shot him.'

But that morning, it was not Pier but his son who did the milking. When Pier discovered that his son had been killed, he went berserk.

A night or two after that, dozens of people from the area were rounded up, including a relative of ours who was a prominent leader in the local resistance. (See notes on Schuilinga in the Supplement p. 315).

Their bodies were found the next day, dumped along the roads in various places.

I was riding with my uncle in a milk truck shortly after that when he stopped at the side of the road, some twenty miles from where we lived, and pointed to where our relative had been dumped, mutilated, and shot in the head.

Everyone was horrified, terror struck, and in deep mourning.

And the moral question has persisted: at what price resistance; is killing even the evil one justified when its consequence is the death of so many innocents?

Among my most traumatic wartime memories is liberation day.'

Yes, war did end.

But even on liberation day, in May 1945, there was death.

I remember now that Sunday, the joyous liberation day that all had pined for, when in early afternoon my brother and I made our way to the part of our town where action was expected: when the forces of the underground came to pick up collaborators with the enemy, and even those who were mere suspects, including the brother of Pier Nobach, whose land lay next to us.

When father, son, and mother refused to come outside, their captors tossed a hand grenade.

Then they went in and found the father and a neighbor dead with a bullet in their head, the mother dead from the hand grenade, only the wounded son survived; his hands were bound, and then he stood before the crowd whose wartime anger, long pent up, was now unleashed; some slapped his face, others spat upon him, all taunted him who had just lost his dad and mom; and these were good Christian folk, whom I had seen in church that very morning, praising God for an end to war and death.

***

Yes, liberation came, but the joy was mixed with hate and grief.

I have visited Margraten more than once, the military cemetery in the southern part of the Netherlands.

I walked among the 8300 American soldiers who lie buried there, young vibrant lives cut down by a crazed enemy bent on destroying the freedom of others.

You cannot walk among those graves and not weep for those lost lives and their loved ones who never held them again.

***

That brings another memory, one that goes back to the downed crew of the Allied bomber:

I remember now the day

I met a man from far away,

walking down the main street of our town;

his hair was thin and white, his beard was long.

He asked how he might find the way

to the gravesite of his only son.

I showed him where the churchyard was,

but I did not invite him home with me,

I did not seat him in our best chair,

find the prettiest cup and saucer on the shelf

and make some tea for him.

I did not invite all the war's survivors

of the town to come and thank this man,

thank this broken father for what his son had done;

for I was too young then and did not think of that.

But I would like to thank him now,

and all the others who gave more

than what we ever have a right to ask.

***

If you let them, memories come flooding back, as they have for me:

Wartime memories, regardless of which war or where, have much in common:

> I learned while very young
>
> that there is evil in the human heart;
>
> the dreams of innocence were shattered,
>
> I always looked through broken glass.
>
> Even after all these years, my vision has not been restored.
>
> For me there's only hope, grounded in faith,
>
> that there will be a day, when in a new
>
> and transformed world I will know peace,
>
> and shalom will have come at last.

(see Supplement for more WWII details and the experience of Jews)

***

But there are good memories too.

Close family bonds, for we were in it together. Seated around the table playing games at night in a dimly-lit kitchen, standing around the pump organ in the living room singing hymns and patriotic songs.

And sticking close to big brother Sietze.

During the early war years, I loved to go out in the fields with my brother early in the morning, before breakfast. The dew would still lie heavy on the grass. Our footsteps left a trail across the silent fields, footsteps searching for the silver strips tossed from allied planes to jam enemy radar. Sometimes we would be able to gather a big bundle of these strips and pass it on to underground resistance, for silver paper was much in demand. But to me, the best part of those occasional early companionship morning forays was the silence of the still slumbering world. The bond with my brother could make me forget in those mist-shrouded hours that the world was at war, that the enemy ruled the land, and that danger was never far away.

Sometimes I would sit close to my brother on the hay wagon in the backyard, looking out over the fields that were slowly fading in the descending dusk. We would talk about war, the war that was raging in nearby lands where the German enemy was pursued by soldiers from Russia and England and Canada and America. Even then we would hear the steady drone of planes overhead on their way to bomb Germany. I listened intently when my brother began to talk about his dreams.

"I'm going to tell you a secret. I know you're good at keeping secrets. And this will be our secret, nobody else's. I'm building an airplane, with my friend Steffen. Someday I'm going to fly it, just like the pilots are in the planes above us. And I want you to fly with me. I want you to be my navigator. That means you will sit next to me, in the co-pilot seat. You will study maps and help us find the way. We will fly all over the country, maybe all over the world. And if the war is still on, we will drop baskets of food for the hungry people."

My eyes grew wide, and my imagination nearly exploded: flying a plane, sitting up front beside my brother, becoming heroes for feeding the hungry from the air. Suddenly, in the chill of early evening, I felt warm and good all over. The future had lost some of its mystery. My brother and I, we would be part of the future and part of an exciting adventure that now became my dream too.

"When is the plane going to be finished?"

"I don't know. It's a big job."

"Can I watch you build it?"

"No, I'm afraid not. Nobody's allowed in the building where we're working on it."

"All right, but will you tell me about it again sometime?"

"Oh yeah, we'll talk about it lots of times."

"That's good. I think I'm going to bed now."

"Sweet dreams."

And they were. That night I dreamed about floating through the air, dropping food to the hungry people, and watching the children race to find white loaves of bread and oranges and candy bars—all the things they had not eaten during the years of war.

I looked up to my brother, though I also knew I wasn't like him. I sometimes followed him from door to door when he would try to sell garden seeds to the people of their town. I didn't really follow him all the way to a customer's door, though. Instead, I would stop at the hedge or a gate or the walk that led up to the house, and there, at the edge of the yard I would stand, watching Sietze in awe for being so daring as to just walk up to a stranger's house, knock on the door, and try to sell something to whoever came to the door. I knew I was much too shy to ever be able to do anything like that.

When I was a little older, I even followed my brother chasing girls. Well, maybe not chasing exactly. There came a time when Sietze asked a girl out for a walk. The girl, too young for a real date, had her sister come along. So Sietze had his little brother come along too, as a convenient companion for the younger sister, of course. Thus, one summer evening, a boy of barely fourteen with a girl of about twelve walked hand-in-hand along a sand path on the edge of town. At a discrete distance, the young brother of ten followed with the younger sister, but not holding hands, though he really wanted to. But the boy knew they were too young for such boy-girl intimacies. Still, there was a feeling of future anticipation and the ways of a boy with a girl.

Though my older brother functioned as a model in many ways, there were times when this younger brother strongly disapproved.

When Sietze took interest in another girl temporarily staying in town during a severe famine toward the end of the war, his younger brother was flabbergasted. For he thought the girl had the shape of a big bag of potatoes, with the face that looked like it had been dipped in a can of lard but featuring fiery eruptions on cheeks, chin, and nose.

One day the girl was invited over to visit with the older sister. In the evening the parents went out to visit friends and the sister, Lies, had another friend over. This provided Sietze of course with an excellent chance to practice his romancing skills. He and Miss Pimple soon paired up and looked for some privacy. They thought they had found it in a corner of the kitchen with the lights turned off.

Unaware of all of that, I opened the door to the kitchen. The first thing I noticed was the penetrating smell of somebody's armpits, and the second was Sietze and smelly Pimple hunkering in the shadows in a close embrace. I scurried out again in a hurry, but it took me a while to raise this brother back to his former level of esteem. Perhaps, I thought later, my brother was simply an equal-opportunity admirer of the opposite sex, regardless of smells, lumps, or complexion.

Post War

The post-war years, when at last they came, were hard. The country had hardly recovered from the Great Depression of the Thirties when WWII broke out. The Netherlands had suffered severe losses in life, in property, in production, in its economy.

Dad's side business had lost customers because of the church split, and everything indicated there would be some very lean years ahead.

Brother Sietze in the meanwhile was trying to work up his own business, in partnership with another who was equally interested in the emerging field of consumer electronics.

He acquired a tape recorder (maybe he was the only one in Opende who had one of these new inventions), played around with acquiring and selling old radio parts, and one day placed an ad in a national trade publication that brought two gentlemen all the way from Amsterdam in a car that consumed very costly fuel to our modest farm door, looking to buy hard-to-get radio parts. Sietze was not home, neither was his dad, so little brother had to tell the rather bewildered gentlemen that the little farm did not feature a radio shop.

Lucky for big brother that he was not there, for he would have gotten an earful of imprecations and vituperation that would have left burn marks.

Part Two: Emigration and New Beginnings

Departure and Arrival

Not so long after the terrible war years, people began to talk about emigration. Some feared the threat of Russian communism, and others did not want sons sent into an Indonesian war. Many lived near the poverty line and the future looked bleak for raising a family toward prosperity. Opportunities in other lands like Canada, America, Australia, New Zealand, and South Africa looked tempting. In fact, one in every three Netherlanders considered leaving the land of their birth. Eventually more than half a million left the fatherland behind.

The Baron parents were eventually bitten by the emigration bug too. In retrospect, we can only wonder what exactly moved the parents to slowly but surely solidify their decision to pull up roots and emigrate to America.

Maybe contact with others, some who became friends and who made the big decision; maybe the perceived threat of Russia's communism invading western Europe; maybe dissent with the government's handling of the prosecution of egregious collaborators with the Germans; maybe not wanting their older son to enter the military in the near future and fight an ignominious war in Indonesia; maybe the cumulative dismay experienced in Opende through the church split and the break with Crescendo before that; maybe the bleak economic outlook; maybe the encouragement of the relatives in America – maybe all of these, or maybe something else that clinched the breakthrough. But it meant to let go of the little farm taken over from parents and built up through three decades of hard work, expansion, wise and diligent planning and maintenance; to let go of the fields you walked, you fenced, you plowed, you seeded, you harvested, you pastured your cows in; to let go of church leadership that had always been so much a part of life; to let go of interaction with dear brothers and sisters and relatives and lifelong friends; and at age 52 and 45 to face and embrace the challenges of a foreign land with its own language and customs and traditions, to start over with no property and no money in the bank and no clear sense of future employment and benefit to self or children – looking back on all that and taking the Big Step is mind boggling.

Once the decision had been made, the months flew by with preparations:

Family trips to The Hague for medical examinations; selling farm, cattle, chickens, equipment, furniture, and much more; parents beginning rudimentary language lessons with my ULO English teacher; buying some new stuff for the new country, like bikes (bad plan), musical instruments – a sax for Sietze and a trumpet for me (also bad plan because it came too late for us); having a tailor lady make me a heavy gray woolen suit with long pants, for in the new country boys my age were all wearing long pants:

Much correspondence with the Mom's cousins the Lankhaars and Tjoelkers in NW Washington; inoculations; formal family picture to be taken; trip reservations – to Rotterdam, to New York, to Chicago, to Seattle.

For me there were many interruptions in regular classroom attendance, and toward the end I was exempted from doing the Dutch, French, and German lessons so I could concentrate more on English, and that's when and why I also pulled back on diligent homework in algebra and geometry. Then there were all those last visits with many relatives, even some we hardly knew, coming from the big cities to the south.

Henk Boersma and I spent more time together now, and he would accompany us to Rotterdam.

During the last few months before the May departure, nearly every day and evening were busy with visitors at our place, sometimes staying for the night, always sharing meals or teatime. And if they weren't hosting, Dad and Mom were off for final visits with all kinds of friends and relatives.

I wonder now how they could handle all that "drukte" – excitement, stress, emotions, fears, and tears; did they feel that it was a final parting? I'm sure they did. For Dad it was.

By now I was a teenager, and my experience of this enormous change in life was similar to Suketu Mehta, who in his Maximum City, wrote:

"Each person's life is dominated by a central event, which shapes and distorts everything that comes after it and, in retrospect, everything that came before. For me, it was going to live in America at the age of fourteen. It's a difficult age at which to change countries. You haven't quite finished growing up where you were and you're never well in your skin in the one you're moving to."

Except that the time would come eventually when I did feel well in my skin, when the new country began to feel like it was my own.

What were the last hours like in the only home I had known and now would leave forever? I kept a diary of that last day and night in Opende, and of the journey that followed, that time in May 1948. I called it The Crossing, covering the last hours at home, the early morning's ride to Rotterdam (picture of arrival below), the last farewells, and the adventure of the ocean voyage on the Veendam and subsequent train rides to our final destination. This lifechanging journey is included in the Supplement p. 321.

Veendam

(The story of the Baron journey to the Promised Land is also found in Cruel Paradise, originally written in Frisian by Hylke Speerstra and translated into English by me.)

America – The First Summer

What did it mean for this 14-year-old boy to find himself after a journey of 16 days and 15 nights in a place wholly unlike the place he came from – cars instead of bikes, hills and mountains instead of a flat horizon, homes unattached to barns, no smoking for anyone younger than 18 (that quickly cut my smoking to zero consumption), and so much else.

I relished the newness of everything – language, people, learning to drive Uncle Gilbert's tractor and doing field work for him, exploring the Nooksack River that ran around the Lankhaar place, developing an eye for shiny, beautiful cars like Uncle Gilbert's Pontiac.

I was less impressed when we eventually moved to the Knutzen place where Dad and Sid would work. Our new dwelling place would be an unpainted shack that had been abandoned for some time. Mom and Tante Jeannette Lankhaar had tried valiantly but vainly to make a kind of silk out of a sow's ear, but when at last the crates with our furniture arrived, it began to feel a little more like home, especially after acquiring another pump organ and we could make music again.

But the place was too small to accommodate all of us, so Sid and I needed to make our nightly lodgings in a trailer, which I actually came to like. It gave us privacy and lots of opportunity to spend time together as brothers.

I became aware of the challenge and hardship that brother and father faced daily, working from 6:00 in the morning till 7:00 at night for a crude, rough, profane, and half-drunk farmer when English was still a foreign language and even milking, now by machine, had to be relearned.

Thoughts how it must've been for Dad came later – a man in his 50s who had been his own boss and employed others now slaving for another he couldn't understand and who often cussed him out; the hard work must've been physically exhausting and the disrespect emotionally humiliating.

All but baby Marijke Janke, now Mary Jane, went to work that summer of 1948.

Let the memories come:

- The berry fields waiting for pickers, first strawberries followed by raspberries, and then later in the season, beans; the fields Mom, Greta, and I headed out to every morning to gather the crops that were ripe for harvest

- The fields with my language teachers, kids my age who talked all day long and began to build my vocabulary and tune my ears to the sound of English; kids who sometimes took advantage of my ignorance and taught me words I didn't know the meaning of but was eager to learn and eager to please them too, maybe because I wanted their friendship; so when they asked me to deliver a message to the field boss, I left my place in the row and walked confidently up to Pauline Knutzen to deliver the message I didn't know the meaning of: "fuck you"

- The session with Pauline, who lived across the street from us, in her home where she in great kindness and patience explained to the shamefaced boy the meaning of what he had said; I was not as keen after that on seeking friendships with my deceivers who had exploited my language deficits; actually I had been that kind of victim many years before when my big brother sent his very young ignorant brother to the hardware store asking for a pound of spikerkoppen, nail heads; the storekeeper, a family friend, told me with a smirk that unfortunately he was all out of nail heads; the raucous laughter provoked in both instances smarted a little and likely made me much later too sensitive to possibilities of losing face or dignity

- The Orange Crush treat on a hot summer afternoon after berry picking when a bunch of us piled into Pauline's '36 Chevy and headed for the country store and its icy water-filled pop tank with a promise that it would make us forget sunburn and sweat and aching backs by putting a cold bottle of Orange Crush to our sun-parched lips; it made me feel lucky to be in America

· The trailer parked behind our family's unpainted home that became the private residence for the two Baron brothers, allowing us to share personal impressions, jokes, questions about the future, and maybe what I looked forward to the most each week: the Saturday evening ride to Hinote's Corner, the gas station/store owned and presided over by old Mr. Hinote in a solid rocking chair set right smack in the center of his cluttered store from which  he watched both the customers that might wander in and his aged wife as she shuffled around waiting on them; Sid and I were there every Saturday night to resupply our candy stash; it felt good to become more closely bonded with each other as brothers who were strangers in this new reality

· The 1937 green Ford V8 that became our transport, our fuller entrance into this new mode of living for us but so common to others all around us; Sid was the only licensed driver in the family, but Dad was trying to learn and I became keenly aware how much it meant to him when he finally obtained his license too; when he would drive to town on Saturday afternoons, he would look like he'd just won the lottery, a smile of satisfaction replacing the stressed look of the work week, sporting a tie with his striped bib overall, a hat covering his balding head, and a cigarette or cigar dangling between his lips; sometimes he'd take his eyes off the road, admiring the cow-spotted pastures, inadvertently pulling the steering wheel in the same direction as his gaze and coming to an unintended sudden stop in the roadside ditch; but he learned and went on to love driving the '48 Chevy after the Ford and later the '50 Pontiac with automatic transmission.

School and Farm

Lynden Christian 8th grade: our parents were advised that I should enroll in 8th grade to advance my English language education and to get an 8th grade diploma as a kind of minimal future job requirement; (a fragment from Mom's letter: "The kids ride to school in big yellow school busses. They attend school in Lynden. We have to pay a lot of tuition for that, for the Christian schools get no help from the state.")

I was eager to get back in a classroom, and when on the first day of school I went through the swinging doors and was greeted by Ken Vander Griend who had been posted to welcome me because he could speak a bit of Dutch, I did feel welcomed, and I was very eager to arrive at a feeling that I belonged, belonged in this new country, belonged in school; maybe I had always wanted that feeling, a feeling of belonging which I had felt at home but not always among the classmates at school; still that first day did make me taste the sting of being new and especially being an immigrant kid, as I told the audience in De Harmonie, the city theater and concert hall in Friesland's Ljouwert in 1999, translated here:

"So, I went to school. But first shopping with Mom for some new school clothes. We couldn't afford much, of course, for it was slim picking at first. But Mom wanted her son, named after Grandpa Hoekstra, to be well dressed. That good-looking wool pants with the nice-colored thread was a bit more expensive than the ordinary cotton pants, but OK, her son needed to make a good impression, after all.

But that turned out quite the opposite. All the boys had cotton pants, while I was in my dressy pants that was good enough to wear to church. As a new young fellow going to a foreign school in a foreign land you want to be as inconspicuous as possible. But I wore the wrong kind of pants. Everything went wrong. It was a situation something like Joseph and the many-colored coat. The 6th grade boys teased me mercilessly. So poor Mom had to go back to the store to buy new cotton pants.

For young folk between the age of 12 and 18, the quest to belong is especially an urgent and important one. That was often a problem for children of immigrants. In the first years for me too."A couple of other immigrant boys were in the 8th grade with me. That was good for some company, on the one hand. But there was another side: the more you would hang out with other immigrants, the more you were separated from the other kids you really wanted to be a part of.

And then there was sport. You really wanted to participate in their sports, of course. But the sport wasn't soccer but basketball and baseball, and you knew nothing about those sports. All you could do was watch kind of helplessly, and the teachers didn't have time, naturally, to start teaching you some of the basics. So, the quest to belong was frustrated here too.

And then the girls. I already had an eye for cute girls. But most of the cute girls didn't want to have much to do with immigrant boys. Those girls had their own quest to belong, to be sure, and because immigrants were pretty low on the status totem pole, the cutest and best looking turned their backs to "us."

(But I must add something here: I did catch the eye of Sylvia who was cute and maybe even somewhat flirtatious for I did get her smiles, and that was enough at the time; I also felt good about not needing the supplemental grammar lessons offered to new immigrant kids by young Language Arts teacher Lee Vander Ark; in fact, I don't remember struggling with English and soon was able to do very well in all the work others were doing, except for Current Events whose base was still foreign to me; and the other teachers – the plump Mrs. Geleynse with the red hair who brooked no shenanigans and whose animated gestures would often give her arms a good work out, their sagging flesh swinging with each movement that always succeeded in holding my attention; her sister, the classier Mrs. Heusinkveld who lacked her sister's fiery temperament and was a welcome contrast, though I remember liking both; but I came to appreciate some of my classmates especially who were smart and mature and from whom I felt that I did belong and with whom I wanted to continue beyond the 8th grade.)

More from the 1999 presentation:

"Most Frisian immigrant farm children at that time were finished with their education after 8th grade. Though I wanted to continue, I too quit school. It was a difficult time for my parents, and as children we had to help out. But, of course, that also meant that you hardly had anything to do anymore with the young people of your own age who were still in school."

I was needed on the farm. First it was the Buitenzorg farm (worry-free—an ironic name as it turned out) on the Sunrise Road in Custer—where we moved from the Knutzen place in the fall of '48, a move I liked because we would now be on our own, running a big place (180 acres) with some 100 purebred Ayrshire and more than a thousand chickens, a place with two tractors and its own gas pump, a place with a decent and roomy farmhouse, a place that made me feel like we were moving up a notch and where Dad could again make his own decisions.

But that wasn't quite the case, for this was a 50-50 arrangement with the owner, lawyer Ralph LeCocq, who turned out to be a tight-fisted dictator who often gave Dad more grief than pleasure or profits. I became the "chicken and egg" man on that place, keeping busy after each school day gathering and cleaning eggs and more eggs, baskets full of eggs, a dull, boring task when what I really wanted to do was driving tractor. But there was much work to do, and Dad increasingly felt the pressure of really needing me on the farm fulltime, planning to possibly take me out of 8th grade after the Christmas break. Somehow Principal Bernie Koops got wind of that, and one early evening came to Buitenzorg with high school student interpreter Frank van Zanten to visit Dad during cow milking time. To my great relief then and my lifelong gratitude for that interceding on my behalf by Mr. Koops, I was able to stay in school and graduate from 8th grade and receive my first "non-terminal degree."

While living at the Buitenzorg farm I recall with pleasure the Saturday afternoon rides with Ray Tjoelker in his new Kaiser automobile to Lynden to attend catechism class with Rev. Verbrugge at First CRC. I liked the rides and the chats with Ray, the father of Margaret who would marry brother Sid, as well as the catechism instruction.

LYNDEN CHRISTIAN SCHOOL!
Grade 8 · 1949

And what did all these changes and adjustments mean to the parents?

There was first of all the loss of independence, being responsible to someone else who saw their role more as a superior looking down on a lowly immigrant who, they thought, needed to be told what to do and how to do it, though they had far less experience and knowledge than Dad; and all of this humiliation exacerbated by the embarrassment of not understanding the language.

But they kept their hardships mostly hidden in their correspondence with the relatives they had left behind.

(see Supplement Letter Excerpts p. 333).

Dad was happy when he got a chance to leave LeCocq and the Buitenzorg place behind and exchange it for the Thompson farm in Everson where he would build up a place and herd that had been rather neglected on another 50-50 contract; I was generally less happy – milking cows coming in with mud-caked udders when too much rain had turned dirt to mud, pushing wheelbarrows full of manure up the steep, rainy or icy slippery "gang plank" to the top of the manure pile, hoisting heavy bales of hay in summer's heat onto the hay wagon; doing tractor work was more to my liking, especially when we acquired a new Farmall C with a manure loader attachment.

Wedding Bells and Winter Woes

When brother Sid married Margaret Tjoelker in December '49, I was happy for them but not so happy for myself; it wasn't so much that I lost my brother for we stayed close and saw a lot of each other and still did a lot of stuff together, but I lost out on a continuing education, for I was now more than ever needed to help Dad run a farm; and farming was not in my genetic makeup – I lacked interest, and I think I lacked the physical constitution or frame for strenuous farm labor. I had wanted to go on to high school with my 8th grade classmates and had dreamed of a chance at higher education, and now the door to that seemed shut and left me wondering what that would mean for my future.

And yes – weddings, for sister Betty was married the same month to Bernie Steiger who followed her from Opende to NW Washington. The parents weren't so happy either, as a fragment of one of Mom's letters to relatives indicates: "And now Sid wants to get married on Nov 4 and go on his own. We're not happy about that and wanted him to wait a couple more years; he would still be young then. But we don't want to force him either, so 'foetsie.' He's willing to continue to help us out because he realizes his help is needed, but we can't afford to hire him. And when he marries, he has to take care of his wife and own household. So, we don't want those favors, but let him go free. They often don't appreciate what has been sacrificed for them."

Sid and I never talked with Mom or Dad about their "sacrifice." Neither of us, I think, saw their emigration as a sacrifice for us. We would have been happy to stay where we grew up, though later on we were happy about where we had come.

Then came the winter of '50 – when we found out the power of a Northeaster we had never dreamt of in Opende. For a whole month snow and frost had us in their icy grip. Roads became dangerous if not impassable. At times our yard was a sheet of ice that made it hard to stay on your feet and easy to take a nasty fall. Our dog Fritz got caught under the milk truck and was badly hurt. Some days the milk truck couldn't make it through, leaving dairy farmers stuck with too much milk they didn't know where to put. Churches closed and so did schools.

Sid, married now, took many a risky drive to come over and help out. Some days the winds would blow so fiercely as to cause whiteouts and power outs and blow the snow roof-high, stopping all traffic, and freezing pipes. Sid and Margaret temporarily moved in with us.

We had to dig a path through the snow to get from our house to the road. Sometimes freezing rain made us take ten minutes to get from the house to the barn. Five thousand homes were isolated in the county. It took Betty and Bernie five hours to drive to their home in Mt Vernon.

By the end of January all were sick of this kind of Washington winter – kids were eager to go back to school and families eager to go back to church. But the winter of 1950 would not be forgotten.

Part Three: The Teenage Years

Finally, Dad had a chance to become a self-dependent dairy farmer when he was able to rent a place from Pete Heutink on the Trapline gravel road west of Everson. He could take his own cows along as well as some of the equipment, like the Farmall. I think it gave Dad and Mom a much-needed ego boost and dose of optimism that slowly but surely the road ahead began to look more hopeful for the future than the first few years had promised. Now Dad was able to focus on building up the herd into first-rate milk producers by recording each cow's history (birth, feed intake, milk production, breeding record, etc.) and performance, something that his love for recording and improving crops and cows and his expertise in bookkeeping could be exercised with pleasure and satisfaction. I remained the farm hand who watched Dad's intelligent diligence but took no personal interest or pleasure in it.

But most of my daytime teenage years were spent helping Dad on the farms (Buitenzorg on Sunrise Road, Thompson farm in Everson, Heutink farm on Trapline Road) we happened to move to. I enjoyed tractor work in the field and would often give orations and practice singing while driving.

I commented on that in my Ljouwert Harmonie speech (tr.) I was asked to give in a 1999 emigration program in Friesland's capital:

"I recall that time of the immigrant adventure still very clearly. Sometimes when I'd be working in the field with the tractor, my thoughts would wander back to the fatherland, to the fields around our farm where I knew every gully and thorn bush, and to the relatives and friends we had left behind. It would catch me by surprise, but all of a sudden the tears would come and a profound feeling of homesickness would momentarily weigh on my heart. Maybe that's why I started to write letters to girls in Friesland and other places in the Netherlands. But it's not easy to stick a date inside a letter, so that finally went nowhere."

I especially liked loading manure with the Farmall manure loader, perfecting a continuous motion moving into the manure pile, loading the scoop, raising it, backing up, swinging around, moving forward to the spreader, dumping the load, backing up, swinging around, moving forward with the scoop lowered – clutch, gear, steering wheel and hydraulic levers all smoothly coordinated characters in this manure ballet.

I found heavy manual labor hard on my frame. When I was less needed on the farm, I did other work.

I got a job in the Everson Kale Cannery where I made a good enough impression to be offered a permanent job, if I joined the union, but our minister (Rits Tadema at the time) advised against it.'

And other jobs: Bellingham Stokely Van Camp cannery; field work, like pulling beets; selling Raleigh Products for Sid which later included floor waxers, glow-in-the-dark ornaments, address labels (but I was not born to be a salesman, especially not the kind that needs to knock on doors and offer products rather than waiting on interested customers). Union Printing in Bellingham became another short chapter in my life when its owner came to talk to Dad during milking time one evening and received his permission for the company to groom me for a good future in the printing business. I started clerking (for $35 a week) in the store part that sold stationery, office furniture, etc. I loved being in the heart of the city on Cornwall Ave. which felt like I belonged there. I would sometimes stay in the evening to attend a movie (off limits for young Calvinists at that time, and I think it was the first one I ever saw – "To Hell and Back" with Audey Murphy) or a musical performance. I know now that I enjoyed the cultural opportunities there more than the job of waiting on customers in a rather un-busy store, though I liked that work far more than farm work. But I think the boss observed in time that I lacked passion (and training, for they never talked to me about the printing business and how to go about selling all they had to offer), and so Union Printing let me know, after a bout of viral pneumonia and pleurisy landed me in the hospital for a number of days and many more days of recuperation afterward, that I need not come back. I don't remember being heartbroken, but I did need a job, for I now had a car to maintain and pay off (more about that later). So, I took the job they offered and became a delivery truck driver in Bellingham, a job I actually liked better than store clerk, though I knew it didn't have the same level of prestige I thought I had when I had to dress up for the store position.

The Heutink place holds a number of memories for me, two of which may be especially worthy of sharing.

I'm not a very daring person when it comes to dark, spooky, dirty places that may hold some scary, creepy surprises.

But one afternoon I came home to the news that our cat had found a way to deliver her litter in the crawl space under the house. I was designated by the family to retrieve that litter and thereby saving the "poor little beasties."

Well, if our cat could get under the house, so could other critters, like rats, even skunks maybe. That's what I was thinking, and the prospect of somehow worming my way into that dark stinky hole of terrors led to a vigorous protest – which fell on deaf ears. The consensus was that it had to be done, and who would be there to do it if not the skinny teenager! So, I screwed up my courage, of which there was little, crawled into my personal inferno, and met my enemy – fear. I battled that enemy with pounding heart, crawled on my belly over dead bones, fasted my eyes only on the baby kittens, put them in a bag, and resurfaced, shaken and dirty, but didn't I feel a bit of a hero too? I smile now as I think of that foul adventure.

Another memory was an equally unanticipated homecoming. I had been out and came home late that night, a bit after midnight. I would usually enter the house through the front door, very quietly traipse through the front room to the stairs to grope my way to my bedroom upstairs.

This time I saw Dad and Mom's bedroom light on and Mom in her pajamas emerging to meet me. She seemed distraught as she croaked out something about a dispute and then hoarsely whispered: "Dad's in the barn, trying to sleep there. Will you go there and ask him to come back in?" I felt pain and remorse in those words, and they touched me deeply with their sadness and the wonderment evoked in me: what can happen between a husband and wife that stirs such hostile emotions for one to escape to the barn to sleep among the cows?

I went to the barn under the moonlight, flipped on one light so as not to disturb the sleeping cows too much. I spotted my dad in a "bed" of hay, not asleep, and turning to face my coming. "Dad," I said softly, "Mom wants you to come back in. Will you do that?"

He nodded, got up, and followed me back to the house. Not a word was said. I went to bed, burdened with confusing thoughts, yet also feeling relief and even a tinge of gladness that Mom and Dad were back in their bedroom, together, hopefully forgiving each other for what had come between them, for what might have been said that shouldn't have been said or even felt.

I hope I prayed for them that night before I fell asleep, but I don't remember. I know it was years before I told any of my siblings. And never was a word spoken about that night between me and my parents. I felt secure in their love for me and the love I knew they had for each other, imperfect as it was.

Social Life

While working in Bellingham I had spotted on a used car lot the car of my dreams: a '47 maroon convertible Chevy coupe.

Dad loaned me the money ($750) and I became the proud owner of what for a time became a kind of idol to me, something I could feel proud of as a teenager who tended to feel a bit forlorn as one without a high school diploma but with academic ambitions. I think I spent too much of my pocket money to embellishing my baby – mud flaps with lights, a lighted rod on each front fender, painting the tires into whitewalls, Hollywood muffler, backup lights, a neon-lettered message on the back bumper that warned all followers: "Speed Kills," and more. Unfortunately, Washington is not known for sporting many super days of convertible temperatures, so I didn't wear out the slick top-down mechanism.

The car had a spotlight and one of the worst pranks you can do is to tie a red handkerchief around it and use it as a pretend police car with a blinking red light and a voice that makes sounds like a siren through an open window, but one night that's what I did and stopped a speeding car by the Lynden Fairgrounds – much to the scary surprise of me and the buddies with me. We took off, turning the headlights off and the fog lights on so that the back license plate would not be readable. We got away with it, but we weren't finished: later that night we saw Edna Van Dyken (whom I had dated a few times) speeding down Front Street on her way home, even running a stop sign. When we caught up, the red light stopped her, but then she took off again and fast; we kept at it till she slowed and gradually came to a complete stop. Ron Heeringa got out, wearing the mask which I had in the car and a little black hat, making quite a frightening sight. He walked up to her window and pointed the little water pistol right in her face. That made her take the fastest take-off she had ever managed. We left Ron standing on the road and took off after her, hitting 70 before the next tight corner. She blocked us successfully from passing her and giving us a chance to explain and make things right, if that were even possible. She slid into her home's driveway, blasted the car horn, jumped out and, totally traumatized, tore inside the house while the car was still rolling.

Poor Edna! We had been terribly mean and insensitive, but we realized that only later, and at the time we laughed our heads off, turned around and picked up forlorn Ron, still wearing the mask and hat….

I did most of my hanging out, especially before my dating days, with other Frisian immigrant kids, like Fred Boonstra and Bert Tjoelker, but we also had what we called the Everson gang – some lively fun-loving young ladies like the Vogel sisters, Betty Woudstra, and Jeannie Scheffer. We'd go just tooling around, sometimes have them over to the house and play games, on holidays maybe go to Cultus Lake or to B.C. or to Birch Bay. But Jeannie warrants a special bit of space here.

I don't suppose that all teenagers (and beyond) develop romantic crushes, but I was caught by surprise – I had had a consuming one on Jeannie Scheffer. I remember vividly a sunny afternoon when I stood close to our house on the Thompson farm yard and looked longingly southeastward where I knew Jeannie lived and was maybe at that moment picking in their berry patch. I held her image close to me in my imagination, and I suppose when you have a crush it's honest to say "in my heart." But I had never talked to her or even met her. Besides she was dating a "high-ranking" fellow student at Lynden Christian High, so she was unattainable. Maybe crushes are at their most intense when their object is unattainable. But as time went on, behold – she did become attainable. Her romance with Ken Hoving terminated when he left for Calvin College, and suddenly Jeannie was available; not only available, but interested in dating me. I think I discovered that a crush is at its best when created and embellished and indulged in the imagination, and it becomes something else when the imaginary succumbs to the actual.

I wonder now if I would've jumped at the chance of dating her if I hadn't had such a strong crush. I did date her but not for very long. Something kept me at an unromantic distance, and I've never quite figured out what did. She was a fine and fun young lady, but she was apparently not "predestined" to become more than a friend, as she had not been for Ken, who went on to a PhD and a prestigious academic career (years later, when I talked to him at a Calvin event, he confided to me that he might have married Jeannie if it had not been for going into different directions after high school). In my diary of that time, I notice now that I might have dated Jeannie again after she returned from working at Pine Rest during the year if I hadn't seen another side of her when she flirted what seemed to me outrageously with a couple of rough Bellingham dudes. Maybe she had become hard up and maybe that explains why she eventually ended up marrying the wrong man.

One time when Ruth and I were back in Lynden, I arranged to meet part of the "Everson gang" at the Fairway Café where we talked a bit about our lives (Ruth Vogel had never married, Margaret got divorced, Betty had a hard life, and Jeannie had had much sadness in her life), after which I gave a goodbye hug to each and was surprised by the special "rocking hug" I got from Jeannie, but we know each kind of hug tells its own story.

Jeannie wasn't the first date, but before the dating game began for me, I had been busy finding young ladies in the land of my birth to be in contact with; later I added young ladies in my present land too.

For a while it became a busy writing life with pen pals (but also letter exchanges with former teachers, friends, and relatives). But the one who remained a constant was Ali Talma, the girl I had sat next to in the ULO, a farm girl from Oostermeer with curly hair and a cute, dimpled smile. We wrote for maybe six years or so, sending little gifts on each other's birthday, and not so occasionally subtly hinting at our curiosity about the other's romantic interests or activity. There may have been an underlying assumption that sooner or later there would be a meeting between us, but that began to fade when, hidden from the other, each of us had begun dating. Ali will surface again in this story.

The dating I did was not seriously intended as if I was actively seeking a future wife, but I had a good time enjoying female contact. That included (somewhat more seriously) Ida Van Zanten who had been an 8th grade classmate and also a member of First Church, Shirley Tjoelker, and her best friend Edna Van Dyken.

But that changed when one evening (July '54) while at Sid and Margaret's place I screwed up the courage to drive from their place to the nearby Sunrise gas station-store and used its public telephone to call a blondie I had never spoken to by the name of Ruth Bosman. She was a cute young lady I had had my eye on (but never expected to date, really) since I had seen her standing next to a car parked on the side of the road with a flat her dad was trying to change. She must've been around twelve or thirteen at that time but looked older. I'd seen her around in later years too and continued to feel an attraction. Later still, Al Vander Griend, a friend whom I knew had dated her fairly seriously, recommended her highly to me.

I still don't know what made me able to cut through my diffidence and confidence deficit, but I called and to our lasting surprise she said "yes." As they say – the rest is history, though there's always much more to it. We double dated, especially with Fred Bierlink who was seriously dating Shirley Mellema, we went to our first drive-in ferboten movie (The Parent Trap, I think), went to Theater Under the Stars in Stanley Park, Vancouver, and enjoyed "Oklahoma" and other colorful musicals there, all the while wondering whether our dates began to hint at something more serious than a passing fancy. And then came the Army interruption.

Church

Another big part of my teenage years was church.

The family initially attended the First CRC of Lynden. Most of the recent Dutch-Frisian immigrants joined this church because it offered a Dutch service in the afternoon besides the English service in the morning. We had been members of the Gereformeerde Kerk Art. 31 or Vrijgemaakte Kerk (Liberated Church) in Opende after the Gereformeerde Kerk split into two denominations, but there had not been a similar split in the CRC. Now Dad had to decide whether to join the CRC which was in ecclesiastic fellowship with the Geref. Kerk Synodaal and not with the Geref. Kerk Liberated. Just across the Canadian-American border, five miles north of Lynden, was the fledgling beginning of a Canadian Reformed Church, the North American version of the Liberated Church in the Netherlands, and there was much pressure from friends for us to join that church. We went to check out that congregation by attending their service a couple of times. I was aware of Dad's internal struggle – he was a man of integrity and spent much time with the pastor, Rev. Verbrugge, seeking assurance that the CRC did not hold to the doctrinal position that had caused the church split across the ocean.

I was happy when Dad came to the decision that we would join the CRC and First Church in Lynden. I think Dad had always been grieved about that terrible 1944 schism and saw this as a possible chance to find and offer his family some spiritual stability and tranquility. His friends back in the NL and across the border might have seen the decision as a betrayal, but I know his children thought it was the right choice, and I've always been truly grateful that we became members of the CRC.

In time I became quite involved in First Church as an usher, leader in Young People Society, member of a men's quartet, missions, etc. This compensated somewhat for missing high school, especially the social part, forming friendships with other young people like Fred Bierlink, Al Vander Griend, Micky Vander Griend, and others.

Looking back on those early years, I realize now that I was a pretty serious-minded church boy on a rather unreflective level, especially when I now read my entry in the Young Calvinist Oratorical Contest held in First Church. On the one hand I wonder where I got the boldness to enter this contest, since I tended to retreat into a pretty self-conscious mode when speaking in public, all the more so since I wasn't yet perfectly confident about my English. On the other hand, I grimace a little about the content of my speech, "Prepare to meet thy God," composed with too many thoughts and phrases I had been programmed with through reading and listening and which had not yet been filtered by either experience or informed reflection. But I was quite serious about this event, for I had promised God that if I won, I would take it as his calling me to the ministry. God wisely led me to take second place in that contest and my friend Al Vander Griend first place. He did go on to ministry, and after his retirement, to a prayer ministry that took him all over the country as a prayer leader. God's leading, yes?

And then there was Seabeck.

CRC young people would come from all over the state and even neighboring states to spend a summer week of making music, Bible study, panel discussions, prayers, presentations by youth leaders, playing games, boating, swimming, hiking, goofing off, romancing, and what else – at a place called Seabeck Conference Center on the Olympic Peninsula, 15 miles northwest of Bremerton along the southeastern shore of Hood Canal. I attended twice and loved it – the loveliness of the spot, the chapel in the woods, the devotionals and singing, the food, the panel on pop music in which I participated, the games, the interaction and discussions with other guys and gals –

including the young ladies on the staff who wanted us to tuck them in the last night we were there (even kept corresponding with a few of them for some time, and for the first time felt a mutually close connection with an attractive and serious young lady named Judy from a remote place in east central Washington. We had some evening walks and serious talks about life and faith.

Seabeck made me feel rejuvenated by this time of intellectual, spiritual, and social stimulation and growing maturity that I had missed by not being in high school.

94

Part Four: Pursuing the Dream

What haunted me in those early teenage years was the slow death of my dream for an education. As the unrealized high school years slowly passed, the burden weighed heavier – what was I going to do with my life with not even a high school diploma to show for. Then one day, in 1950, I spotted an ad in one of Sid's magazines, Opportunity. And there I discovered the chance I had been praying for – the opportunity to earn a high school diploma through correspondence courses offered by American School in Chicago. I jumped at the chance, seeing it as God steering me to idly look through that publication. I enrolled and began to spend many evenings after the day's labor studying various subjects that were going to lead me to a diploma. I greatly enjoyed being back into learning, doing lessons in history, psychology, basic math, Latin, even typing (which turned out to serve me well in a future temporary Army job and many a college paper). And especially literature, which included reading "Our Town" for the first time and being powerfully moved by it, especially the dramatic closing when Emily Webb, who has died in childbirth, returns posthumously to her little New England town of Grover's Corners to relive a single day from her life — her twelfth birthday. Overcome at the experience, she cries out:

> "Oh, Mama, look at me one minute as though you really saw me....We don't have time to look at one another...So all that was going on and we never noticed. Take me back — up the hill — to my grave. But first: Wait! One more look. Good-bye. Good-bye world. Good-bye, Grover's Corners...Mama and Papa. Good-bye to clocks ticking...and Mama's sunflowers. And food and coffee. And new ironed dresses and hot baths... and sleeping and waking up. Oh, earth, you are too wonderful for anybody to realize you."

> She then asks the Stage Manager, a semi-divine narrator-character, the poignant question: "Do any human beings ever realize life while they live it — every, every minute?"

Jared Ayers reminded me of that scene recently in his Reformed Journal article *All Saints, A Little Early: Remembering Michael.*

It turned me on to more literature ever after. But progress was slow because a teenage male working full time and looking for some leisure time fun finds only so much time left for cracking the books, and I finally ran out of time to complete the course load. Nevertheless, American School had reignited my dream for an education, and I would not let it get close to dying again. More importantly, I think, the correspondence courses stimulated my mind by opening it up to expanded ways of thinking and understanding and learning that I found enriching, deepening. I longed for more of it.

I became a U.S. citizen on January 9, 1954, when the Naturalization certificate describes me as a 140 lbs. blond young man with blue eyes!

Looking back at some diary entries now, I find to my surprise that I felt reluctant to turn 20, like I didn't want to exit my teenage years.

During my 19th year I had made public profession of faith (July 12) when I appeared unannounced before the unexpectant elders. I had not told my parents either, but I was very serious about it. During that year I also had a pretty serious bout with viral pneumonia, took part in the Oratorical Contest (April 1), enjoyed dating (including Ida, Jeannie, Edna), the Bible Conference at Seabeck, bought my first car, took a weekend trip to Yakima, was elected vice-president of both the Boys Society and the YPS, joined our First Church quartet (Fred, Leo, Johnny Heutink and I) began studying with the American School, found work in Bellingham, and more.

Did I feel some reluctance because the rather carefree upper teenage years were going to become more complicated in the 20s?

I wanted to go to college, was in consultation with Snapper and Koops (even applied at Calvin(!) but did not qualify without having finished high school, or as Dean Ryskamp offered later – at least 11-12 units of credit and passing the GED, and that made me impatient to get to that point sooner rather than later. Besides, there was the real possibility of being drafted by the Army.

It was a busy summer – on the farm, trying to get more studying in, quartet singing dates, hanging around with the "old gang," a party at Ida's home with lots of young people, an occasional date with Edna and Ida, first dates with Ruth (went to Alvin's place with Alvin's date, Mary Lou Likkel, and Rich and Doris, and the next Friday night with the same bunch to Birch Bay for a wiener roast), often going to hang out at Sid and Margaret's place, celebrating my new citizenship status with the Bellingham Kiwanis Club at a dinner in the Bellingham Hotel, riding with Fred Bierlink, Micky VanderGriend, and Gerard De Koekoek to Seabeck, dating Ruth again after Seabeck (for some reason didn't even interact with her at Seabeck), took my Amateur Radio Novice Class License exam with Jake Meenk, did the milking for Sid when he was too busy with his TV business, went as doubles with Al and Mary Lou to Grouse Mt. chair lift and in the evening took in "Oklahoma" in the Theater Under the Stars in Stanley Park, Vancouver, a fun show but which I at that time in my un-reflected faith wondered if such secular entertainment should be acceptable to Christians.

And I was rather tensely awaiting the next phase of my life. On August 21, I along with others had volunteered for the draft, not an easy decision to make.

The parents advised against it, but I felt the inner urge to do it, after much prayer and soul searching. It would keep me out of college, though I was especially hoping that it would become a means to secure my college education through the GI Bill. And the army experience would constitute another kind of education, I was thinking. As I put it in my journal at the time: "In the army I hope to learn to know myself, to evaluate myself, and to learn exactly what God wants me to be." I honestly believed that it was God's will for me – would I discover otherwise? And I remembered what "Seabeck Judy" had said to me: "If God is for me (and with me), who or what can be against me."

I had one more double date, this time Ruth and I with Fred and Shirley, and after spending a fun night in Bellingham, Ruth and I waited for Ken to come home from Phyllis's place, which wasn't until close to 2:00 a.m.!

I had one more date on August 30 with her at her place, and found it hard to leave on time, to let her go when I maybe really wanted someone steady in my life while

I would be in the army away from home. As the day of leaving came closer, I felt more torn about it because I deeply loved home, church, friends, and place.

One of the last nights, I felt moved to play our church organ for an hour, an intense joy. I sold my piano and camera, but I couldn't sell my car.

Had lots of family get-togethers, tightening the bonds before departure. The last night home I played the pump organ and sang along, especially "His eye is on the sparrow, and I know he watches me."

Army and Nightmare

On Friday, September 3, at 8:15 a.m., we (Johnny Orange, Gerard De Koekoek, Lamar Vander Griend, Ken Bosman, and I) were at the Bellingham bus station, with parents and siblings standing close by, to catch our ride to Seattle, where we took our physical again. Gerard was sent home because he was ¼ inch too tall!

When I told the doc that I had had viral pneumonia for six weeks, I was told to go to bed and go to sleep. Later they took my blood pressure twice and then declared me fit to enter; I was in.

We took off from Sea-Tac that night (my first airplane ride), stopped in Portland, and arrived in San Francisco at about 3:30 in the morning where we had an early breakfast that had me eating my first fried eggs, sunny side up "too yet."

Then by bus to Salinas and Fort Ord, where unfortunately I was separated from my buddies. Had an instant exposure to cursing and dirty stories and callous hearts – as I wrote at the time: "I have come to find out already that life is hard on a sensitive person," so I was determined to try to lose some of that sensitivity. We had to get up at 4:00 a.m. and to bed at 9:30 p.m. Got stuck with a terrible demanding corporal with a face sculpted in cold steel and a voice like a resounding canon shot who made one poor kid do 100 pushups (I made it "only" to 65).

Dream's End?

The Army Hospital was not the home I had anticipated, but it didn't take long (Sept. 10) to become its reluctant but necessary pneumonia patient with a fever of 104. I seriously questioned God why I was separated from my Lynden buddies, why I got so sick so soon and now wouldn't be able to finish basic together with the others. Will "all things work together for good?" I tried hard to make myself believe that.

I was soon "demoted" to the Isolation Ward with a TBC sign hanging on the outside door. I was held there for observation, and I made my peace with it, leaving it all in God's hands and feeling confident that I had no TB. There I endured many tests that were often unpleasant, like the gastric test and the procedure of removing fluid from my lungs.

I spent much idle time wondering, imagining, thinking of home and yes, of Ruthie too. I had a visit from service pastor Harry Dykstra and lots of letters, all of which were much appreciated. By October 8 I graduated to convalescent ward 8; later I was able to hitchhike to Alameda on a 36-hr. pass, where I went to the Service Home and attended worship service on Sunday.

By Oct. 18 I was on the way to WA on a 14-day convalescent leave and loving it; and loving those days at home and at family and friends' places and at church and with Ruthie – physically, spiritually, and romantically richly experienced.

Returning to CA was hard, now alone and knowing something of what was awaiting. I spent the weekend in the Alameda Service Home, then back to Ft. Ord. I had a 36-hour pass to spend sweet time with my hometown buddies, and after a week in holding pattern before assignment to a basic training unit, I found myself back in the hospital Isolation Ward with a TB sign on the door – the sputum specimen tested positive!

To come back to that diagnosis was hard to process, for I had been feeling increasingly fit, and the stigma of TB was staining my soul, shaking my faith, and making me despairing about the future. TB had no known effective treatment except complete bed rest (which we know now is a very bad treatment for almost any disease). I felt very much alone. I cried. Friends will pity me, I thought, and girls will avoid me, shattering any romantic dreams and hopes.

But after an emotional and spiritual struggle, I committed myself to God's way with me, though I didn't understand it. I wanted to come to see it as an opportunity to grow spiritually and intellectually. With time the pain and sadness began to fade and a more optimistic view took hold, especially when it became clear that I had a very mild case, with X-rays showing no sign of active TB. Something in that unanticipated and unwanted circumstance gave me the impulse to record the experience in verse form, something never tried before, untutored, unsophisticated, sometimes rhyme-forced, sentimental, but it tried to tell my truth at that time, with a dose of self-pity:

> I looked outside and sighed,
> The clouds were dark, 'twas raining hard,
> And 't was no use to try to hide
> The tears and sadness in my heart.

Five days ago my name was called
And out the room I went
Wondering why; I could've "bawled"
When to the hospital I was sent.

I wasn't sick, but feeling fine!
Strong, happy, and well.
Hope and ebullience had been mine;
Now this – my spirits fell.

I thought – it can't mean much,
Perhaps a checkup or an error.
But when I heard the news as such
It coldly swept my heart with terror.

TB? Who! Me?!? – that couldn't be!
Such thing could never happen.
To others maybe but not me,
Impossible to think of even.

Would there be days, yes, months ahead
Which I would have to spend
Lying lonely on a bed –
Days – months – almost without end?

Friends would pity, perhaps shun me,
Blame them if you think you can –
Who has use for one with TB?
Very few, if any, man!

It was unbearable to think of,
Deep down I felt a hurtful sting –
Had I not gone through quite enough?
Must I yet bear this awful thing?

A TB victim – there I lay
Refusing to believe it.
But then – I knelt to pray
"Dear Lord, do as thou seest fit.

Grant me patience and obedience
In whate'er thy will may be.
Be it health or be it illness
I know thy way is best for me.

May thy heav'nly peace reign o'er me,
With thy presence always near.
May this bring me closer to thee,
Take away my load of fear."

I looked outside again and smiled,
The clouds were gone – bright was the sunshine.
Bright was my heart and mild –
Dear Lord, thy will be done, yes, only thine!

The Army decided to send me to its main hospital especially equipped to treat TB patients, at a time when Denver was considered an ideal place for treatment because of its elevation. On Nov. 23 I left Ft. Ord on a wild ambulance ride, going 120 mph at one point (the driver was just having his fun!!), heading for Travis Air Force Base and from there, after several days waiting, on a military plane to Denver and the Fitzsimons Army Hospital in Aurora, my "home" for the next three+ months.

And it turned out to be a good place, if one needed treatment and healing.

I gratefully accepted admission to an experimental ward where patients would be allowed fairly regular activity, and even outside privileges in a restricted area. This was revolutionary, for TB's history goes back thousands of years and in all that time no treatment was found for this epidemic disease.

Now we were treated with the experimental drugs streptomycin* and isoniazid** (coming with the warning that it would cause hearing loss – and it did!), which meant daily shots and oral intake, some rest periods, and regular checkups – all of which became the standard treatment for TB and virtually ended its pandemic history. I enjoyed my ward buddies (DeChaney, Hunter, Jensen, Taylor), learned chess, exchanged tapes with Sid having back and forth conversations with those at home, and even with Ruth on occasion, had long conversations with some remarkable people, read a lot, developed more depth of thought, played games, pulled pranks, read much in my Bible (lots of underlining and marginalia in my King James Bible presented on my 8th grade graduation on May 24, 1949) grew spiritually, made friends and had long theological talks with Jensen, a Mormon, wrote a lot of letters and really appreciated mail call, and gained weight. (What I don't understand now is why I didn't continue to pursue American School courses when I had the time to do it; that foolish neglect confounds me now!)

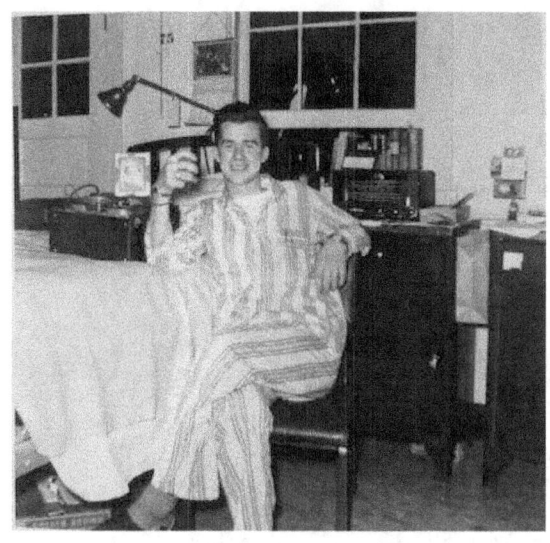

But all this came to a sudden and unexpected and unwelcome ending when the Army decided they would get no future use out of me and effected – over my protestations which went to a kind of jury trial by the P.E. Board – a non-service connected medical discharge, claiming that I had TB when coming in, and therefore I would not be eligible for future benefits.

Dreams don't always turn into reality. I had to do some faith searching again and regain some peace about it all. The VA would now become my host.

***

There were however some serious limitations to the use of streptomycin. These included the fact that it needed to be painfully injected, and after long term therapy the development of resistance took place. There was also a particular toxicity of the drug which led to a loss of hearing or the sense of balance in some patients.'

**isoniazid In 1951 in an amazing coincidence, three pharamaceutical companies Bayer Chemical in Germany, and Squibb and Hoffmann-LaRoche in the United States almost simultaneously made the discovery of what was to be the next major drug for the treatment of TB, isonicotinic hydrazide, soon to be renamed isoniazid. It was ten times more potent than any previously tested drug and it appeared to be nontoxic.
Combination Therapy:
By the time that isoniazid became available, attention had turned to how the drugs needed to be used in combination in order to avoid the development of resistance. Triple therapy of isoniazid, streptomycin and PAS became the standard triple therapy for the next 15 years until the availability of rifampin in the 1960s.

After a plane ride back to Travis, and staying there for two days, I arrived at the VA hospital in Portland on March 6 and was given my own private room to my sweet satisfaction. It turned out to be a good place to make new friends, to read and study (but not enough) and think more deeply (reading my journal entries of that time now, I note how the substance and style of my writing changed and matured in comparison to my pre-hospital life), to learn to do some simple knitting (a brown sweater for somebody), to file and bend and polish a stick of silver into an engraved bracelet, to sneak out of the hospital one evening and go on my first and last bar-hopping expedition in Portland with a fellow "inmate" friend, to take the G.E.D. test, to write journal lines like these:

"So many people are caught in the wild treadmill of life with no time to think – for those kinds of people a stay in a hospital can be a life-saver. Here they have time to come to themselves – to find their own true self again."

I received with great appreciation a 72-hour pass that allowed me to catch a flight home on March 25, where Mom had been able to keep my visit a secret so that I could surprise the rest of the family and especially Ruthie, whom she had persuaded under false pretenses to come home from school with Mary.

During this time in the VA, I was also grateful to have sister Betty visit me one day when she had to be in Centralia for treatments; to keep reading and studying and recording in the journal: "My mind has broadened in many respects …. Intellectually I think I've also gained"; to get Ruth's welcoming going steady (on my May 2 birthday) while enjoying a 6-day hospital pass.

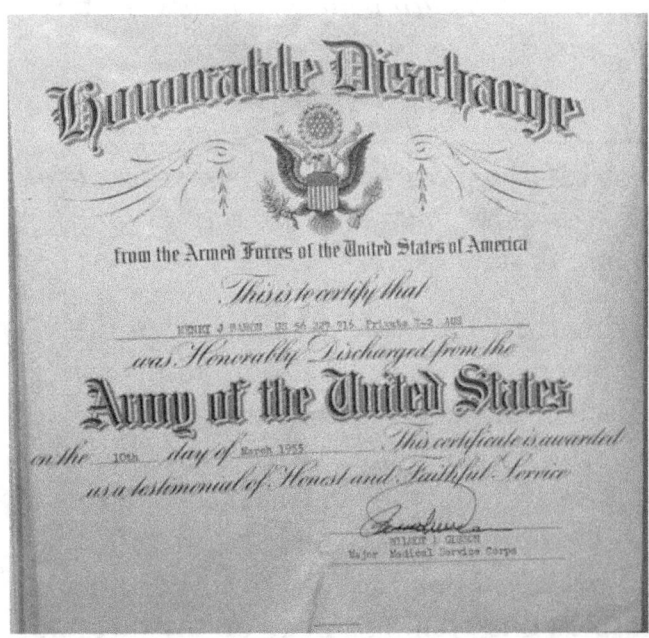

But I couldn't help but wonder and worry about a future I felt clouded by the expectation at that time that having had TB would disable me from many jobs and activities and have its effect on me the rest of my life.

I was back home in late May on another 6-day leave and took in Ruthie's high school graduation. That was soon followed by an unexpected early discharge which saw me coming home on June 3, exactly nine months after induction.

Recovery and Death in the Family

My beloved Chevy had lost its charm, maybe due to some negligence during my absence, its rattles now moving me to trade it in and go with a '50 Studebaker.

Twice a week I had to get my strep shots in Bellingham. I was not supposed to do anything strenuous and enjoyed going to Sid's radio shop where he kept me pleasantly occupied with little jobs. He was working on setting up a side business of Baron's Sound Recording, and I became more involved with that as time went on – in fact it delayed my plan of starting Western Washington College in the fall. Regrettably, I didn't do much reading and writing as I had been doing while hospitalized, and I blame myself now for not exercising the needed discipline to continue my self-education.

Ruth and I spent time together too, of course.

One time after attending a Horace Heidt Show at Western, we stayed out too long and she got restricted to an 11 o'clock curfew for the rest of the (short) time before she would leave for Calvin on September 5. There had been mostly ups in our relationship, with an occasional down – our communication modes differed, I tended toward moodiness, the strep shots were not exactly kind to my nervous system, and becoming more critically analytical would sometimes generate a cloud or two over an otherwise sunny sky, no doubt to the undeserving dismay of my steady. And I had some anxiety about her departure and wondered how we would be able to navigate such a prolonged absence.

September did not start out well: Cultus Lake on a lovely day with my love, egg sandwich, vomiting, flu that proscribed a lovely last weekend with Ruth as well as serving as Groomsman for Fred & Shirley's wedding – aaagh!!

Ruth left for Calvin on the 5th, Labor Day, leaving me with a kind of lonely feeling. What makes me wonder now too is the re-mention in my Journal of that time when

I began to think "all that hospital time did not fail to leave an impression on my mental or nervous system." Or was it something else – like some anxiety about my future, education, progression of the romance, side effect of strep shots?

A lot of letters went back and forth to and from Grand Rapids, though seemingly neither of us was pining away from loneliness, yet both looked very much forward to Christmas break when Ruth would come home.

Mom must've had some concerns about my future that made her contact the Lynden bank president for a possible job, and he kindly agreed to give me an interview, which I didn't take because I still had my heart set on a college education (I could've become a banker??).

In the last week of October Mom had to have minor surgery which I remember worried Dad considerably When Mom had to stay in the hospital overnight, he asked me to stay home with him, and to this day I feel remorse that I didn't. Mom had not often been sick, and he really had some anxiety about it, there being a chance that the surgery would uncover something more serious, like cancer. But it all turned out well. My closing lines in the Oct. 29 entry quotes 2 Cor. 9: 8: "…we know that God is able to make all grace abound toward us…."

(This is the last picture of them together.)

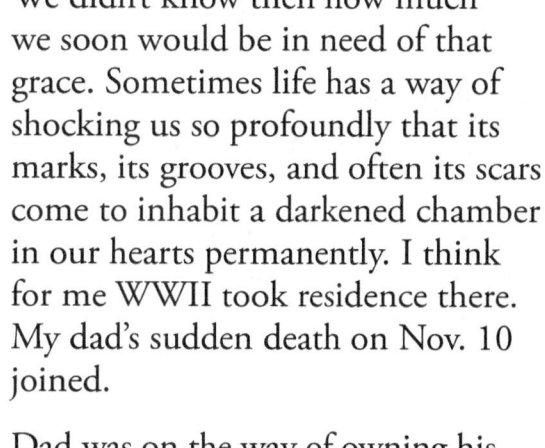

We didn't know then how much we soon would be in need of that grace. Sometimes life has a way of shocking us so profoundly that its marks, its grooves, and often its scars come to inhabit a darkened chamber in our hearts permanently. I think for me WWII took residence there. My dad's sudden death on Nov. 10 joined.

Dad was on the way of owning his own place, his own livestock and equipment, in an ideal location three miles from the Canadian border and with a full view of the Canadian Coast Mountains and the Cascades.

Mom and Dad had celebrated their 25th wedding anniversary a couple of years before.

Now they were beginning to relish the anticipation of visiting the homeland, the relatives, the old familiar places that were still rooted in their hearts. But in that second week of November, Heit's (Dad) work on earth was suddenly cut short.

It took me a year to finally try to put into words my response to that bitter loss – it's recorded on sixteen pages in my journal. What follows are some fragments from that account and something shorter written much later:

"I woke up from the noise downstairs – anxious voices, hurried steps from one room to another, a loud groaning…I hurried downstairs dreading what I would encounter…Dad in the bedroom groaning from intense pain…Mary leaving for school…did she say goodbye to Dad whom she would never hug again?...called an ambulance when Dad started hemorrhaging…watching in near shock as he was being placed in the ambulance…following him to Bellingham in silence…endless hours of waiting in the hospital, hours of torture, of uncertainty, of hope, of fear, of tears and prayers…waiting, waiting, waiting…as the hours dragged on our minds became dull with fear, with tension…an hour and a half after the operation started, Dr. Graham reported that the blood pressure had taken a sudden drop, leaving little hope for survival…after praying hard the faith grew in me that God would hear and answer, even miraculously…my faith grew even more certain when Dr. Graham next reported that shortly after the operation the bp had suddenly gone up…took turns being in the room with Dad after the surgery, to hold his hand, to moisten his lip, and just to show him that we were with him…at times the flame of life glowed very, very low…I asked Dad "Is everything alright? Is heit bereid?" (Are you prepared?) …Dad heard me and squeezed my hand and managed a slight nod…Mom and Bernie stayed at the hospital that night…stumbled upstairs in a daze at 12:30, exhausted physically and emotionally and tried to sleep, feeling a dull ache, a sense of unreality …waking up from a nightmare to the ringing of the telephone downstairs, filling me with the dreaded, hopeless feeling that there had been a turn for the worse…Sid picked me up, and I never felt worse or more dazed than during the race to Bellingham …when I stumbled out of the car I was almost unable to stand…when I heard that it was all over there came a feeling only those know who are told of a loved one's death…the full realization of that great earthly finality, of the many nevermores, comes only slowly but with ever increasing clarity and intensity and sorrow and pain…but in our efforts to comfort Mom we found comfort ourselves…but there were times when you could stand it no longer, and fly upstairs, and sob your heart out, and then there was Mom to comfort you… not much time of talking then, not even of praying, but times of silence, of tears, of doing what had to be done, and of nothing…and always there was one missing – a face, a voice, a step, Heit…in the Gillies Funeral Home nine-year old Mary comforting Mom: "That isn't really Dad, Mom, Dad is up in heaven"…friends who looked into your eyes with heartfelt sympathy…

Ruth's phone call…the funeral…the terrific tension of emotional restraint for Mom's sake…a violent burst of emotion, refusing to part with a loved one… being pulled away…a last look…and the closing of the casket… "but the trumpet shall sound…and the dead shall be raised, incorruptible!"

Last Words

Written later:

"Sixty years ago today, Dad suddenly died.

Sixty years dims and erases many a memory, as if a shade were drawn over it.

But not this one.

What happened that day, Nov. 10, 1955, will always be an indelible part of my being.

That morning Dad had done the early morning chores as usual.

The dawn had come promising a crisp but beautiful November day.

According to Greta who had helped with the milking, Heit had been in a good mood, maybe more talkative than usual.

Could it be that, after seven years of extremely hard immigrant labor, he especially enjoyed the sweet taste that morning of finally being on his own place and improving the quality of his own livestock?

The pain must've hit him suddenly when he was in the silo. And it was excruciating. Somehow he managed to climb down, to leave the barn, to make it to the house.

Did he sense even then that it would be the last time?

I was still recovering from TB and exempt from farm work.

The ominous sounds downstairs woke me up that morning – agitated voices, rushing footsteps from one room to another, and the frightening moans of someone in great pain.

When I came down, my mom and sister's faces told me that something profoundly serious was going on.

Heit was in the bedroom now, his moaning growing in intensity. Mem hurried back to tend to her husband. I stayed in the kitchen, afraid to go to the bedroom, afraid of facing a father in agony.

But when Mem came back to tell me that Heit wanted me to come to him, I had no choice.

Still I hesitated.

Feelings between fathers and sons are often complex, confused, even strained, especially in those uneasy years when sons grow uncertainly toward adulthood and express their insecurity through a sharp-edged critical faculty.

I had hardly been a rebel, but maybe a self-righteous idealist is worse.

We had sometimes been hard on each other, more often through silence than through words.

So, I hesitated. I was not prepared.

When I entered the bedroom, my insides told me that I was about to step into a new dimension of being.

I saw Heit, stretched out on the bed, his face contorted with the terrible pain that was wracking his body.

His eyes turned to me. Those light-blue eyes spoke of intense pain, but it wasn't the pain that struck me. It was a tenderness, a gentleness I had never seen before that reached my soul.

He beckoned for me to come closer.

He took my hand; he stroked it gently.

This was not the Heit I thought I had known, but my heart told me now that I had always wanted, I had always needed his tenderness, his gentleness, his love.

Then he pulled me closer to him.

In between spasms of pain, he tried to say something: "You are such a dear boy."

He pulled me closer still, put his arms around my neck, and tried to speak again: "I've sometimes done you wrong, will you forgive me?"

Too choked to speak, I could only nod.

"And if I don't make it, will you promise me that all of you will take good care of Mom?"

Then he kissed me.

When I stumbled out of that room, I knew that I had been on sacred ground.

My father's faith became real to me that day.

Heit died in the early hours of the morning, after surgery for a bowel obstruction.

The next day I hid in the barn, among the bales of hay, and wept as I had never wept before.

I wept with grief for the years in the past when Heit and I could have been tender and gentle with each other, and weren't.

I wept with grief for the years to come when our love for each other would not be a part of life.

But I wept too with gratitude for the heavenly gift of grace that had hallowed those last minutes with my dad.

Grace that had softened a sometimes stern, proud spirit into a loving father who asked his son's forgiveness.

That was the Father's gift when Heit, my father, died sixty years ago.

And that gift became my lifelong blessing.

For on that day my Dad's faith became real to me."

This is a fragment of what Mom wrote to her family back in the NL afterward:

"… at first I thought I wouldn't be able to go on; later I realized I still have work to do and must go on. It's very hard at times and sometimes I'm afraid of the future. Each day I must live by faith."

Thanksgiving later that month was hard. We, gratefully, had each other. And brother Sid often reached out to me, spending time with me, going to church together. But I envied my married older siblings who had their spouse to share the grief.

Christmas was still clouded by our loss. I very much welcomed Ruth's coming home during Christmas vacation. When she returned to Calvin, I really noticed for the first time how much I missed her.

Part Five: Continuing the Dream

WWCE

On January 3 I became a college student, a long obstructed desire finally becoming a reality!

The bit of money I had managed to save and the small support allowance I received from the State Social Services made it financially possible. Willard Hiebert did the milking chores and Bernie (the Steigers had moved onto the Dewey Bajema's place in the meantime) helped out too when necessary. But Mom couldn't hold on to the farm, of course, and eventually sold it to Martin Anker, a more recent immigrant.

I liked the new experience of finally being a student again, enjoying the classes and working hard on the load of homework. I often carpooled with other Lynden students like Marv Beukelman, Alvin Bajema, Gareth Bouwman, and others, and enjoyed the social interaction. As a commuter student I didn't get to know fellow classmates really, and that was a loss. But I did join the Glee Club and enjoyed the practice and the performances that kept me singing.

I remember a nice sunny day coming out of the library after a heady study period in that impressive facility and, walking with Gareth, hearing myself say to him: "I like this, I think I'm going to stick with it all the way to the PhD." I would never forget that moment of exhilarating fantasy and the sweet feeling of living a dream that gave rise to it.

In March we moved to 1106 Front Street, with Mom now working part-time for Mrs. Spaan and at the Christian Rest Home, which much later became the Lynden Care Center, both job contacts really accelerating her English facility – her new language that as the years went by she would learn to read and write almost flawlessly as well as speak it fluently. Ruthie and I continued to pursue our "correspondence romance" through which one perhaps learns things about the other that in a normal romance don't necessarily surface. But by the end of May she was back home, and it was good to be together again.

I decided to keep going to school during the summer, and since Ruth did too, we went together every day. In fact, she switched to Western and we would both be attending in the fall too.

Since I had not had four years of high school education that would have included more than basic courses in math and science, I struggled when I had to dig into those subjects at Western and keenly felt a lack of preparation. And when I enrolled as barely a sophomore in a Shakespeare course intended for majors and found myself among mostly seniors, I felt more like a pygmy among giants. But I hung in there, though sometimes thinking I should have buckled down harder exercising my brain during those long hospital days. Yes, college often challenged my mind, but it also challenged my faith.

Faith Crisis

I had always been pretty serious about faith. I liked church, the Bible stories Dad read at mealtimes, Boys Bible Study, Catechism classes, etc. I remember praying, as I have mentioned, when I was maybe eight or nine in the doctor's office waiting room that Dad's problem would not be serious, and praying as a twelve-year old when one Sunday afternoon I was babysitting little sister Marijke Janke who wouldn't stop screaming her head off – which after some time managed to make me so upset that I pleaded with God to please stop her crying and I would thenceforth live gratefully for Him. No doubt I prayed more often, but those I remember, including the visuals of the location. When I reread my earlier journal entries now (which unfortunately cover only a few years, and sporadically at that, age 20-21), what strikes me is the frequency and intensity of my faith expressions. I had done a lot of Bible reading and underlining, read religious periodicals, books about faith, and enjoyed discussing faith subjects and issues with others. I remember that in my upper teens I began to wonder how we knew that Christianity was a true religion when those of other religions thought the same of theirs. But I had always simply assumed and accepted that all I was taught and read in the Bible was pretty literally true. And because I had always taken our Christian (and Reformed) faith seriously, I would also take seriously an attack on religious faith. But I hadn't been challenged and therefore wasn't prepared for it.

It came with a vengeance at Western, particularly in a sociology class taught by a brilliant, articulate, authoritative, and vehemently anti-religious sociology prof. Taylor. I felt my faith shredded. Up to this time I think my faith was fact-based, in the same way that my grasp of WWII was fact-based: the Genesis account of creation was factual, the immaculate conception of Jesus was as real, if not similar, as the conception of my little sister Mary; but I had to learn the difficult lesson that fact-based knowledge is not the same as faith. And that would take the rest of my life. However, at this time in my initial immersion in college education and thinking, I felt unmoored. I couldn't get past the thought that it's humanly possible to imagine objects or forces or creatures into gods and by perpetual reinforcement over a period of time gain the acceptance and worship of the masses for that "god." I remember sharing a bit of my turmoil with brother Sid, standing by Mom's house and pointing to one of those majestic trees that line Front Street, saying, "If we told people long enough that it's a special tree, a tree we should come to regularly and speak to it and chant songs and bring offerings, in time we would begin to accept it as a god because we begin to imagine its divinity."

I felt emotionally and spiritually battered, I reached a low point of depression, but I did not reach out for support and counsel, maybe because I felt betrayed but ashamed to share with pastor or counselor, or I didn't think I would get the kind of understanding ear that I needed.

Had I gone through Lynden Christian high school, I might have reached out to someone like Spud Snapper. As it was, it became a solitary burden. Though my faith came close to the breaking point, faith was rooted too deeply into my soul to simply discard. God didn't let me go, but my faith life was never the same it had been, and in retrospect I'm grateful for that. As my studies continued at Western, I felt my mind grow and many ideas, viewpoints, and beliefs broaden. I became much less certain of many aspects of religion and more inclined to doubts and questions. I was especially bothered by the church's unwillingness to address or its dismissal of the theory of evolution, glossing over it as a scheme to prove there is no God. I've come to accept a critical, analytical mind as one of God's good gifts, a gift that discerns complexity where others see simplicity, a gift that makes believing harder but also deeper and richer. Doubt became a familiar and often uncomfortable companion, but I came to accept that faith without doubt or questions is not really faith, and that has always made me give a ready ear to students and others who struggled with doubt. What I hoped for then and ever since was a deepening of faith, hope, and love – a more comprehensive love for God and fellow human beings, a faith that does not function as a limiting factor in knowledge and wisdom but as a complementary one.

The Woman in My Life

1956-'57 – Ruth and I continued at Western, one quarter after another, including summer quarters, I trying to make up for lost time, heeding Robert Herrick's admonition – "Gather ye rosebuds while ye may." As I got into the swing of college classes and overcoming the high school education deficit, I found myself earning better grades (3.6 GPA in my 6th quarter) and loving learning and thinking. I wasn't sure what I was preparing myself for – through a biology course I had felt an interest in genetics, but my academic strength pointed more to the humanities, like literature and psychology, than to the sciences, and the profession of teaching attracted me. Ruth and I had been together long enough now to make plans for our future, a possible summer marriage.

Marriage Licenses

Donald Jack Altman, 20, Ferndale, and Ora May Byer, 18, 1421 Meridian Rd.

George Papuc, 24, Rt. 2, Ladner, B. C., and Marie Louise Solomon, Point Roberts.

Allan G. Hunter, 21, 3026 Birchwood Ave., and Donna Dee Brighton, 19, 1206 Samish Highway.

Henry J. Baron, 23, Lynden, and Ruth Bosman, 19, Rt. 1, Sumas.

Norman H. Shelly, 20, Rt. 3, Lynden, and Shirley L. Swank, 19, 923 Iowa St.

We had a couple years of college left and no money in the bank, so when an opportunity came for both of us to teach at Sumas Christian School, we came to the decision to accept the offer, though I was concerned about the interruption of my educational dreams – dreams I knew would persist and I would not abandon, for I had the determination to finish college in '58-'59 if at all possible.

We became engaged on May 5, a Sunday night, exactly two years after we agreed to go steady. A wedding date was set for August 7.

I bought the rings through one of Sid's catalogs, rings my Ruthie has worn for more than 60 years now, still shining with the beauty of love.

Yes, love is "a many-splendored thing," but for me the approaching seal of marriage sometimes gave me some mental perturbations – an analytical, critical mind can do that and raise the questions of "am I mature enough to be ready for this, are we really right for each other, is our love strong enough to see us through to whatever may come our way, will our differences become barriers, will we really be able to communicate our hearts to each other?"

120

I had been introduced to Shakespeare by now, and Sonnet 7 came to mind:

How soon hath Time, the subtle thief of youth

by John Milton

How soon hath Time, the subtle thief of youth,
    Stol'n on his wing my three and twentieth year!
    My hasting days fly on with full career,
    But my late spring no bud or blossom shew'th.
Perhaps my semblance might deceive the truth,
    That I to manhood am arrived so near,
    And inward ripeness doth much less appear,
    That some more timely-happy spirits endu'th.
Yet be it less or more, or soon or slow,
    It shall be still in strictest measure even
    To that same lot, however mean or high,
Toward which Time leads me, and the will of Heaven;
    All is, if I have grace to use it so,
    As ever in my great Taskmaster's eye.

Ruth intuited something of my occasional struggle, and that was hurtful. And to this day I feel the sometime painful tensions of that young man who didn't want to make a mistake of a lifetime and a wish that my present self could have come to him with a message in his dream: "Do not be afraid, you will not regret joining this wonderful woman who loves you, and this bond of mutual love between you will, yes, be stretched, but only grow stronger as the years pass."

Marriage is a Bungee Jump

by Walter McDonald

We'd checked the charts, the geology of cliffs
and canyons, but no one knows which fibers split,
which granite ledges crack. On the edge of hope
for nothing we'd ever done, we tugged at the ropes,

both ropes, blessing the stretch and strain
with our bodies, a long time falling to the pain
and certainly of stop. Hand in hand we stepped up
wavering to the ledge, hearing the rush

of a river we leaped to, a far-off
cawing crow, the primitive breeze of the fall,
and squeezed, clinging to each other's vows
that only death could separate us now.

We married in the Sumas Christian Reformed Church on a rainy day in August, spent our honeymoon night in a Bellingham motel, went on to Seattle for a couple of honeymoon days, settled into Mom's home at 1106 Front St. since Mom and Mary were going to be in the Netherlands for six months, and began to prepare for our teaching adventure without ever having had teacher education courses. We found it helpful to take a Christian teacher workshop in Lynden with Prof. Flokstra from the Calvin Education Department in August.

Teaching

We became commuters, sometimes carpooling with Mrs. Vander Stoep who was the first-grade teacher at Sumas Christian. I found myself standing in front of twenty-two 5th and 6th graders while Ruth faced thirty-eight 3rd and 4th grade boys and girls!

Was I ready? Not really, though I didn't recognize that then – after all, I had started practicing already when I was five or six, right? But now we were preparing lessons for all the subjects for two different grade levels, so we newlyweds had our hands full five days a week and nearly every evening plus most of Saturdays preparing, grading lessons, trying to stay a day or two ahead of the students, with Ruth doing the cooking and on Saturdays the cleaning, baking, laundry, etc. besides her own teaching preparation tasks (a wonder woman whom I should have teamed up with on chore duty too). We were busy but we were young, and we liked the classroom teaching, the kids, and the principal Ben Boxum. Sometimes after school we would go swing a while on the school swings and feel like kids ourselves who happened to be suddenly cast into adult roles of teaching the young. We were inexperienced, we had not finished college (at that time many taught without a degree because of a teacher shortage, especially in private schools), but we were together, and albeit our salaries were small (Ruth $2400 and I $2600 – (yes, women's salaries were less than men's then, too), we managed to save enough that first year to buy a new car – a '58 Beetle with a sunroof for about $1800.

Besides teaching, we were also expected to prepare our kids for the annual school Christmas program – which we did, all new experiences and tasks that somehow we managed to be equal to, including my being pressed into the challenge of preparing an 8th grade girls choir for a program number, the beginning and end of my music director career.

But I was embarrassingly less prepared at reffing a playtime basketball game that Boxum asked me to do one noon hour, for I had never played the game and was quite ignorant about the rules. I was not surprised (and not disappointed) that he never asked me again.

When Mom and Mary returned from their Netherlands stay in the spring, Mary joined our commute and, temporarily, the 6th grade class to catch up with the learning she had missed, and so the poor sis had to adjust not only to a different language again (she had attended school for a while in NL and became fairly fluent in Dutch), but also to a different school and a brother for a teacher.

Also in that spring of 1958, Ruth discovered that we had conceived a new life, not something that had been in our plans, for in the meantime I had been accepted as a transfer student at Calvin and Ruth had an offer to teach at Baxter Christian School in Grand Rapids. We had to reorder our plans, but we were excited as well as a bit anxious at the prospect of becoming first-time parents. The intent of finishing my college education had to be put on hold, and instead I accepted the opportunity to succeed Ben Boxum as principal when he decided to take the offer to become principal of Lynden Christian High School. It was a bit much suddenly – an underprepared teacher with just one year of experience under his belt becoming a teaching principal with the responsibilities of leadership as well as teaching all the subjects of the 7th and 8th grade classes and facing parenthood to boot??

We had enjoyed sharing Mom's home on Front Street and stayed there after they returned, but we found a place for the summer when Walt Lankhaar and spouse were going to spend much of the summer in the NL, asking us to stay in their small country home on the Hannegan close to the Wiser Lake Road and take care of the premises and the dogs. I also took in a similar workshop that the previous summer Ruth and I had both attended, but this time it was with Prof. Jaarsma from the same Calvin department.

It was the first introduction I had to teaching Christianly and I greatly relished these workshops and immediately went to work to implement what I had learned in my teaching and wanting to share this with the other teachers when I would be principal. I also continued to help sister Mary catch up that summer on her preparation to join her former classmates in 7th grade, a task I enjoyed, for this little sis I had babysat back in Opende was and always would be special to me.

When the Lankhaars returned, we moved closer to Sumas in what was known as the Country Home Motel, an old establishment that now served mostly as apartments. It was small and rather neglected (to the pleasure of the mice who didn't welcome our intrusion), but the price was right and its location made Sumas Christian only a short ride away.

I would now face 7th and 8th graders; the 7th graders I knew for they had been my 6th graders, but I quickly found out that the 8th graders were on the whole a bit more challenging than the kids I had the first year, especially when they included a naughty set of twins and a liberal sprinkling of slow and reluctant, unmotivated learners.

What do I remember most vividly from that year? The pleasures of having an office, having Marjorie Visser as a delightful and stimulating colleague who took Ruth's position, the responsibility and mostly satisfying feeling of "being in charge" and enjoying a bit of wry amazement that this undereducated immigrant boy in seven years' time had become head of a small Christian school.

And the less pleasurable? Having to use the principal's discipline "rod" occasionally (which now indicts me with the question of why I didn't use gentle words of reproof and counseling, but alas, my action reflected common practice at that time and my own unexamined impulse); overhearing a teacher yelling at her young charges for being sinful by making mistakes, and discovering that this veteran teacher at the school had no college credit to her name, which I subsequently brought to the attention of the Board, but they found out that the teacher had no intention of taking a college course; discovering that a zealous parent periodically went through the sparse library collection in the principal's office and crossed out all the goshes and darns she could find as well as other "offensive" words or concepts, thereby inciting my censorship-averse ire, for the books that had been acquired, most of them many years earlier, needed no sanitation; that the Board expected me to not only bring a report to their monthly meetings but also a snack, and being dismissed after having delivered the same as if their business deliberations needed no hearing or input from their principal; the Saturday janitor duty of cleaning the whole edifice, including the toilets, waxing the hallway and floors, etc. – for I needed the extra pay to augment the $3600 I was now making since our income had been reduced to one salary, and we had a child on the way and much education left to complete.

A Birth

I don't know if one ever feels ready for parenthood. You know it's coming, and it's a thrilling thought while at the same time there's a tinge of anxiety as you watch the body grow with the mystery of another life whose being springs from your own and whose presence will change your own.

(It would have been good to have someone whom you can feel close to sit you down and plant this question in your mind and heart: what kind of a dad do you want and hope to be to this child and to however many others may come after? Dads-to-be [and moms too] need to ponder that question and re-ponder that often as the years go by and children fill the home, and a question equally important for the groom-to-be.)

Our first-born arrived later than expected, too late to become our special Christmas present, too late to become a tax deduction for 1958, but not too late to be welcomed with gratitude and joy as we received Cynthia Rose on January 7, 1959, a healthy-looking baby who had been well fed in her mother's womb.

Her first home was the humble Country Home Motel, (visited here with Cindy all grown up) but we felt blessed to have her share it with us, and we eagerly welcomed all the nearby family members to come and join us in wonder and admiration.

The winter and spring months passed by rapidly for us, busy with teaching, parenting, future planning that gradually fell in place with me intending to finish my college education at Calvin and Ruth procuring a teaching job at Creston Christian in Grand Rapids, preparing for an 8th grade class outing and graduation program, and keeping little baby Cindy at the center of our attention as she was teaching us how babies grow.

Calvin College

That was hard, really hard – leaving family behind, and friends, and especially to me to leave my widowed mother and my little sister Mary who as a young teenager now could use her older brother's presence and support when needed. That weighed rather heavily on my heart, and I remember having a hard cry that first night in the Montana motel. But it was only going to be for a year, that's what was understood by us and by those we left behind; so, we packed the little VW Beetle with our possessions, and placed our most precious possession as a queen (or baroness) on her throne on top of the boxes, her head close to the ceiling, making an excellent lookout spot for her.

We took Highway 2 across the country through many desolate places but also much beautiful scenery.

It was a long and tiresome trip in a small car whose much maligned heating system was fortunately not needed and whose cooling system definitely was needed but absent. But we were young and hardy, and Miss Cindy was mostly peaceable and lovable. So it was that we at last reached Grand Rapids and enjoyed the welcome of the Bakers – sister Greta, Wayne, and twins Bobby and Lori.

Why had I had this dream that became an unswerving decision to become a Calvin College graduate? It would've been so much simpler to continue teaching at Sumas, stay close to loving family, keep taking courses at Western for the bachelor's degree, maybe sooner or later join Boxum at Lynden Christian as a high school English teacher, and raise a family in beautiful Western Washington! From whence came that urge to go outside my comfort zone, to stretch the limit of our financial means, to leave the place and the people I loved for a "foreign land" – Grand Rapids, Michigan? Maybe because at that time many Lynden high school graduates would leave for Calvin, and I wanted to belong to that group? Maybe because Calvin was then regarded as the flagship higher education institution of the CRC, and my ambition reached for the best? To this day I'm not sure and can't help wondering, but I think more and more that the inner voice that urged me on to Calvin, never even open to considering a more reasonable alternative, was a providential nudge that I've always been grateful for.

We settled initially in the home of Uncle Pete Bosman on Worden St. as the Bosman family was spending the summer in Washington. It was an easy walk from there to the Calvin campus as I started my summer school studies. And it was a gratifying feeling to be actually walking the campus and sit in the classrooms of the place I had had my mind set on for quite some time. Summertime was a good time to get started with small classes and a more relaxed atmosphere.

I found out from the Dean and Registrar's office that I faced taking heavy loads if I hoped to graduate in a year's time, for not everything from Western would transfer. But I was on the way.

What I needed now was to find some part-time work to keep bread on the table and baby food in Cindy's tummy. I found a warehouse job at Acme Insulations. following Trent De Jong who was graduating. Trent was a tall, well-built, strong fellow, whereas I was a skinny runt who had done little physical labor since the TB diagnosis (I was still taking shots regularly at the Kent County Hospital), so there were times when the company boss, Raymond De Jonge, would have to help me out, who as a sympathetic and quality person he did readily. My main job was filling orders, loading, and unloading. Besides that, I also picked up some hours at VanderSys Carpeting downtown. All that left no time for boredom (in fact, I'm not really familiar with that state of being).

The fall semester followed, with us having moved to 1049 Baxter, a nearly all Black neighborhood that once had been mostly Dutch, where we would pay little rent in lieu of serving as caretakers for the upstairs apartment housing four Calvin girls. Ruth now started teaching at Creston Christian, Cindy would be in the home and care of good babysitters, and I would occupy a basement spot as a study. Though the load was formidable, I still needed a part-time job and found one as a school bus driver for Plymouth Christian.

I enjoyed driving that big bus, double clutching and all – I had always wanted to be a Greyhound driver, but this would be as close as I'd come. I enjoyed Calvin too, though it took me a while to adjust my expectations, which had envisioned a heavier religious layer. I even toyed with the idea of writing a Chimes article that would assume the identity of John Calvin, delivering a barrage of critical observations after visiting the college named after him. But that would have been ill advised since I was still very much a newcomer to the campus and still sorting out my faith positions.

I liked my classes, especially taking lit classes with Prof. John Timmerman, Sr. with the gaudy ties, the New Jersey accent, the big laugh, and the contagious love for literature he blessed me with. My course plan was now solidified – I would as a secondary education student major in English, minor in German and Speech. I had always been attracted to the stage, so I tried out for Thespians and was accepted, there too very much as a newcomer.

But camaraderie tends to be strong among would-be and seasoned cast members, and I really enjoyed some close friendships there, especially with Roger Heerspink, a consummate actor, a fascinating introvert, a master of German, a deep thinker who could also display a brilliant wit. I tried out for "Our Town," the story that had touched me originally with the spark that ignited my love for story, but a four-year member of the group and a favorite of director Ervina Boeve landed the role I had tried out for, and rightly so, for Mrs. Boeve had never seen me act, and, though I thought I could do a bang-up job in the role of Stage Manager, in fact I had never been in an ambitious stage play. But I did have a leading role in two one-act theater-in-the – round plays, and that was more than I could rightfully expect.

I also joined the Chapel Choir (at that time daily chapel was still mandatory) and the Calvin Oratorio Society to sing in the annual "Messiah", which I had done in Lynden once or twice as well.

Two required education courses were taught by Professors Flokstra and Jaarsma, and I quickly discovered that my Lynden experience and appreciation of these gentlemen were not shared by my classmates – in fact they were the butt of many jokes, some of them deserved, as I came to find out.

In the spring I had to do my student teaching, a prospect that didn't faze me the way it did many others, for I had had two years of rather challenging classroom experiences. I was assigned to teach junior high English at Kelloggsville Christian School, grades 8 and 9. When I showed up in stage make-up in preparation for a performance right after class, I think I sort of won them over from the start, for even when I later made the 9th graders read Jane Austen's Pride and Prejudice, they tolerated it peaceably.

In the spring prospective teachers needed to start the job application process, and needy schools began to contact placement offices to look for teachers. I must have sent out some inquiries too, and I remember stopping at the principal's office at GR Christian High. I wasn't offered a job there, but I did hear from Mark Vander Ark, the principal at Lynden Christian which might possibly have an opening in junior high with my former teacher Lee Vander Ark scheduled to leave his slot in Language Arts open. But I also was wanted by a rather new small Christian school in Fort Lauderdale which needed a teacher for grades 4-8, and a small school in Langley, B.C. which needed a teaching principal for grades 6,7, and 8. Closer by came an offer from South Christian High School to teach the senior English courses.

Yes, we had intended to return "home" to Washington and the beautiful Pacific Northwest – but we were expecting a second child in June which would complicate traveling and which also meant that Ruth did not teach the second semester (ouch!), and obviously we needed financially the best salary package offered, and that turned out to be South Christian, my choice also because it would mean I would be teaching high school seniors and that appealed to me.

When I found myself among the graduates at the ceremony in the downtown Civic Auditorium, it was an immensely gratifying feeling – yes, the first college grad in the family, but more so because the road to the A.B. degree had not been typical (no high school diploma, no financial support, no campus residency with dorm living, no college clubs or parties or dates but marriage and a growing family) and certainly had not always been assured. I felt much appreciation for my dear Ruthie for the support she had been during this whole challenging adventure, and we were very grateful that my mom and brother Sid and sister-in-law Margie came all the way out to help us celebrate.

Another Birth

In June, daughter Judy was born, and her birth's joy gave way to angst when we discovered that she was born with spina bifida and subsequent hydrocephalus. No parent is ever prepared for a child's compromised medical future, and we certainly were not. We prayed, we sought out a good pediatrician, we consulted with a neurosurgeon, we leaned on family, we worried, and we knew Judy would always have special needs that would require our sensitive awareness and support.

(Ruth's response to this unexpected and unsettling event is in the Supplement p. 335).

Part Six: Practicing the Dream

The South Christian Years

I felt I was in the right place from the start.

Though the big belligerent senior boys who were not on the academic track challenged me initially, they soon found out that this young teacher they were going to send through fiery trials took quick command and was not hesitant to impose penalties when rules were broken. When other new colleagues joined, like Don and Alyce Boender, Harry Boonstra, and Ed Start, we meshed quickly and became life-long friends – in fact now, '20-'21, Don, Ed, and I still meet every week for coffee (sadly, Harry passed a few years ago).

In the seven years I was there, my teaching load did not always stay the same: I functioned temporarily as librarian for one or two periods a day, always taught college prep English lit., not always non-college prep Senior English, in later years German I and II, and Advanced Composition, a course I had introduced, and added to that in the last two years or so the supplemental Driver's Education teaching. I was asked to coach Forensics and direct the senior play (which the Boenders took over after me) – my speech courses and drama experience had prepared me well for these tasks — and I honestly enjoyed doing all that was asked of me.

The teaching week would usually end with a family supper trip to McDonald's, then a babysitter for the kids, and parents off to a S.Chr. basketball game or a travelogue in the gym and to a coffee place afterward. At Christmas time some of us would trek together with the kids to a Christmas-tree field to chop down a festive winner, and on New Year's Eve we would sometimes go roller skating or bowling or just hang out, which soon became an annual event with a small group of friends, a tradition that continues to this day.

There were also times that the teachers would put a skit together, supplemented with some band instruments with which musical colleagues were eager to show off their unpracticed skills. On Shakespeare's birthday we hosted a Shakespeare party in our home, asking the participants to come dressed up as a Shakespeare character (which the others would have to identify) and deliver a few chosen lines by that character – it was a smashingly enjoyable success, which we should have repeated every ten years or so, but never did.

Some of us who were drama lovers felt that a dramatic stage presentation cannot only please the audience with good entertainment but that it also can touch all of us with serious social or moral issues, like racism. Racism was alive and well in the S. Christian area when redlining was often covertly practiced. Harry Boonstra and I were going to direct a poignantly moving faculty play that focused on racism in the South. In those days the Board had to approve plays put on by the school, and when they read the play we had chosen, they sent word that it was not approved, no reasons given. I sent a letter of indignant protest and sought a meeting with the Board, to which they never responded.

Not only could drama get you in trouble, but so could literature. I was using a paperback of Great Short Stories in which one story had its setting in Africa where native women didn't cover their breasts. One morning after the class had just started, the principal knocked on the door, came in, and told the students they had to march to the bookstore down the hall and turn in their sinful books by order of the School Board. Again, there had been no conference about the issue, simply a command.

Yes, racism and censorship raised their ugly visages in this Christian school, maybe not so much as a present vice among Board members as it was their sensitivity to and fear of possible parent criticism and subsequent withdrawal of financial support. In the case of this "dirty book," I found out later that the complaint to her parents had come from a student who, oh sad irony, at the time of the complaint was pregnant. I'm not a public crusader or fighter by nature, but such encounters did reinforce my convictions about the purpose of literature in education. I wrote about that in articles but also a small piece in the school's student paper:

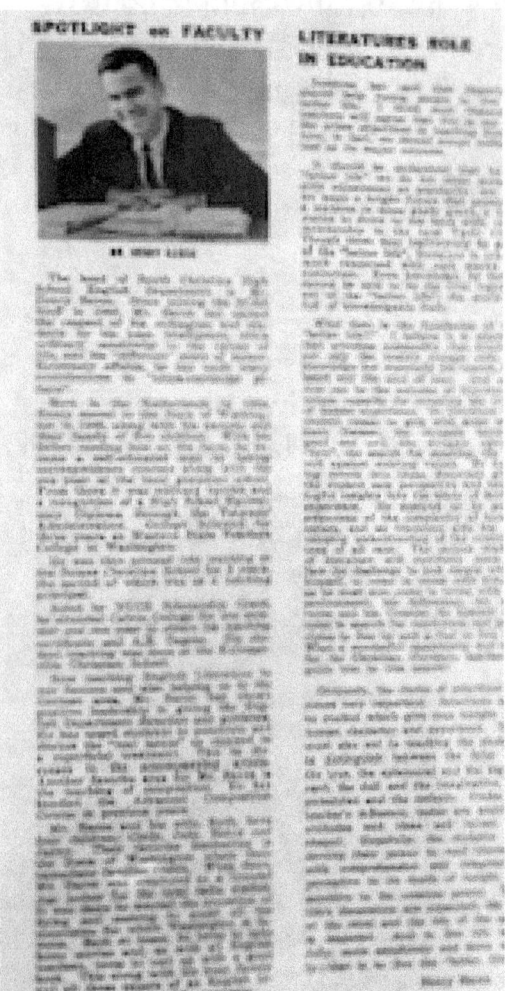

There were many students I taught in my classroom I still remember vividly, especially those who left a story attached in my memory, stories that would fill pages. But they'll keep in the pages of my memory, some very good ones, some not so much.

I should mention the occasional Pine Rest students I had, students who were there for mental treatment of one kind or another but who were well enough to take some classes. I had a special feeling for them – they were not home, and this wasn't their school. They were loners but often more sensitive to language and literature than the "normal" students. One such student was Marti, serious and silent. But her soul absorbed the meaning and beauty and emotion of literature, and she was grateful. At the end of the semester, she sent me a card and gave me a gift that has been a special presence in my office/study ever since = Rodin's The Thinker.

I will always wonder what happened in the rest of her life; I fervently hope she not only survived but thrived!

But we didn't live in the classroom – life for many includes home, family, friends, finances, arts, children, summer vacations, and more. In February 1962 Ruth and I invited S.Chr. friends over to our Baxter place on a Sunday night to sing from the CRC blue hymnal, and we liked it so much that we decided to do this once a month, taking turns hosting and serving a potluck feed, agreeing that we would sing through the whole hymnal, skipping only the unsingable numbers, and having little idea at the time that almost 60 years later we would still be singing as a group with seven original members still included and harmonizing. And we also have lovely memories of our extended outings to Chicago, Toronto, and California.

Also, in 1962 we moved from Baxter to our first purchased home – 1040 Alexander, close to Neland

Church that we would join and remain members to this day – where Jayne and Lisa would be baptized, where I would serve many terms as elder, including chair of elders and chair of council, teaching catechism, and much committee work. Ruth too would become quite involved in Neland organizations, including several terms as a Pastoral Care Associate. And our oldest daughter would one day become Pastor Cindy at Neland.

It was also around this time that I began to work toward an M.A. degree by taking U of M extension courses offered in Grand Rapids. I fulfilled the language requirement by passing the German test, which enabled me to complete the degree in a fairly short time of taking extension courses and a fulltime summer session in '65 on the UM campus in Ann Arbor to complete the M.A. degree in English Language and Literature, (while Ruth and the children boarded a train in Chicago to take them to WA for a summer with family in Lynden). I had a very enjoyable time of traversing the beautiful campus to classes every day and staying with others in the "Dutch House" with excellent food and accommodations. The internal drive to academic advance was still very much in motion – there was never a question of should I or shouldn't I, and for that too I've always been grateful. The degree was awarded in April '66.

Earlier summers during that seven-year span included cross-country trips (sometimes car, sometimes train) "back home" to the Washington family, where Sid the first summer back (1961) gave me a job as disc jockey and announcer for KLYN-FM. Other summers I worked with Harry Boonstra as ceiling light fixture cleaner for GM and then on the floor feeding buttons into a stamping machine; or painting houses with John Verstraete; or polishing antique clocks for the Pastoor Antiques shop on Eastern; as well as painting our own Alexander home which seemed to need a new coat nearly every year.

During the school year I needed to make some extra pocket money to feed a family of six and pay Christian school tuition for the older children, and so I found myself trying to fit shoes on mostly women's feet for Nobil Shoes for .75 cents an hour, and later finding the right shirt or socks for gentlemen for $1.00 an hour for Rogers Department Store, where the only renown I gained was as an amateur graphologist who analyzed some staff members' character through their handwriting.

The summer of '66 was spent in Ripon, CA when I was awarded an NDEA fellowship for an 8-week session at the University of the Pacific in Stockton.

I had also received a fellowship at Cornell University, a more academically prestigious institution, but I felt the pull westward, which could include a side trip "home" to the Lynden family.

CHOOL

teacher? This year, for several members of our faculty, summer meant classes. Earning nine hours of credit beyond his masters. Mr. Baron spent eight weeks at the University of Pacific in Stockton, California. All fifty teachers in his institute had been awarded scholarships. Mr. Baron's courses included a Seminar in Myth and Symbolism in Fiction, classes in Criticism of the drama, Rhetoric of the Critical Essay, and lectures on Modern Critical Methods. The requirements for the courses included: reading 23 plays, 6 books, and writing 7 critical discussions of the readings. When asked why he took these courses, Mr. Baron replied, "I thought it would be helpful in interpreting modern literature, and it was — to some extent."

The Europe Trip

But there was also the summer of '67 when I was accepted as a chaperone for mostly East Grand Rapids high school seniors who would go on a four-week tour of Europe sponsored by the World Affairs Council. It was a long and maybe wrong time for leaving the family, with Jayne just four and leaving Ruth in solo charge of the whole brood, but at the time I thought it would broaden and enrich my future teaching, and I was also very eager to finally reconnect with the fatherland for the first time since 1948, as we would spend a bit of time first of all in the Netherlands.

I remember now: cousin Tine waiting for me as we arrived in Amsterdam; quick trip to Oudwoude and Tante Janke with Tine; the beautiful quaint German villages and the translator role I often had to fill; one student's lost passport and the day and night I had to spend with him in Munich with unexpected help from a German encounter in the central station; the soul-stirring beauty of Austria and Switzerland; the Sistine Chapel ceiling; da Vinci's The Last Supper in Milan; the awesome Michelangelo's David in Florence and the evening's romantic outdoor Pitti Palace concert; the sculpted gardens of the Versailles Palace and the midnight moonlit walk through Paris boulevards from the streetcar termination point all the way back to our hotel, stopping on the way in the bar frequented by Hemingway back in the 20s – yes, memories – that also include long, long bus rides, teenage hormones, fatigue, and missing my dear wife and kids.

But all this while my thoughts had also drifted now and again to what lay ahead, for I had applied for an NDEA TTT fellowship offered at the University of Illinois aimed at improving high school English teaching through leaders such as English department chairpersons and curriculum directors, and I had been accepted. I had already been quite active in such leadership at S.Chr. and I was eager to gain more background and expertise in that area. S.Chr. granted me a leave of absence for a year, so all lights turned green for a challenging change in our lives, a change that would alter the course of my direction.

The U of I Year

And thus we packed the stuff we needed to furnish an empty apartment into a U-Haul truck, rented our home to a seminary couple, and off we were to a new adventure in Champaign-Urbana, Illinois. With four small children, the sense of responsibility weighed pretty heavily on me: would this be the right move for all of us? Would the study load be reasonable? Would Ruth's part-time job in the Montessori School be a sufficient supplement to my fellowship stipend? Would the three oldest find a friendly classroom atmosphere?

We were grateful to discover a "yes" to these wonderings and others. It was a good experience for all, though son Henry found the new school adjustment a bit challenging initially. But the 3-bedroom apartment, the cornfields across Mattis, the Hessel Park Church and its non-traditional minister Boelo Boelens, a parcel of great new friends, the congenial group of 20 that made up our TTT Fellows (including Grace Huitsing, English teacher at Grand Rapids Christian High, whom I had known for some time) and our gentle mentor/leader, but widely known and highly esteemed Dr. J.N.Hook, the political and cultural whirlwinds that were swirling across the nation and roiled university campuses into demonstrations and protest actions, the stimulation and challenges of the academic studies we had come for – all of this I found energizing and gratifying. I felt blessed to be there, to have this opportunity that opened up and that continued to advance me on the path I had dreamed of and had chosen to pursue. What made the U of I adventure even sweeter was a TTT fellowship bonus – all of us would attend the National Council Teachers of English convention in November, and this year the convention would be held in Honolulu, Hawaii!

It turned into an amazing treat of traveling together, seeing Hawaii for the first time, getting picked up for church by Ruth's cousin Linda Terpstra and her husband, attending many, many wonderful sessions, chairing in an associate role to which I had been invited in a session on "Literature in Academic High Schools" (my first official function at an NCTE convention but with many to follow in the future), and so much more.

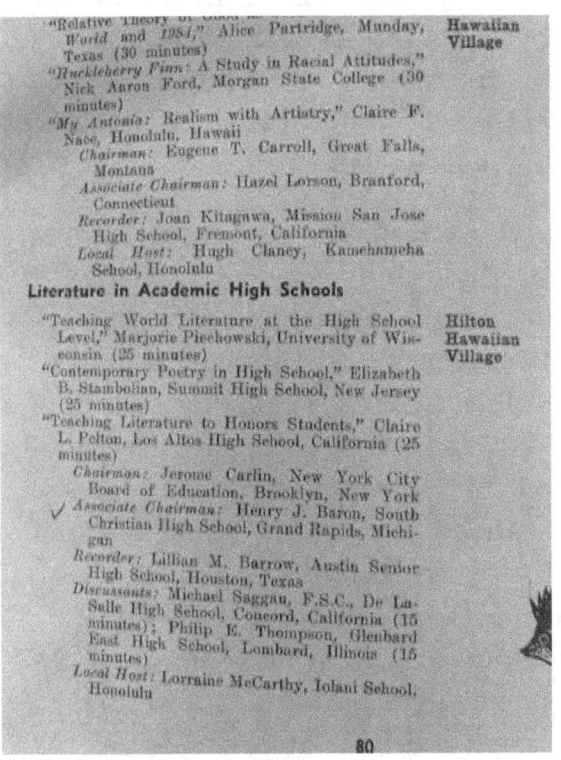

One memory of that year has remained vivid and deep: the night I spent at the hospital with our son who was under observation for meningitis, a possibility that fills a parental heart with a measure of dread. Blessedly he slept through the night, aided by sedatives, and I was blessed by a thrust of inspiration that enabled me to write the core of a long project paper for Dr. Hook, "A Thematic Framework for the Teaching of Literature" – yeah, he gave me an A, called it "brilliant," and asked a copy for himself.

This new direction I was following by being at the U of I and immersed in academics (but balanced by family and social and church life) continued in an unexpected way when I received a note from Prof. Ken Kuiper from the English department at Calvin, asking if I would be interested in applying for a position there since he needed help in teaching and supervising students preparing to become English teachers. At S.Chr. I had had several Calvin student teachers with Ken as their supervisor, and one semester he had even invited me to make a presentation to one of his classes. I applied, received an invitation from chairman George Harper for an interview, made the trip to Grand Rapids, and was interviewed by the department and later by the Board.

President Spoelhof, separately, demurred because he feared that I would not be able to go on to the necessary PhD level after earning an Advanced Certificate (a kind of Specialist Degree) which would come with my fellowship year at the U of I, so I became designated as a Visiting Instructor which would allow them to terminate me if indeed I couldn't go on to the next academic level expected of college profs (but I had already been assured by the university that I could). I accepted and was accepted, and now I would not go back to S.Chr. but had an agreement with principal Kool that if I found college teaching not my thing, I could come back to teach high school. We would return to 1040 Alexander, but much for me would change.

A Calvin Beginning: 1968-70

The dream to graduate from Calvin came true, but I had not expected to someday teach there, and so when in the fall of '68 I did, I pinched myself, as I would many times in future years. I had an office, a student helper (Sandy VDZ), and a reasonable load of classroom teaching. Fewer classroom hours than high school teaching, yes, but the preparation time was no comparison, especially since everything had to be planned from scratch and expected to be more substantive.

I liked it, including the supervision of student teachers, one of whom took me to a pretty much all Black inner city high school (South High) where she faced the challenge as a teacher to motivate reluctant and even resistant learners and as a young white person to gain their respect and cooperation. It was an eye opener for me too and I felt limited in my coaching skills in a classroom so different from the all-white classrooms of South Christian.

Understandably these first two years of college teaching was a learning experience, but a good one. There were occasions to interact with Education Department folk, and I favored communication about our shared interest in teacher education, but I would find out that my partner and friend Ken Kuiper was all about keeping a rigidly observed distance from that department – his domain of English teacher education was sacrosanct and not to be diluted by possible influence or expectation from the education department staff. My friendliness toward that staff would come back to bite me.

I had a two-year appointment, and I knew that I needed to enter a PhD program for continuing college teaching. I had been encouraged to enroll by its education department at U of I, and I checked out the possibility at Michigan State; and then came the call from J.N. Hook that there was a spot open in yet another government sponsored PhD program out of the English department at U of I, and he offered it to me! He had spoken to me back in 1967-68 about pursuing a PhD and given my age, not to put it off too long to tackle the academically formidable challenge. And here was the opportunity, once again unexpected, and accepted with joyful gratitude. Calvin offered a two-year appointment as Assistant Professor and granted a two-year leave to enable me to go on for the required doctorate. I received some funding ($2,500) from the Grand Rapids Foundation, and besides the fellowship stipend and salary Ruth would receive as a teacher in the Urbana Public Schools as a 1st and 2nd grade teacher, we should make it financially, especially since our kids would be in the public schools at no tuition. So, once more we rented out our home on Alexander, packed a truck, and landed back on Mattis in the same apartment building we had lived in before.

The PhD Years: 1970-72

This was it – I was where I needed and wanted to be, not without some apprehension but especially with fervent hope for a good outcome and gratitude for this God-given opportunity. It was a lot of work, and now and then I'd find myself in a course for which I lacked sufficient background, exacerbating the load. Much had to be crammed in, for I'd given myself only a year for the required course work (fortunately, some of the credits from the '67-'68 year transferred to this program), preparation for the prelims, choosing a dissertation committee and a topic, needing to teach a poetry class as a TA, and doing some workshops in schools with Bruce Hekman who had been one of my student teachers at S.Christian and was now in the same program with me.

Yes, there was pressure, for Ruth as well with teaching and mothering, but there were good friends on campus and in Hessel Park Church, "and all things worked together for good." I passed the prelims (huge relief), my dissertation plan was accepted, and we would move back home to GR where I would do my dissertation work, kids would go back to Oakdale Christian, and Ruth would continue her education at Calvin, this time, as a faculty wife, free of charge. But there did come a fly into the ointment: a rather angry letter came from Ken Kuiper expressing his total disapproval of my cooperative spirit and attitude toward the Education Department colleagues and therefore terminating my participation in the English teacher education program. Yes, that was a big blow, very upsetting and dismaying. I was advised by chairman Harper that I had two choices – I could look for a position somewhere else, or I could come back teaching but with no involvement with student teachers. I had several opportunities for changing directions (working with the NCTE, teaching English Education at the University of Illinois at Chicago, English department chair at a prestigious academic high school near Chicago), but I didn't pursue them. In spite of this unforeseen change, I felt an internal nudge not unlike one I had felt at Western in Bellingham and one that made me want a Calvin degree and that had wanted me to stay in Grand Rapids rather than return to Lynden, and that now made me feel the Calvin choice was still the only right one, also because the family could resume the life they were already comfortably familiar with, including church and school.

The Summer of '71

That summer became a special one for all of us. We drove from Champaign to put the children on the plane in Chicago for their flight to Seattle, where Dad and Mom Bosman would pick them up for a stay with them in Lynden while we went on to GR to join a DIS flight to Amsterdam where Sid and Margaret would join us on a nostalgic journey to the dear places and people the Baron family had left twenty-three years earlier.

It was really the first time back for me, other than the quick stop and fleeting visits with a few in '67, and it was deeply emotional.

The four of us made the rounds to all the surviving uncles and aunts, plus more than a few cousins.

I wonder now what they were thinking when they saw me again – I'd been a young boy of 14 with hardly one ULO year behind me when they'd said their goodbyes in 1948, and now I had returned as a 37-year old with an AB, an MA, an AC, and a year away from having a PhD behind my name. Maybe they didn't give that a thought, as I don't think I did – we were too caught up in the joys of reunion.

The beauty of it was that in 1971 not so much had changed yet – not so much the church we had been baptized in, not so much the farmhouse and buildings that had been our home (after church we were invited by cousin Grietje and husband Folkert, who had taken over our place in '48, to come to D219 for dinner, and thus once more I sat at the kitchen table in the place of many memories, now freshly revived), not so much the schools we had attended and the towns we had lived in and next to, not so much the people we had known and loved and loved still. And when Sid and I drove the narrow sand path to the Komize Bosk, got out and looked across the fields at our former place in the distance, thoughts flooded back to the years that place had been our home through times of fear and fun, those fields that had been ours to roam and explore, those woods behind us that had been our destination for adventure, and all of which had sometimes in the intervening years in a place more than 5000 miles away pressed tears of remembrance and nostalgia to our eyes.

We stood there, the two brothers, falling silent and yielding to the feeling that all this had been a close and dear part of our lives and still was.

After "doing Holland" we ventured into Germany, our WWII enemy, where I needed to rely on my fading German facility at times and where we thoroughly enjoyed its landscape dotted with charming, picturesque villages and towns with cobblestoned roadways and half-timbered buildings dating back to the Middle Ages, its many imposing and impressive castles and cathedrals, idyllic lake scenes and the Rhine of romance guarded by the 433-foot high Lorelei – this and more proved to be a wonderful icing on the family reunions cake we had enjoyed in the fatherland.

We flew back to our adopted land and to our young family which had been in the good care of their grandparents, and the Great Northern took us all back to Chicago and then on to Grand Rapids in time for the start of the new school year.

It felt good to have the children back at Oakdale, two blocks from our home, to have Ruth back at Creston Christian, to be back at Neland, a block from our doorstep, and for me to buckle down on the dissertation project which would take me to several high school English departments as a consultant, but would have me working more intensely with the English staff at Illiana Christian High School in Lansing, Illinois.

My dissertation title would be "An Investigation in the Consultant's Role as an Agent of Change in the High School English Program." As the high school English teacher I had been, I had always been on the alert to what the English curriculum and practice should look like at its best and what new developments and ideas one should know about in the teaching of literature and grammar and composition, but I also knew that many a classroom teacher developed his or her own tradition of thinking about and practice of the subject and is loath to change.

The Illiana principal wanted the school's English teachers to be challenged by some new ideas and eagerly accepted my offer to come and present that challenge. I would work with the teachers, especially the chairman and leading teacher of the English department, Vern Boerman, on a continuing basis, conducting sessions with them at least once a month. The process and the outcome would become the substance of my dissertation. My hopes were high, but I also knew it would not be an easy stroll among gentle slopes of a sun-smiling landscape – it might become more of a rocky climb on some steep mountain paths.

Which it did.

Fortunately, the teachers became more friends than adversaries and the chair cooperative, though somewhat disorganized. I would make the long drive to the busy Chicago expressways, turn off on Torrance, have our session, often go home with the chair for supper and become familiar with a remarkable family whose level of thought, imagination, and conversation became the most interesting and impressive and enjoyable part of my Illiana visits. And when night fell, the principal had a bedroom for me, and so I got to know that family too and enjoyed many a serious conversation with the principal's wife.

When I wasn't on the road to Illiana or more nearby Christian high schools, I had an office space at the National Union of Christian Schools (NUCS), which later became Christian Schools International (CSI), where I did most of the writing and planning.

And when not away, I would be home at noon to welcome the kids home for lunch which I prepared for them – and that remains my favorite memory of that project year.

A close second would be turning in my dissertation in the spring, then defending it before a committee, hearing positive comments, even the mention of possibly

being publishing worthy, then leaving the committee to decide, and soon afterword being welcomed back in and congratulated on earning the PhD!

When I was back outside, I was walking on air and I wanted to share this feeling most of all with my family – Dad and Sid especially, but Dad was no longer there, and I wasn't sure how much my brother had tuned in to this whole project. So, I drove back from Urbana to Grand Rapids, thinking back to that campus moment sixteen years earlier at Western in Bellingham when I had felt

that flush of pleasure and promise of having started on an academic track at last, and I heard myself say, "I think I'll go on to a PhD!" It had been a long and strenuous haul and not without doubts and tensions. But now, heading back north over the expressways toward family and a possible future at Calvin, I felt a need to celebrate my blessings – maybe a bar party with campus buddies? (But they were scattered all over the country now.) A home party with family and friends with good drinks and gebakjes? (But everybody was busy and who could make the gebakjes?)

Oh, but Don and Alyce Boender orchestrated a Calvin campus party at the Knollcrest Manor House with invitations to some Calvin administrative staff, faculty friends, and colleagues, and it felt wonderful. I felt blessed, but I also knew that a PhD comes with a barrel full of expectations and responsibilities in academia. When someone in an organization or institution is promoted to CEO, the honor is relished, but the new status isn't going to make life easier and more relaxed. But again, I welcomed the challenge with still relatively youthful enthusiasm.

Part Seven: The Calvin Years – 1972-1997

Where does one begin when reminiscing and trying to remember the many years of teaching? There are drawers full of files that hold memories, and that makes you wonder.

Memories – which do you want to highlight, and why? Which do you want to leave out, and don't explain why. What did what you taught mean to you? What did the students you taught mean to you? What did your colleagues mean to you? What was expected of you? What influenced and shaped you? And what besides academics was an important part of your life during those years of your thirties which became the forties and then the fifties, and oh dear, even the sixties?

Teaching

I looked forward to resume teaching at Calvin; I had enjoyed those first two years and I gratefully anticipated many more.

Looking back, I wonder now – did I feel nervous? And I'm surprised that besides first day flutters, nerves didn't attack the way they did for some, and I'm not sure why not. Maybe because of my early years preschool practice on the front yard of our humble Opende home? (That makes me smile now.)

I liked most of the students too. They were there to get an education and, though some more than others, worked hard at it.

They tended to be rather passive and quiet, though.

I wanted their questions, responses, interaction – but it was sometimes hard to get them to open up. Maybe the fault lay with me; maybe I set too formal a tone or didn't open myself up enough. Maybe I should have done more bridge building between their world and the world in literature. Maybe I didn't tell enough stories or needed to present a more jocular persona. And though sometimes, with a congenial set of students, I managed that and enjoyed it, I probably didn't present that persona consistently, but I don't get to do it over. I was encouraged, though, by the positive evaluations I got from many students.

I spent a lot of time preparing for each class, especially those first years when for a new course everything was done for the first time. Much reading and planning went into the lessons I would write out for the most part. But I greatly appreciated the student assistants I was privileged to have throughout my teaching years. They helped with library research work, checking objective parts of quizzes and tests, running off handouts, etc. Sometimes a student assistant would need a listening ear as well, and they found me willing to lend it.

I enjoyed the subjects I taught (which included Composition, Intro. to Lit., American Lit., Canadian Lit., Young Adult Lit., Teaching of Writing, a number of special Interim and M.A.T. courses, (and, together with Ken Kuiper, a Rapid Reading course), and the interaction I had with students who came to my office for conferences and mentoring. Often the conversations turned to the personal, to issues of the heart that harbor pain and secrets and confusion; but also hopes and faith and joy. A number of those students stayed in touch with me long after they graduated, and a few became lifelong friends. I found that one of the great blessings of teaching. When I look now at student evaluation comments in my files, I feel a warm wave of gratitude for the privilege I had, through the courses I taught, to touch a life positively, even if it was only for one class session or for the duration of a course. The teaching of language and literature allowed me to share my appreciation for disciplined and creative use of language and for the ways that good literature can plumb the depths of human feelings and motivations.

But sometimes it takes only one student to eclipse a teacher's sunlight and cast them in a moonless darkness. I had one such student in freshman English. She started out well. I knew her mother with whom I had had a pleasant conversation when I did a presentation at a Seattle Christian school evening event. I had conferences with the student and was happy to have her in class. But as the semester went on, her performance went steadily in decline; she failed the required departmental grammar test and became increasingly uncommunicative. Her preparation for the final research paper was badly deficient and I began to worry about her chances of passing the course. That's when I received a letter from her mother, addressed to me, as well as to the department chair, the academic dean, and the president. It was a poisonous letter, saturated with false reports from her daughter and judgments about me that lowered me to the status of a monster who should not be teaching. I felt like I had been cast into outer darkness. Depression closed in on me in a way it had rarely done before. Subsequent conversations with the chair and the dean helped to bring back some light. I had the record of the student's attendance, her scores, her papers, her absences. I received the support and encouragement of my superiors, and that was a balm. Eventually I was ready to respond to the mother's letter of attack in a reasonable and civil manner, laying out the facts of her daughter's performance slide. And in time I recovered the joie de vivre essential to wholesome living and teaching. But the soul-shaking experience was never forgotten.

How did I see my task as teacher, though?

I wish someone at some point in my preparation had challenged me with that question, challenged me to think that through and thereby make my teaching more intentional in plan, purpose, and performance.

I think I always wanted to connect what I taught to a student's life – the way we use language, the words we choose to get closer to the truth of an issue or an experience or a feeling. And through the literature to get closer to what it means to be human in search of a sense of significance, pursued in all kinds of bad and good ways, in all kinds of times of agony and loss and times of peace and joy. But a more reflective intentionality might have informed my preparation and enhanced my performance. For I wanted my students not only to become more competent writers and readers, but I hoped that they would also grow in their awareness of and love for words that through the imagination connect mind and heart and make them larger, grow closer to the human experience shaped by history, culture, race, home, faith and more, toward a greater understanding of self and others.

Colleagues

What makes the years at Calvin and the English Department such a pleasant memory include the colleagues I had the pleasure of getting to know and work with.

Row: S. Wiersma, J. Timmerman, W. Vande Kopple, J. Vanden Bosh, H. Baron, G. Harper, J. Cox, H. Ten Harmsel. Row Two: K. Kuiper ... le, P. Heuvelink, P. Oppewall, C. Walhout, M. Walters, C. Otten, I. Krose. Not Pictured: E. Ericson.

Not only to work with but also to play with. Most of us in the department at some time or other played at first handball and later racquet ball together, and some of us played regularly once or twice a week for many years. We would play a foursome, which made the court a bit crowded but proved a great workout for our powers of concentration and reaction time. It was a very enjoyable way to maintain some physical conditioning.

A game or two of tennis supplemented the exercise for heart and lungs and arm and legs. It's a game we played till I was well into my 70s.

But there were also the social get-togethers, picnics, celebrations, making music, and the memorable hours of lunch time in the department meeting room early on when Wiersma, Tiemersma, and Harper were still regaling us all with enthralling stories of military service, former memorably idiosyncratic colleagues and staff members, while smoke from cigars and cigarettes gradually shrouded us in a haze.

I can't think of department colleagues, though, without remembering with much sadness even now those who passed too soon and so unexpectedly:

Henry Zylstra died well before I joined the department, on an Amsterdam street, at 47; Harmon Hook at 39, Howard Conaughy at 34, Stan Wiersma at

55, Lionel Basney at 52, Bill Vande Kopple at 63, Ken Kuiper at 68 – all gifted and wonderful people whose passing left a deep hole and for whose permanent absence we grieved but whose memory and influence still blesses us, blesses me.

Moonlighting

Calvin's pay scale was modest; the beginning salary was perhaps even a bit below what I would've made at South Christian. So, I looked for some moonlighting opportunities, with Ken's help; all four of our children were in Christian school now and the tuition took a big slice out of my $8,100 salary. Both Ken and I were needed to teach an evening course at Grand Valley University. I enjoyed not only the chance to make a few extra bucks but also the difference in class atmosphere and student diversity. The same thing was true of classes at Grand Rapids Junior College where I also did some evening teaching. There the range in age and job preparation and personal background made it especially interesting.

But there was also the opportunity for summer school teaching, offering both regular college courses but also in-service teacher seminars for teachers looking to expand and enrich their professional preparation. I greatly enjoyed getting to know a number of English teachers from different parts of the country.

Consulting

Other opportunities for augmenting the income in other teaching modes surfaced as well. I had started doing work for NUCS while at South Christian already, writing "An Instructional Guide to Teaching Literature Thematically" for both junior and senior high teachers, published in 1967. When I started teaching at Calvin I was appointed as the CSI Language Arts Consultant, following Nel Vander Ark who had been my colleague at So. Christian.

NATIONAL UNION OF CHRISTIAN SCHOOLS

865 TWENTY-EIGHTH ST., S. E.
GRAND RAPIDS, MICHIGAN 49508

HENRY J. BARON
Language Arts Consultant

Phone (616) 245-8618

That appointment kept me busy many a subsequent summer, initially writing a monograph with the fetching title of "'Dirty' Books in Christian Schools" which went through several printings and acclaimed as a Christian Schools International (CSI, formerly NUCS) best seller (even though it made a case for *Catcher in the Rye*, a perennially censored classic). Censorship was alive and well, or maybe I should say was contorting and eager for combat in a number of schools. Some of my most challenging visits were to those schools where a mass of parents gathered usually in the school's gym, sometimes ready to fire teachers who had introduced their children of the covenant to offensive language or actions or leanings in literature. The tension index was high in such meetings.

My view of Christian education as preparation rather than protection was not shared by all. But I did my best to convey my convictions in as non-confrontational a way as I could, through talks and articles in the CSI magazine "Christian Home & School," as well as in the "Christian Educators Journal" in which my most direct defense of a much-censored book, *A Wrinkle in Time*, titled

"Wrinkle on Trial" appeared. I also wrote a great many short reviews of Young Adult books for a CSI publication. But many other projects followed as well.

It was a privilege for me to gather and direct teams of good teachers to work with me in putting together a five-volume literature series (Soundings) for junior high and a four-volume series (Touchstones) for senior high students, along with teaching guides, as well as several other language arts and media instructional guides. And we had a good time doing it, having fun as a team working with each other and confident that we were doing something valuable by introducing junior and senior high school students to engaging literature and valuable language learning.

As consultant and projects director I was often invited to do teacher workshops in various Christian school settings and conferences, places that included Pittsburgh, New Jersey, Edmonton, Calgary, Iowa, Ontario. And during one interim period I spent most of a month on a kind of Chautauqua tour, going to many schools doing chapels, teacher groups and classroom presentations, wearing myself out but happy the tour included California and Washington.

The most surprising CSI "assignment," however, sent me to Tasmania as keynote speaker at an annual Christian Educators Conference, a conference that included Christian school teachers from all over Australia and New Zealand.

Brother Sid decided to come along, and we had a great time visiting Sydney and environs before taking a flight to Tasmania. There we were warmly welcomed among teachers and leaders who were much closer to pioneers than teachers in the U.S. where Christian education had been a going enterprise for nearly a century. But they were seriously dedicated and eager for moral support and guidance.

Sid too felt very much at home among them and delighted the group with his crazy sense of humor and storytelling charm during conference breaks.

The most lasting "legacy" of that contact was meeting Nel Van't Wout, a struggling teacher from Dunedin, NZ. Struggling because she felt underprepared for

Christian teaching and because her school was small and underfunded. Her dream was to come to Calvin College to augment her education and preparation. So, we had some long talks. That was the beginning of our lasting association as a family with Nel, for she eventually did come to Grand Rapids, did earn both a bachelor and master's degree from Calvin, and became thoroughly integrated into the extended Baron family as well as in the Calvin community. Her school in Dunedin not only survived but eventually under her dedicated leadership grew and became more solidly established.

Nel had a sister living in New York state which brought her back now and again, never skipping Grand Rapids in those travels. And our first retirement trip took us to Dunedin, NZ!

Academics

I've never thought of myself as a scholar really, or as particularly scholarly. Yet, I was always attracted to academia, the place for research, education, and scholarship. I had of course taken several scholarly courses in my master's and PhD programs. And those courses demanded scholarly course papers, most of which I had enjoyed crafting and in the course of which I discovered that I loved research. But I never found enough time to do a great deal of it as a professor.

Education – of course! In fact, teaching was central at Calvin, and hopefully still is. When I attended Calvin as a student, most of my profs were primarily teachers who were not required to conduct scholarly research that led to publishing. And when I joined the faculty, that mode was still mostly in place. It began to change in the 70s, though, when academic activity beyond teaching became the expectation for faculty if they were reaching for tenure. And faculty delivered! There's been an impressive outpouring of first-rate scholarship in the form of articles and chapters in prestigious publications, and a good many books making valuable contributions to the academic disciplines in higher education. The college supported its scholars by granting leaves and financial help.

So, what did I do? My activity beyond teaching centered mostly on English education. That had been my avid interest as a high school teacher already and had been furthered by my program at U of I. I joined the professional organizations like the National Council of Teachers of English (NCTE), MCTE, and English Education. I attended most of their national conferences (which had started in Honolulu), and gave presentations at many, both on the national and state level. I became involved in state leadership workshops and wrote reviews and articles for professional publications.

Most of my academic writing was in the form of reviews, most of which were published by Salem Press for such publications as Masterplots, Cyclopedia of World Authors, Cyclopedia of Literary Characters, Cyclopedia of Literary Places, etc. I wrote reviews on such Canadian authors as Rudy Wiebe, Alice Munroe, W.O. Mitchell, Mordecai Richler, Earl Birney, and Margaret Laurence. But also on others such as Jonathan Edwards, Walter Wangerin, Meindert De Jong, Antoine de Saint-Exupery, Jonathan Swift, Reynolds Price, Jonathan Swift, John Keats, E.E. Cummings, and Joost van den Vondel.

I wrote for non-profession-oriented publications too. Calvin is a denominational college (now a university). As such it encourages faculty support for the denomination and for its tradition of Christian education on all levels. I reached out to the readers of the denominational monthly, "The Banner," by contributing more than a dozen submissions.

(Our department rag would now and then feature a profile of a department member. Colleague Bill Vande Kopple wrote mine, included in the Supplement p. 337; also, material in two ring binders document many of my activities during those nearly 30 years as a Calvin prof.)

CEJ

"The Christian Educators Journal" also became a fairly prominent part of my Calvin years.

Before I was appointed to its Board, I took an idea to its editor, Prof. Donald Oppewal. It had been brewing in my noggin for a while. The CEJ went out to Christian school teachers all over North America; there were subscribers in other countries as well, like Australia. I had been a faithful reader during my high school teaching years. And during that time, I had developed a pretty strong sense of the faculty room as a kind of asylum, a kind of retreat from the trenches as well as a place for the expression of some occasional inspired wisdom and madness. I thought a regular column would be cool that featured a faculty lounge where teachers would gather and chat and argue and joke about their students and courses and issues that would reflect convictions and direction, all of which could be engaging and helpful to frontline Christian educators. It would have a regular cast representing a range of personalities, viewpoints, and functions. And the author should be anonymous to let the focus be on educators and education itself, rather than on the columnist.

THE "ASYLUM"

A BEGINNING
H. K. ZOEKLICHT*

It was comfortably warm and peaceful in the faculty room of Omni Christian High. The Stromberg wall clock indicated 12 o'clock, time for the teachers to start meandering in for their noon break. The aroma of freshly-percolated coffee added to the atmosphere of anticipation that pervaded the empty room.

coming in now, and banter befor The first four mahogany table Each contempla tary lull in the John carefully fish sandwich.

Oppewal liked the idea but wasn't sure he could sell the anonymous part of it to the Board.

He managed to do just that, though, on a trial basis.

And thus, in 1970, "The Asylum" under the pseudonym of H.K. Zoeklicht was born.

The K stood for Ken Kuiper, for after a couple of columns I was eager to have a partner with whom to brainstorm and produce. "The Asylum" became the most popular feature of CEJ and ran for 22 years. I intended the column as a means of placing in the spotlight poor, good, and better ways of doing Christian education.

Out of more than 70 columns, 18 were chosen for the special April 1992 CEJ issue.

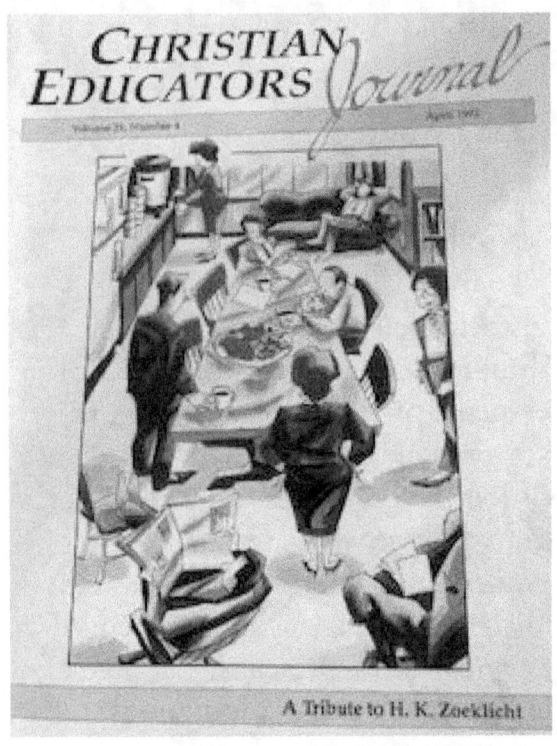

A Tribute to H. K. Zoeklicht

Don Oppewal wrote a wonderful guest editorial for that issue on the column's literary and educational contributions.

And in the April issue of 1997, the year of my retirement from Calvin and the CEJ Board, the cat finally came out of the bag through an interview with Lorna Van Gilst, the editor of CEJ at the time.

(Also at that meeting, the Board surprised me again with a beautiful big plaque that found a happy place next to an earlier one in my study.)

Yes, I had been on the CEJ Board pretty much since the early 70s, most of them as chair, preparing for its quarterly meetings, organizing the occasional conferences when at-large board members would join too, and when a new editor was needed, persuading wonderfully qualified people like Lillian Grissen, Lorna Van Gilst, and Bert Witvoet to commit. As I said in that April issue, "I look back on all those years with a good deal of pleasure. I think I have worked with more than sixty board members, some of whom made tremendous contributions. Some had to come from afar, like from Ontario and the Chicago area. They volunteered to give up a good chunk of a Saturday to guide and supervise the work of CEJ without compensation. I'm grateful to have been associated with them for so long.

And I still am.

Department Work

What does that all include?

Teaching surely, and the preparation for teaching, like "lesson plans," making up and grading quizzes and tests and exams, reading and grading a never-ending influx of student papers, student conferences, keeping up on professional reading, and much more. In addition, directing the Freshman English Program and the Rhetoric Center for several years kept me focused. And when advising and mentoring graduate students working on their MAT was added to the load, plus committee work (among others I served on the Graduate Studies Committee and for a time was faculty mentor of the controversial Film Arts Committee) and department and faculty meetings, the workday hours often needed to extend into the evening as well. Especially when you initiate your own committees, like the College-wide Writing Committee and the Faith & Writing Committee (more about that one later) I formed and chaired. Both were intended to nudge the college to add to its quality program. One to improve student writing in all subjects that require composition, and the other to connect the English department to readers and writers of faith far beyond the campus. I've always been rather diffident about "putting myself out there," preferring to let others take the lead, but comfortable leading when asked. Now I took the lead to persuade others to a vision and action, and that was a stretch, but I saw it as a necessary one. Still, I can't help wondering now and then what gave me the confidence and urgency to take a lead. I know it wasn't an impulse; I tend not to go on impulse. My flaw is rather that I overthink actions and decisions. But I think it was the growing conviction of a need that called for attention and the always mysterious inner nudging.

1980 Sabbatical

Climbing up the academic ladder went smoothly – from assistant to associate to full professor with tenure. And you don't have to scale that mountain all in one strenuous stretch; if you give due diligence, you may qualify for a sabbatical. So, in January of 1980, Ruth and I packed our car, gave "little Lyske" and Jayne a place in the back seat, and we were off to our home state of Washington where we had rented a cabin on Lummi Island.

I would immerse myself in Canadian literature, since I had been accepted in a 1978 NEH 8-week intensive summer seminar at Michigan State University that introduced us to Canadian culture, history, and literature. Canadian literature had never been a part of the English department offerings, and since we had some 300 Canadian students on campus, it was past time to honor our northern neighbor and its students. I had volunteered to teach an introductory course in Canadian literature. And the sabbatical would enable me to read widely and deeply, taking advantage of the resources at nearby universities.

Jayne stayed with Sid and Margaret in Lynden that allowed her to attend Lynden Christian High School. And Ruth and I enjoyed the peace and beauty of the island, walking our two-year old along the quiet woods-lined path, listening in the stillness to the doxologies of birds, breathing in the unpolluted air, and filling with wonder at the glorious sight of Mt. Baker on a clear day.

Transitioning to a more bucolic lifestyle was at once soul-refreshing for me but also challenging. "The woods [were] lovely, dark and deep/but I [had] promises to keep…." I needed to impose the discipline that would put me at my desk each day to steep myself in the literature of nearby Canada. I found the groove after a while and focused especially on the image of the Christian church in Canadian literature, aided by library trips to nearby Western Washington College and across the border to the University of British Columba and Simon Fraser University.

Chopping wood to keep our woodstove burning on cold wintery days was also a blessed change from grading essays or sitting through yet another tedious committee meeting.

But I wasn't altogether disconnected from the department colleagues. They kept me informed of campus happenings and even concocted an elaborate practical joke. Someone bumped into a Time magazine whole-page ad for Wolfschmidt Genuine Vodka that featured a man clad as a Czar persona, holding a glass of vodka. The Czar had a face that upon a cursory inspection seemed to resemble mine.

CALVINIST CONTACT   MAY 9, 1980

WANTED: Information on the whereabouts of H. Baron, alias Baron Van Sneek, last seen writing postcards on island somewhere in Puget Sound. Responds to "Hank." Notify: English Dept., Calvin College, Grand Rapids, Mich. 49506.

That triggered the joke impulse, no doubt in Ken Kuiper's office. The unholy trinity of Ken, Dick, and Tom made a plan: post an ad in the "Calvinist Contact" publication, write an immigrant's Yankee

Dutch letter to Provost Peter De Vos with a scathing indictment of the college's heretical liberalism in general and now personified by this communist-drink professor posing in liberal magazines as a Russian Czar! Somehow, brother Sid got lassoed into writing that hilarious Yankee Dutch letter under the name of Mrs. Lena Snuiver, posing as a Lummi Island storekeeper who had recognized that sneaky communist spy coming into her store now and then.

The joke was extended into my return to Calvin in the fall when the faculty program at the start of a new school year included a special appearance of this vodka-loving Czar telling his story, which I did.

Our stay on the island and so close to WA family became memorable. Cindy, Henry, and Judy came out to join us during the Calvin spring break. Ruth arranged an elaborate May birthday party for me in the Lummi Island social building with many area friends from adolescent years as well as family, all taking the ferry ride to surprise me. Later Sid and Margaret invited us to accompany them on an Alaska cruise as an over-the-top birthday gift!

Did I make some special contributions to our English program, on campus and off, I ask myself.

I think I did in a modest way – to English teachers in preparation and in the field, to students by introducing courses in Teaching of Writing, Canadian literature, and Adolescent Literature in the curriculum, and maybe especially by starting what became the biannual Festival of Faith and Writing.

Festival of Faith and Writing (FFW)

It started in 1988 when the Canadian author Rudy Wiebe visited the department and he and I spent some time together. I felt a kind of bond begin to develop between us, maybe partly because we were the same age and both of Frisian and emigrant background, he as Mennonite from Russia to Canada at age four. We talked at one point about the need for serious literary writers and readers of faith to come together, writers and readers who didn't necessarily shy away from encountering dark realities of life as it is lived and experienced all around us, how good it would be for them to have a taste of a special faith community composed of esteemed writers and appreciative readers, as well as aspiring future writers.

That conversation planted an idea within me that refused to leave. More and more I thought about the need to make that happen, to offer serious writers and readers of faith a sense of community, an opportunity to perhaps learn from each other, to be inspired by each other, to be affirmed by literary expectations and appreciation.

To make that a reality, much work had to be done. As I think back on that now, it surprises me again that as one who doesn't easily initiate leadership, especially among peers whom I think more capable, I decided to go for it.

I needed to procure the approval and support of the department chair, of the provost, of my colleagues. I needed planning committees, each with its own focus. And then we needed to find money and sponsors, we needed to select speakers and publishers, we needed to advertise, we needed a budget.

And we needed to find time, lots of time – for committee meetings and people meetings, for lots of emailing and lots of phone calling, all in addition to our regular teaching load.

Somehow all that got done, though I wonder now how we did it and how I kept my sanity as chair to stay on top of the myriad of details a conference entails, especially when starting from scratch, but in the spring of 1990 the Contemporary Christian Writers in Community conference was born and launched in a small, tentative, beginning way.

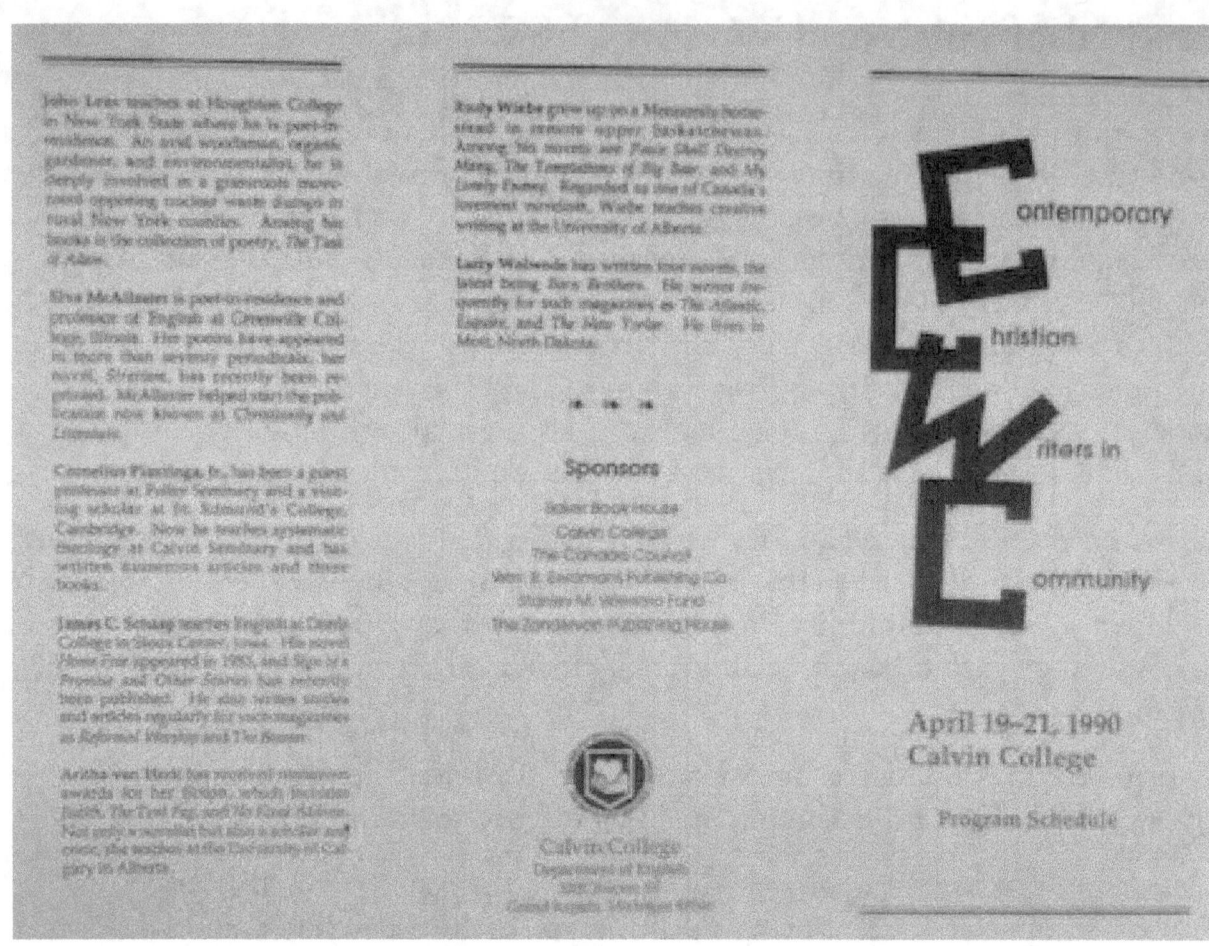

And maybe especially because it was small it started with a real feeling of community.

I remember how gratifying it felt to hear voices say – we need to do this again, how can we stay in touch.

And yes, Rudy Wiebe was one of the speakers, as he was as well in some subsequent conferences.

For oh yes, we did it again, and again, with each time a bigger audience and more authors and publishers and editors, rather quickly evolving from a small but hopeful beginning into a nationally recognized and acclaimed conference, with eventually a fulltime director with assistants and an adequate budget. Much of this growth was attributable to the skillful and knowledgeable leadership of Dale Brown whom I liked and respected and was glad to defer to.

Unfortunately, Covid-19 cancelled the spring 2020 Festival that had been a year in the planning (and again the 2022 Festival for the same reason).

In 2020 we were going to make the Festival very special in celebrating its 30 years of bringing writers, aspiring writers, readers, librarians and word lovers of all kinds together, in later years some 2000 of them. (I say "we" but I haven't been directly involved in most of the Festivals.)

But the Festivals have been an ongoing source of deep satisfaction for me to have had the initial vision, and I expressed my gratitude for its growing contribution to Faith and Writing by honoring it with a Henry and Ruth Baron Family Endowment. Attached to that is the privilege of choosing one of the plenary speakers to be sponsored partially by the Endowment and having dinner with the chosen speaker. Among the "chosen ones" was Yann Martel who wrote *Life of Pi,* and Chimamanda Adichie, author of *Purple Habiscus, Americanah,* and others.

Frisia

It was in the early 80s when the land of my forebears began to occupy an increasingly more serious spot in my academic life. Sometime before that I had met my erstwhile Calvin German professor at a local Frisian service. We were both surprised to discover each other's Frisian roots and interest as we began to speak Frisian to each other. Up to that time I had never been seriously interested in engaging my Frisian background. I was born just across the Friesland-Groningen border, on the Groningen side. So, though both parents were born in Friesland and their ancestors went back for centuries in that special province, our Frisian heritage other than the language did not figure strongly in our upbringing. So, I didn't have a strong sense of Frisian identity; nor of Groninger identity. You're not in the center, you're on the border, and rather ignorant of its history, its unique traditions, its nursery rhymes, its folk songs, its literature.

But I had read one book in Frisian, a language I spoke but had not learned to read. Someone gave the book to me as a present when still in Opende, and I managed to read it, sounding out the words, and enjoying it. That must've awakened something in me, for I took the book along when we emigrated as a kind of roots-reminding treasure. It was like a small candle had been put in place, then waiting for someone to come along and light it. And that someone turned out to be Prof. Bernard Fridsma who had come to this country with his family when he was only five and on American soil had grown into a passionate and intellectual lover of Fryslân , its fervency probably exceeding that of any lifelong Friesland resident.

As time went on, our relationship grew stronger. In fact, Fridsma became an unofficial mentor who encouraged me to learn to write Frisian (a challenge that initially intimidated me totally), read Frisian literature, and eventually persuaded me to take over his work as a reviewer of Frisian literature for *World Literature Today,* an American quarterly publication of international literature and culture that presents essays, poetry, fiction, interviews, and book reviews from all over the world. I retired as a reviewer in 2018, and by that time I had more than a hundred reviews published, now archived in the Frisian Academy in Ljouwert (Leeuwarden). Many of them are included in the Free Library [https://www.thefreelibrary.com/ Baron%2c+Henry+J.-a12701]

In the summer of 1984, an alumni grant enabled us to arrange a home-car exchange with a family just outside of Drachten. I spent time in Friesland researching its literature in the hope of finding a novel worthy of translation into English. That search led to many contacts with authors and people knowledgeable about their literature, including one of its most popular and prominent authors, Rink van der Velde.

Some of those contacts grew into long-term friendships that significantly enriched my knowledge and appreciation of my heritage. And I also greatly appreciated when in the mid-90s the Fryske Akademie honored me by making me a member, a rather prestigious distinction awarded to those who in a special way have represented and promoted the Frisian quest for cultural significance.

Looking back on that time now makes me count my blessings. The person of Bernie Fridsma was the center.

He was a widower, living alone in the old family home on Sylvan Ave. In my frequent visits with him, usually in his home (but he would often visit me in my Calvin office too), he became more than a friend. In my eulogy when he passed at the age of 100 in 2005, I said that he became like a father to me. And I felt that he appreciated me like a son.

And what did that initial contact lead to?

Yes, much reading and reviewing. Some articles in Frisian publications. Some submissions on Frisian literature in Britannica Micropaedia, The New Princeton Encyclopedia of Poetry and Poetics, and in The Reader's Advisor.

But also much translation work. Rink van der Velde's De Fûke became The Trap in English and led me into a joint self-publishing partnership with Clarence Hogeterp.

This experiment sold nearly 2000 copies. (And this little classic WWII novel came out later in a hardcover edition in 1997 when it was bought by The Permanent Press.) That was followed in 2000 by Lowland Tales: Stories from Friesland, published by Friese Pers in Ljouwert.

Next came the translation of Hylke Speerstra's It wrede paradys into Cruel Paradise, published by Eerdmans in 2005 and more recently by Mokeham Publishing. The book featured true world-wide Frisian immigrant stories, including our own.

After translating a couple of books, including Ecclesiastes for Managers, and several theological chapters for Calvin's Heritage Hall from Dutch, the last Frisian translation project featured another Hylke Speerstra book, De Treastfûgel, in English The Comfort Bird, published by Mokeham Publishing in 2018. Each of these projects has its own story, some of them rather interesting and worth the telling, but maybe somewhere else.

Since all of this so far comes under the rubric of Academics, I need to mention also that the Frisian heritage became a part of my classroom too: I taught "Introduction to Frisian" to interim classes and "Introduction to Friesland" to CALL classes.

It's already becoming clear by now that my Frisian-ness found itself increasingly active. A few of us began to gather for a weekly Frisian lunch time in the Calvin faculty dining room in the late 80s. We often had more than a dozen joining at a round table, practicing our Frisian tongue on each other.

In the 30 years that we continued these meetings, we would usually spend some of each lunch time focusing on the language, history, literature, and current events of Friesland. And we would have special gatherings when I arranged for a storyteller or singer from Friesland to come and present a program. We also enjoyed an annual post-Christmas dinner that would include a short program and much singing from the Fridsma song book with his excellent translations of hymns in Frisian. A Frisian summer picnic was added later.

And in the summer of 2009, it was Friesland Day on Governors Island, with a number of Michigan Frisians in attendance, It offered a chance for me to talk a bit with the famous Frisian bard, Tsjebbe Hettinga, a blind poet who drew large audiences as a Dylan Thomas-style oral performer.

Fridsma also got me involved in the annual Frisian service that had begun in 1958, including persuading me to preach one year. That was a challenge, but challenges have a way of energizing the challenged, and I felt grateful for the opportunity to share God's way with us with fellow Frisians.

Since I was seen as the leader in all things Frisian, the planning and organizing of these activities fell on my sagging shoulders. But some fine friendships were forged, though there was considerable diversity within the group. Language and our Frisian roots were the cement that melded us together.

This chapter in my life now strikes me as something closer to a would-be book. A life constitutes volumes rather than chapters, maybe. Each volume has its characters, its surprises, its trials, its grief, its peculiar layer that, combined with others, tells the story of a unique life journey. But if the story of this life, my life, is to be told close to its end, as I have often felt it is, I can't even yield to chapters; it would not get done. And the intention is to get it done, D.V. Should there be time enough at the end to offer the bonus of elaboration, I may return to those partial chapters and add some human tales to mere facts.

However, this Friesland segment should not leave out what became lasting memories, some experiences that still hold a special place in my heart.

After "waking up" to my Frisian roots, I became even more interested in arranging for a home-and-car exchange with a family in Friesland. The first one, mentioned earlier, in 1984, found the three of us (yes, lytse Lyske too) on a hobby farm just outside of Drachten. That experience too merits its own story. So does the Amsterdam exchange in 1990, when all the children joined us for a week and shared something of our Netherland experience and appreciation. It was a joy to travel with them to the very southern tip of the country as well as the very northern one, which of course had to include an overnight in Friesland.

And the last one in Fûns, just outside Jorwert, where we got a memorable taste of living in the flat grasslands or clay region of the province with horizon-stretching vistas and Frisian horses, Holsteins, and sheep dotting the landscape.

We had a great view of the flat lands vista that allowed us to spy the Ljouwert tall buildings on the far horizon from the "round house" that had been home to the renowned Dutch writer Geert Mak, now the home of Friesland's first-class cultural ambassadors, Hindrik and Beitske van der Meer.

190

The "Harmonie"

But the invitation that came in September 1999 led to one of my most unforgettable and rewarding experiences. After Speerstra's It wrede paradys came out and generated a firestorm of enthusiastic interest, the leading provincial newspaper decided to sponsor a public program on emigration. The program would take place in De Harmonie, the city theater and concert hall of Leeuwarden and one of the top five large theaters in the Netherlands. (De Harmonie was also the cultural heart of Simmer 2000 and the celebration of "Leeuwarden as Friesland Cultural Capital" in 2018.) I was invited to be one of the three speakers, with all expenses paid. All presentations would of course be in Frisian. The opportunity thrilled and unnerved me at the same time. Face a large Frisian audience and speak to them in their own language? My oral Frisian had been in semi-hibernation for 50 years and had never had much of a chance to progress beyond adolescent facility, even with occasional exposure and practice. (Strangely, I had dreamt of this not so long before the invitation came, and its fear-tinged excitement had woken me.) But of course, I would accept. So, I worked hard on getting my emigrant story on paper in Frisian, aided by some Fridsma editing.

On October 3, Ruth dropped me off at the airport, and after a long KLM 747-night flight, Hylke picked me up from Schiphol. The four-star Oranje Hotel in Ljouwert would be my resting place. Though I had been deprived of good solid sleep for some time, that first night on Frisian soil was not good and solid – jet lag and too much internal stirring of things to come.

The next day kept me busy with phone calls from Frisian TV and radio. Had a Dutch radio network interview; Dutch did not come back to me as readily and smoothly as I would have liked, affected no doubt by some physical fatigue and tension that were exacting their toll. After supper with Hylke and the radio reporter, I headed for the Harmonie. I saw people streaming in from all directions. No one knew me, of course, so I could take a spot in the lobby and watch the young and the old rush in for a good seat. Until I saw the familiar faces of cousins coming toward me: I was thrilled to see Folkert and Griet and Hans and Anita. We chatted till Antje Post from the sponsoring newspaper came looking for me. They had been waiting for me and had begun to wonder if I would be a no-show with five minutes to go before the program's start.

The program did start, nearly 500 people filled the auditorium, and after the introductions, I was on. A welcome feeling of readiness filled me. If I have confidence in my "stuff," I usually relish the opportunity to affect the audience. Something to do, maybe, with a love of the stage, a place both frightening and exciting. I had been afraid of being ambushed by a rush of emotion at points in my talk, but once I started, I felt that I would stay in control. The response I felt from the audience as I went along buoyed me.

And when I spotted Klaas Prins in the audience, coming all the way from his home in Ermelo, well, that animated me even more. (The speech itself is in the Supplement p. 342).

The applause at the end was long and felt warm. Other speeches by Annemieke Galema and Hylke Speerstra followed, then a time for Q & A and a rousing conclusion by a band playing my favorite doxology, "k' Wil U O God mijn dank betalen." The program ended a bit after 10 p.m.

But it wasn't over. I didn't get ten inches away from my seat. People nailed me. I saw family come toward me that included Dries and Geeke Prins and also Tolly Hoekstra. And Rink. But they had to wait. Everybody wanted to tell me stories, ask me questions, shake my hand, give me hugs, telling me how much they had loved my story, wanted a copy of my speech.

It was overwhelming. Most people waiting in line never made it. I made the relatives promise not to run away. Someone brought me a glass of beer. And eventually, by about 11:00, I made it to the lobby. There was still a mass of people there, so I still couldn't get to my relatives. I was kept busy signing dozens of "Paradys" books. Finally, I found a way of hiding behind a plant so that I could become accessible to Baron and Hoekstra family members.

And to Rink who was not well (he would not live, it turned out, for much more than a year) and had been waiting for me for more than an hour. There was all too little time and energy left for family and friends, like Hans van der Veen with wife and daughter Welmoed whom we had exchanged house and car with, Henk Baron, the family genealogist from Drachten, and more. All this time Koen and Reinie Zondag had been waiting, thinking I would come home with them. I told them I would join them the next day and stay with them till my return home.

It was nearly 12:30 when I got back to the Oranje Hotel, higher than a kite and unable to go to sleep. Finally got a couple of hours, then wide awake again. But eventually Mr. Sandman found me and kept me under his spell till the telephone woke me at 9:00. A lady from a newspaper wanted to schedule an interview. When I discovered it was 9:00, I panicked. I had agreed to meet Geart de Vries from the Frisian TV downstairs in the hotel at 9:00, from where we would go to our old Opende place where a film crew would record whatever memories of mine would resurface as we walked around the place that once was home. Stumbled to the bathroom, threw on some clothes, packed, and made it down in twenty minutes. Had I been in a more refreshed and relaxed state of being, I could have made the film they shot dramatically engaging, for I thought later of several interesting stories and colorful recollections I could have recalled. But the energy and the right roleplaying mode were absent. And it would have had to be roleplaying, for I had made that Opende home visit too many times by then to have much of a nostalgia reserve.

When later that day I had a live interview on Frisian television, I was not able to generate enough pizazz to give the viewers an impressive sense of an Americanized Frisian emigrant. What inhibited me especially was my lack of oral Frisian fluency, partly due to a too tired brain. But the good writeup in the next day's papers of the Harmonie program was gratifying.

That wasn't the end of the week in Friesland, but what remains a vivid visual and stirring memory is the Harmonie evening. It jonkje fan De Peen (The little boy from Opende) spoke in the language of his home to an auditorium full of people and touched their hearts as he told them about one life whose Frisian connection was still intact. The people's response made him feel that he was still one of them, and he felt blessed.

Simmer 2000

Less than a year later, I was back – now for Simmer 2000, an event in the summer of 2000 in which Frisians living outside Friesland were invited to return to it heitelân (the fatherland) for a reunion. ‹Frisians om útens’ (Frisians from outside) from other parts of Europe, the U.S.A., Canada, Australia, South Africa, South America and New Zealand returned to Friesland in droves during "Simmer 2000."

Ruth and I wanted to be part of that. My immersion in all things Frisian had been so deep by that time, that I couldn't not be there. Especially when I got an invitation by the Frisian Academy to participate in the publication ceremony of the Frisian-English Dictionary, to the making of which I had contributed now and then. The invitation came with my air travel paid for. Besides that, Rink offered us his waterside cabin for our home away from home. What could be more ideal?

That whole July experience is worthy of its own long chapter too, but the picture album and Ruth's journal will have to suffice as supplements. Still, there's much to include here as experiences that left a permanent benefaction.

During this special Simmer 2000, activities were organized throughout the province, such as countless local festivities like horse races, outdoor drama performances, reunions, music, church services, and photo exhibitions.

Highlights for us? Many, and here are some:

· Not a highlight really, but kind of amusing that when walking the streets in Ljouwert, and sometimes other places too, people we met would occasionally indicate that they recognized me from the Harmonie night and the TV interview, and that gave a little taste how prized anonymity can become for those who've lost it; no danger of that for me

· And there were reporters again sticking a mic in my face for comments

· Seeing the hundreds (thousands?) that streamed to the Wilhelmina Square in Ljouwert for Opening Program on July 1, we among them but seated as special

194

honored guests (arranged by Hylke Speerstra for the subjects of *It wrede paradys* who could attend) on bleachers just a couple of rows behind Queen Beatrix and her entourage; joining in the Frisian national anthem "Frysk bloed tsjoch op" that, coming from the throats and hearts of that great throng of homecoming Frisians, must've resounded throughout the provincial capital

· Being one of four emigrants "chosen" (again through Speerstra) to meet the queen for a short chat after the opening ceremonies; the queen received the first copy of *Het wrede paradijs* from Hylke at that time in a special ceremony

· The boarding afterward on the provincial yacht "Frisian Queen" along with lots of other Speerstra book emigrants, guests, and dignitaries, sailing Frisian lakes and canals while being dined and entertained

Koningin Beatrix spreekt met emigranten bij opening Simmer 2000

· Having the huge surprise of Ali Talma waiting for me with a hug when we disembarked in Grou – Ali, the girl I sat next to in that little ULO building in 1947-48 and with whom I became pen pals for many years after our emigration; both of us had saved each other's letters, which we later exchanged

· Attending an ecumenical service in Wytmarsum where Menno Simons in a farmer's field held his clandestine services after he broke with Roman Catholicism as a priest during the time of the Protestant Reformation and became an influential Anabaptist leader (Mennonites)

· Boarding a special train at 3 a.m. that was picking up Frisians from all over the province to attend the Gluck opera "Orfeo Aqua" taking place at early sunrise on a lake near Workum; we sat tightly wedged among Frisians on bleachers by the water, cold, wet, and feeling lucky to be taking in this special version of the story of

ing Simmer 2000
eboden door de Friese Rabobanken

HEKRADERBOOT 'FRISIAN QUEE

Orpheus's descent into Hades and his fruitless attempt to bring his dead bride Eurydice back to the living world. It was a wonderfully impressive performance, and, as I wrote for a Frisian newspaper (yes, in Frysk), it gave me a special kind of happy feeling to belong to this "tribe" who were not too common-sensical to empty their billfolds, skip a night of sleep, and shiver in a cold, damp, drizzly pre-morning for a unique opportunity to take in some high culture

· The pilgrimage bus ride to the Upstalbeam, with Hindrik van der Meer keeping us singing the familiar old Frisian songs that have remained popular through several generations

· The Upstalbeam was in the 13th and 14th century the place where delegates of the seven Frisian regions would meet once a year on the Tuesday after Pentecost, there to speak (pan-Frisian) justice and to make joint decisions as an alliance; the Upstalbeam is located near Aurich (East Friesland, now Germany); since 1833, there has been a stone pyramid on the prehistoric burial mound; there were speeches, and the mayor of Aurich invited us to see his city and where we were treated to a nice lunch

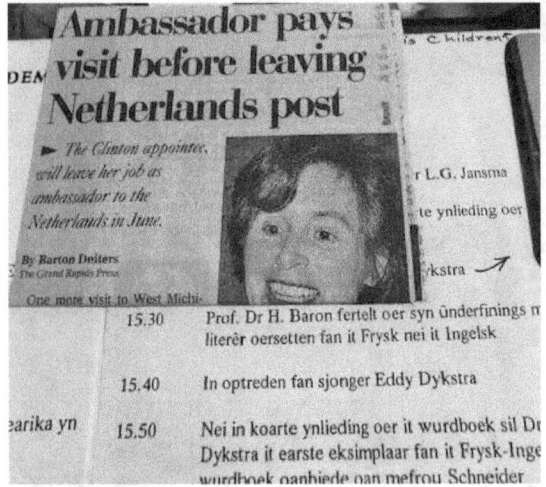

15.30	Prof. Dr H. Baron fertelt oer syn ûnderfinings r literêr oersetten fan it Frysk nei it Ingelsk
15.40	In optreden fan sjonger Eddy Dykstra
15.50	Nei in koarte ynlieding oer it wurdboek sil D Dykstra it earste eksimplaar fan it Frysk-Inge wurdboek oanbiede oan mefrou Schneider

· It felt good to meet my old friend Anne Dykstra again in a special meeting room of the Fryske Akademie where he would be honored for the publication of his Frisian-English Dictionary, an enormous and unique accomplishment that had been years in the making; the book would be presented to the American ambassador to the Netherlands, Mrs. C.P. Schneider, whom I was happy to meet as a former East Grand Rapids resident; in my talk there I expressed my warm appreciation for this dictionary that had already been a significant aid in my translation work

· Walking around in Rottevalle, where 100 years before a young 4-year old must have been walking with his parents, for this was the town where my dad was born; and if he had been walking with us that Simmer 2000 day, he would not have believed it to be the same town of his memory – then oozing poverty, now heralding picturesque beauty and prosperity; In 1953, Rottevalle was declared an 'exemplary village' by the National Agricultural Information Service when Rottevalle functioned as an exhibition village to make modern developments in agriculture visible

· There is so much more, of course; but I should mention the dear memories I have of Rink van der Velde coming to his "wenarkje" (houseboat, which it had started out to be)each morning to join us for a cup of coffee and "koeke", to be chased down by one or more "slokjes" (yes, he was addicted to nicotine and alcohol – which had damaged his cardiovascular system and only months later would kill him); but I never saw him drunk, and his company was most enjoyable; Rink and spouse Mineke not only made this place available to us, but had supplied us with bread

and eggs and koeke for the first morning after our arrival; this was Rink's workplace: this is where the inspiration and perspiration came to him for his many stories, where he could make music on his violin and accordion, where he could set his traps and smoke the eel, where he could enjoy his solitude; we will not forget that solitary place of peace and quiet where nature embraced us as in a dream, where every morning the petgat (peat canal) cuckoo like an alarm clock opened our eyes to a new day and where the view of a graceful swan family gliding on the water in the gathering dusk unspooled our wound-up minds after a busy day in that chilly but exhilarating July in Simmer 2000.

(and though this idyllic place was well hidden, its intrigue proved to be quite irresistible, for relatives and friends made it their favorite destination; when Rink happened to be there at the same time, they felt their curiosity doubly rewarded).

When revisiting in your memory bank this remarkable month that did Friesland proud, it's hard to be selective; but the picture album with comments fills out the story of the places and people and events of those weeks that kept us in motion and stayed with us; so, only one or two to go here:

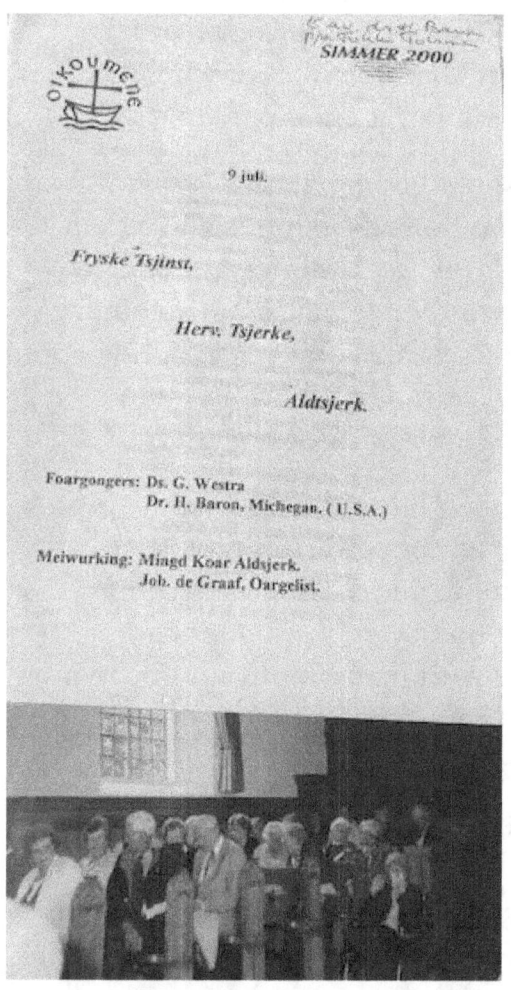

· One Sunday morning in July I walk slowly toward the 13th century church in Oudkerk; Ruth has gone ahead to get a good seat for the service while I lag a bit behind, watching a drove of churchgoers heading for the entrance; I have a sense of surreality – those people are coming to church this morning to hear me preach; I have never preached before, not in English and certainly not in Frisian; but church member Fokko's clever machinations has brought us to this day with everything in place; I enter this ancient church, jittery, dreamlike, but encouraged when noting the more than 20 cousins and friends in the pews; when the time comes, I climb up the preekstoel (pulpit) that rises high above the worshippers in the pews, and I preach (the sermon in translation is in the Supplement p. 342) and I survive; and people say nice things in the coffee hour afterwards; but what makes this special occasion even more special for me is meeting my 2nd and 3rd grade teacher, 92-year old Meester Posthumus who read that I was going to preach and recruited his grandson to take him to Oudkerk.

I sit next to him drinking coffee and enjoying our chat, the likes of which we had never had and never anticipated.

(Maybe I should add here that, yes, this was the first time I preached a Frisian sermon, but it wasn't the last time; I was asked to preach a second one in this same church some years later, plus one at our annual Frisian services in Grand Rapids, and even one in Canada: Woodstock, Ontario.)

· And local family? oh yes, they came too, but when Simmer 2000 was all over, the Lynden Barons and Steigers and Chenoweths came, the Grandville Bakers came, and we had an American and Dutch family evening of entertainment with stories by Hylke Speerstra and music by Bouke van der Woude in our Drachten hotel, as well as a Frisian lakes cruise with many more cousins joining (some of whom we met for the first time) – a beautiful climax to a memorable month in the land of our roots.

When at the conclusion of that unforgettable Simmer 2000 it was time to move on, we felt some sadness mixed in with gratitude. Sadness that comes when all good things must end, in this case the sadness of saying goodbye to Fryslân which had opened its borders and its heart so generously and warmly to its sons and daughters from nearly every part of the world. Sadness too that the goodbye included Rink and Mineke and it "arkje oan de petgâtten" that had made our stay so special. But especially gratitude for the ways in which all of this enriched our lives with experiences and memories that linger still. My continuing Frisian immersion was enlarging my identity, an identity I was embracing gratefully.

China

I wonder now – what stirred me to consider and pursue a China adventure?

I've wondered that too about that first telephone call to that cute blond from Sumas, in spite of my nerves and awareness that I was an immigrant Dutchie farm kid who didn't even go to high school. And also about the will to become a college grad, a Calvin College grad, with inadequate preparation and finances. And about a number of other decisions that led my life to places and in directions which became reasons for gladness and gratitude.

Yes, I wonder about that now, as I think back on these past decades and feel nudged to reflect a bit more personally on the mystery of divine providence. I've been wonted to think it presumptuous for one, at least for myself, to claim God's personal guidance in one's chosen path. To sense that there may have been is an extremely humbling feeling and faith affirming.

But now China – what was it that made me respond to an invitation I read in an English Journal, an invitation to apply for a team leader position of a startup summer program for Christian teachers to teach English to Chinese teachers of English. I had never really thought about going to China, and Ruth and young lytse Lyske were pretty negative about my inclinations. But the opportunity intrigued me and before long had me send for an application to English Language Institute China (ELIC) in San Dimas, California. A visit to San Dimas and interview with Ken Wendling, the president and visionary of ELIC, followed, and to keep a long story shorter – I would be accompanying him as Assistant Director to China in January (with Calvin's approval and someone taking over my planned interim class) to visit four host institutions for summer teams, sign contracts, and work out the details.

And that's what happened: early January 1985 found me back in San Dimas for meetings, staying overnight with Cindy and Ed who then lived in Torrance, and then off to the country whose Bamboo Curtain had parted to welcome American English teachers aiding China's ambition to catch up with the Western world after ten disastrous years of the Cultural Revolution had severely disrupted the country's economic and educational systems. It was a long wearying flight with an overnight stay in Narita, the international airport near Tokyo, where Ken Wendling would join me the next day for the last leg of the flight to Beijing via Shanghai. It felt good for me to come there not as a tourist but on official business with something to offer what they needed.

The "first time" of anything has a way of sharpening your senses, activating your powers of observation, and wanting to take it all in slowly. So it was with my initial entrance to China. But the nature of our visit made everything more rushed than slow – slow would have to wait till summer.

Some quick bites of "first time" impressions and observations – the summer-to-come experience will tell more – and there's much more in the separate Travel Section, for I kept a diary of sorts, as well as in the photo album "Mission to China":

- It's wintertime but many buildings are unheated; we sat for three hours in such a room with outside temps in the 40's which is how I discovered that cold can become more cruel than heat; and the memory of a room that had its windows open, the A/C running (no doubt a recent acquisition to show off to the visiting dignitaries) and two heaters trying bravely to combat the contrary forces and losing the battle

- Most people walk or ride "pack bikes," some with basketsful of geese or ducks or hog's heads, or pull carts with huge loads, and not many trucks or cars and apparently no traffic rules

- Air pollution of thousands of coal-burning fires casting a thick acrid pall over cities with millions of residents, in this case Chengdu

- The typical Chinese banquet with some 15 courses where I, normally known as a fussy eater, sampled nearly everything, including sea slugs and fungus soup, but not enjoyably; maybe, if I were more of a drinker and had imbibed more of their beer and mau tai, I may have eaten the strange foods with more gustatory delight – slurping and lip-smacking and occasional belching, all meant to be compliments to the chef

- Visits to four widely separated campuses (extensive details are included in the separate Travel Secion), each with its own character and ambition to make itself as attractive and progressive as possible in order to attract much-needed teachers from America; the Chinese officials and teachers could hardly have been more welcoming, friendly, and gracious; they knew that I would be headed for Chengdu in charge of three teams of teachers for its summer program there, but that didn't restrain them from trying to win me over to commit to a year of teaching in their fair city

- The mission ended, mercifully for me because I was increasingly in the grips of a China cold, on January 22; after being up for nearly 40 hours, I arrived home minus my luggage (stuck in China?) and sorely in need of sleep; but, as I wrote in my travel diary then, I felt tremendously fortunate to have been chosen for this experience, not only for the places I was able to see and the people I could meet and the treatment I could enjoy but for this country that was so enthusiastically committed to make up for lost time and become a modern, progressive nation; writing this now in 2020 when China has become so advanced and competitive and is engaging in ongoing hostility with the U.S., I can't help but wonder if our ELIC and national efforts to help China get back on its feet is backfiring on us; but there's another side: teachers going to China through ELIC and also ERRC had and have as their mission to plant seeds for faith formation in their students, and that has become a whole other amazing story

Summer '85

That story took shape for the sixty teachers in the summer of 1985. It's a long and for me a very meaningful story. I shall not tell it all but just enough to convey a sense of what impressed, challenged, and blessed me.

The Preparation

- Lots of mailings from ELIC before that summer, all entailing preparation for the challenge ahead in terms of teams, course material, culture info, visa requirements, etc.

- The personal plan – Ruth would come along for the first ten days while Lisa would stay with Cindy and Ed, then Ruth would return to LA and go on with Lisa to Lynden to stay there the rest of the time that I would be in China

- But first the team preparation time at CAL POLY in Pomona – and this is how I experienced that according to my notes of 6-25-54:

  It's been intense. It's been emotional. It's been disturbing and exhilarating. It's been a lot of praying and praising. It's been personal.

  This is no place for a doubter or skeptic. This is for "true believers" only.

  And the experience is not for those who prefer to remain detached, who require privacy, who wish to hide their hearts from others. Team members become your family, recent strangers quickly become intimate, for it is you and they who will need to rely on each other, get along together, pray together, learn together, cry together, support each other, trust each other, build each other up, love each other. We're learning.

It's a new experience for some of us, like me, who haven't been involved in charismatic kinds of "share" groups. I participate, indeed it's my responsibility to be both a teaching and a spiritual leader. But part of me holds back a bit and evaluates and holds out for balance; prefers the occasional silent praying and designated prayers to the pressure of everyone feeling the need to engage in long oral prayers. But the devoutness and Christian fervor impress me deeply. The spirit of God feels very present among us.

(And what we heard today from David Wang and Karen Ray and Carolyn Dirkse about God's presence and working in China also left a profound impression on all of us. The story of the persecution and deliverance and of "Ping Pong" touched us deeply.)

Ruth joined us toward the end and became acquainted with the teams. I feel really blessed to have her join us for the first ten days in China.

6-27

We're on board KAL 617, all 61 of us with 121 pieces of checked luggage and at least as many carry-ons.

I've never had a send-off like this one before. Perhaps not many in this group have either. But then, it's been a couple of weeks like that.

Items:

- The people, ranging in age from 20-70

Mostly young people, with a very active past in campus outreach programs and other Christian witness activities; a very expressive Christian group, much given to singing and praying and "sharing." We've prayed in the meeting hall, in our team compartment, in our own "quiet time" corners, in a grove on Cal Poly campus, on their lawns, in the lounge, in hand-holding circle, on our knees, and tonight before take-off in the LAX ticket counter lobby, lifting our song, "I Love You Lord" and our prayer before the Lord to whose care we entrust ourselves. It's often deeply moving and a spiritual blessing. God is very real among us.

The people – Presbyterians, Episcopalians, Southern Baptists, Christian Reformed, Mennonites, Methodists, Independent Bible Church members, and from many other backgrounds have come in one place for one purpose. and the unity is heart lifting. Tears and hugs have been common and releasing. The loving concern for each other has been felt again and again.

- The sessions, frequent and long

Most of them helpful in preparing us for teaching, for culture shock, for tensions and ways of coping with them; some especially memorable ones, including Daniel Wang's poignant story of his family's painful experiences during the Cultural Revolution.

- The ELI staff: easy-to-like people, from hard-working, seemingly untiring Cheryl Mohr to Gary Lausch, cool, funny, but sensible. The new men acquired in top positions—Don Douglas and Dan—also impress with their competence and Christian dedication.

- The excellent food, in variety, quality, and abundance

- The amiable but punctilious and proper roommate Corban Cornell

The two weeks for most has been a time for seriously facing up to aspects of the reality that will soon face all of us: different cultural traditions, food, customs, expectations; deprivations and restrictions, including loss of comforts; heat and humidity; hard, intense work unfamiliar to most; but also exciting challenges to meet and serve and make friends of many Chinese people. There has been self-doubt, fears and anxieties, but along with that an increasing readiness to assume the challenge and to trust in the Lord.

The Team

· My team: Pat, Cathy, Kathy, Keith, Kim, Wendy, Lynn, Nate, Jerry; more than half of them with strong southern accents

· Once we started meeting, we began to develop a bonding rather quickly

· Over half of us are introverts

· Some have rather strong emotional swings, but all are honest with themselves and the team

· A rather young and inexperienced group: five are not yet finished with college, two have teaching experience, only the associate Jerry Nelson has considerable teaching experience and TESOL training, but a very devout group, and I trust a conscientious one

· We intend to meet often and support each other constantly

The Travel

- Stops in Anchorage (several hours), Seoul, Hong Kong

- Two days in HK; hot but fascinated by frenetic energy of the city, sightseeing: very steep tram trip up the mountain with glorious view of Kowloon and harbor from peak, ferry ride, meetings, Asian smells and shops and food (a HK hamburger and shake in top of revolving restaurant with windows overlooking the harbor and night-lit city)

- Up at 5:00, in bus to train station at 7:00; already hot and muggy and schlepping 70 lbs. suitcases, sweat even soaking my pant legs

- Air conditioned (what a profound relief) train through a fascinatingly variable countryside that had all of us gazing through the big windows, destination Guangzhou – there stepping into an oven with humidity instantly treating you to a hot sweat bath, with luggage once again waiting to be lugged, which completed the process of soaking everything I was wearing

- No one there to meet us; Chengdu's Xiao Xiao showed up late and gave bad news: we wouldn't be going to Guilin, which had been my fondest hope

- Stood in boiling sun long waiting for mini vans to arrive and take us to airport; there the surprise was that we had any sweat left as we once again had to carry (no wheels in '85) all the loaded suitcases many loaded with contraband Bibles) to the luggage hall

- No plane ticket had been included/arranged for Ruth (lapse in communication), quite a hassle before it was resolved (hey, who said this was going to be easy!)

Chengdu

- But eventually we arrived where we were supposed to be – Chengdu and the College of Education and reception ceremonies

· No rest (badly needed) the next day – to placate our disappointment about the Guilin cancellation, the administration planned another treat – climbing 2600 meter high (part way) Mt Emei, sacred for its ancient Buddhist monasteries and famous for the more than 3000 varieties of plants that cover the mountain, more than 100 species unique to Mt. Emei; in the bus at 7:00 for a slow and bumpy seven-hour ride without stopping, during which Ruth became nauseous and through the open window shared her tummy's contents with the Chinese walking along the road, her first gift to China; on to the Mt. Emei hotel which had filthy floors, musty smells, and everything clammy to the touch, no doubt having something to do with the humid climate; as we walked toward the base of the mountain, I was struck by many among the Buddhist pilgrims – old, even ancient looking bent women, apparently toothless and faces with deeply carved grooves, dressed in some tribal clothes, coming from long distances to ascend this holy mountain and worship at one of its sacred temples; yes, mostly old because the younger generations have abandoned their religion in an anti-religious regime which denounces religion as the opiate of the masses

· The next day we did some steep climbing for about several hours to various Buddhist temples and shrines in muggy weather, too strenuous for some; my sweat glands were again working overtime, and I opted not to join those (much younger) who went for the additional 25 km steep hike to the top, most of whom didn't make it all the way

· This "treat" of a strenuous climb after long, exhausting travel wasn't exactly recuperative, but our hosts meant well, and we needed to learn to be appreciative even when their ways would not necessarily be ours

- After that outing my body told me it was being overloaded and gave me the usual dry mouth and the feeling of maxed-out energy, but the following day's more relaxed excursion aided recovery for the whole tired bunch

- As "head honcho," the week's last two days of planning and testing were for me extremely hectic with details, replanning when alternatives had to be found with little time to do it, and adjusting to an unpredictable and elusive Chinese system of decision making; yeah, taxing and stressful, but this was what I had signed up for – and His grace was sufficient

- Some impressions: the first timers among us find all their senses violated initially as they walk past student latrine or any public toilet, as they wake up with the smell of "night soil" in their nostrils, as they see dust and dirt and squalor and unsightly beasties that revel in that dust and dirt and squalor, as they taste fungus soup and sea slugs and esophagus delectables

- The WC's are places to squat, easy to find – just follow your nose

- Housing shortage – college faculty like Xiao Xiao live in one small room for a family of three

- Streets and roads clogged with people walking, riding on bikes, cycles, trucks, tractors, buses, few cars – all merging together and fighting for space to advance

- Riding a bus: shove, push, pull, press to get onboard and become "one flesh"

- The 16-year-old coming in from the street to sneak into a class where foreign experts teach English, relentless in wanting to learn English and who had to be chased off campus more than once

- The architect coming repeatedly with a nearly two-hour bike ride each way, offering to be my guide in showing his city and offering a banquet at his home, all in order to polish his English

- The English Corner where every Friday evening Chinese eager to learn or improve their English from English-speaking foreigners come from all corners of this huge city, like the factory girl, who had lost an opportunity to attend college due to the Cultural Revolution, doing a two-hour commute each way to improve the English she had been learning from TV, nurturing ambitions to become an accountant

- Your students, many lovely, sophisticated, well dressed, charming and often beautiful young ladies sitting in front of you, digging unselfconsciously into noses or worse, expectorating on floor without shame, which hits you like seeing fly specks on a bride's gown, slightly distracting; eventually you get used to seeing proper Chinese ladies on hot humid days lift high their summery see-through dress so they can sit down on their panty only

· Be on the alert when walking or biking for one who gets ready to unload a nose full without the use of a hankie; to these Chinese, blowing your nose into a hankie and putting that snot inside your pocket is really "vies"

The Students

But the reason for us thirty-plus people coming here, leaving home and family and conveniences and comforts for a summer, coming (at their own expense) to an ancient, now Communist country determined to escape third-world status, the reason was the students we would meet and teach and foster relationships that could make an eternal difference in their life.

So, who were these students?

· They came from all over the province, ages 19-55+

· The younger ones at least partly college educated, had optimism, ambition, and confidence, and appeared Westernized

· Those 35 and older felt part of a wasted generation when they were subservient to cadres, the Party, the work unit and sent to places and professions not of their choice

· Many had been victims of the Cultural Revolution (CR), separated from family, sent to remote and primitive countryside places to do hard labor among peasants instead of a pursuit of education and dreams; now tended toward cynicism, bitterness, resignation to no future, all this now coming to the surface with more freedom, long repressed anger vented in late night gripe sessions, in public meetings with officials (as in the farewell ceremony when vice governor of the province gave a speech they didn't like and rudely expressed their disrespect)

· Among them were also some who had served in the Red Guards during the CR when Mao had been their god; some had made a pilgrimage to Tiananmen Square to get a glimpse of Mao Tso Tung, and that had been a mystical experience for them

· Most of them had been deprived of so much we consider basic, who wept when they found freedom

- They took a cautious kind of pride in Deng Xiao Peng, native of Sichuan, who promised a better life ahead, but they expressed a growing impatience with the System for they had been betrayed by the Party and its leaders again and again, and lusted for reform

- They felt sadness for blighted hopes and a dim future, for a people sunk into a deep state of national depression

- They felt a great wistfulness about American freedom to travel anywhere and to choose jobs or switch jobs

- They looked to the Western world for a more hopeful future, and some looked at this group of American Christians and wondered whether the faith in their hearts could also be born in them

- A few students became especially close and dear to me:

- Charles – (on the picture Charles is on my right and Tom on my left) 43 and father of two children, with a heart of gold came one night to tell me of his deep grief of being assigned to teach in a remote place where no one wants to be and that made it impossible for him to be with and take care of his widowed mother as her oldest son; from his meager salary sends her 30 yuan a month; attempts to move back to Shanghai where his mother lives, but has no freedom of choice; grieves his own lost youth because of his father's treatment; asks for a Bible

- Carol – the youngest one among the 360, smart and very good in English, pained that she was assigned to teach Middle School instead of being able to attend college, which she yearned for, because the Party needed English teachers; she was searching for faith and was grateful for a Bible (she later came to the U.S., married a Chinese, joined the church, completed college and earned a master's, became an E.S.L. teacher, and calls us Dad and Mom)

- Tom – one of the older ones, during the CR was sent in exile to a very remote area where he had to endure hard labor, poor nutrition and often no food, physical and mental abuse, and where he had almost died twice from injuries, from neglect, from loneliness (he never completely recovered full health and died well before he had a chance to retire; we kept in touch till his premature death); he despaired of ever being able to enjoy real freedom and opportunity and would settle now just for living in stability and peace with family and friends; cried when he said that he sees this as his last opportunity to learn from a Foreign Expert (as the Chinese call the degreed teachers who come), that we might never see each other again (we did see each other again many years later), that he would try my teaching methods; he gave me a glimpse of the pain and longing of his heart for some sense of fulfillment, and when he grabbed my hand before he walked away, I too was moved to tears; he was very eager for a Bible and read it hungrily, ironic for he was assigned to be a monitor by the administration whose responsibility included reporting on any violation of the rules by the foreign teachers, and Bibles were strictly forbidden and had to be hidden to the public eye; he sat in the front row the cultural evening when we had a "Christmas program" to breathe in the Christmas story, after which he said "I felt a hurt deep inside of me with a sense of something beautiful"; he was the one who persuaded the administration to make a bus available for teachers to be able to attend church services, for religion was an important part of American culture that students should know about; and Tom one evening practiced what he had heard a Christian should do – "do everything in love" when he in a nearby restaurant came as interpreter to the aid of a British tourist couple who didn't like the chicken they had ordered (more bones than meat), paid for their reject dinner (with the scarce money his wife had sent him for necessary expenses) and took them to another restaurant for a meal more to their taste; he came with a heavy heart to me one afternoon with a decision he had to make – whether or not to accept the invitation to join the communist party, which he didn't want to be part of but by declining would forfeit any chance at future promotions which in turn would jeopardize his children's education and future; we talked and at the end he said he would say "yes" with his mouth but "no" with his heart – the Spirit had already taken room in his heart and in the years ahead would continue to expand that space into the "new life" for Tom; in one of his many letters later he wrote to me that it was like a sweet dream that he came to know me and God and the joy of integrating the Bible's teachings into his own teaching

- There was also Ben who had given his allegiance to Mao and communism but felt "a great emptiness in his heart"; one day he said, "I want God to be the Lord of my life," and he had a look of joy on his face when he told his teacher "I am your new brother in Christ"

- And there was Jessie who devoured the NT and said, "A wonderful change has come into my life; I'm no longer alone; we learn not to know but to believe" (sadly, when she came later to the U.S. to live, that wonderful change gradually faded into a penchant for false knowledge)

- Arthur, who like nearly all of them had been programmed to believe that religion is humbug, is bad for you, is for the ignorant and superstitious; we messed them up as a team of educated Americans whom they soon recognized as Christians too, and who modeled (or tried to) the fruits of the spirit; it led Arthur who had been very negative to Christianity to say, "I think it would be good to become a Christian"

- And many others

- But Abram was a special case; he was a minority student from Tibet who had been honored with the opportunity to join this summer program; he was looked down on by the others of the "superior" Chinese ethnic group; one day he found out that his brother in Tibet had died ten days earlier, but his parents were loath to tell him for fear that he would want to come home and jeopardize his once-in-a-lifetime chance to advance himself; he came to me, heartbroken and weeping; we spent two hours together as he told me his story: his father was a Reactionary, which meant that the family had suffered much in the CR; the brother who died had spent six hard years in the countryside, not unlike Tom, and now left two small children; his father was an intellectual who inspired his children to excel, to read much, to listen to the important discussions in the home; Abram had not been religious, but now he went to a Buddhist monastery to pray for his dead brother; Abram wanted me to come home with him to Tibet for a visit – I wished that I could have done just that, and I still wonder with tender feelings for that special person whether he found, if not God, peace and a good future

Many of our students carried physical and psychic scars but they were unbroken and delighted us with their eagerness to feel like children again (had they ever known the simple joys of childhood?) and we had them play games like Blind Man's Bluff, Duck Duck Goose, Drop the Hankie, Farmer in the Dell, and more; they loved it, and loved music and dance and singing and parties (dancing had been forbidden till '79); and they took great pleasure in taking evening strolls which for many years hadn't been possible when nightly propaganda meetings were mandatory.

For many, kindness had not been an experiential part of their lives, and when they observed it among us and received it from us, they were touched for it was their number one admired quality in others, and they were quick to return it; I was almost embarrassed and humbled by it when Tom and Charles took me to a barber in the tourist hotel, after they had scouted our part of the city for a place worthy of cutting this American professor's hair; they even insisted on paying for it; I in turn wanted to show my appreciation by treating them to a good bite and drink in the hotel, but that put them in a terrible quandary for their tradition dictated that they treat their guest rather than be treated, and they didn't have the money to treat beyond a haircut; when I insisted, ignorant of their tradition, they reluctantly obliged but it was painful for them and I'm afraid they didn't enjoy the treat.

It was interesting and sweet to see how quickly the women students took to Ruth, how easily they connected, and how she became a participant in oral English practice among them; they missed her when she had to leave after ten days, but not nearly so much as I hated to see her go; I mourned for a while, feeling the need for her presence and support in my challenging role in a challenging environment; having that dingy apartment all to myself was not a spirit-lifter; and I worried how she would navigate the return all by herself and felt relief when word came of a safe return to Lisa and California.

Toward the end of the program the students chose Charles to take me shopping for a class gift; their kindness touched me as ours had touched them, and so I went into the city with Charles, walking hand in hand with him, for that's what close friends do in China (I couldn't help wondering what my Calvin colleagues would say if they could see me then); I decided to select something that would remind me of China, would be easy to pack, and wouldn't cost them much – so I selected a nice tie; Charles was not pleased and headed for a dinnerware store where he picked out a 40-50 piece set of Chinese plates and saucers and bowls and cups in various sizes – to which I strenuously objected not only because it was expensive but even more because I saw no way of taking that monstrously heavy set home with me; but dear Charles would not take no for an answer and was not bothered by the take-home problem (amazingly, nothing got broken and we still make use of this set).

Later that evening, one of my team teachers came with gifts from her class, after which I wrote in my notes, "I'm so touched, I'm so tired."

The Teachers

- We met often to plan, to debrief, to pray, to problem solve, to encourage, to listen to each other, to remind of the need to be circumspect – to witness by example, by kindness and yes, love but not by testimony

- The team worked hard and most connected well with their students, both in class and out, though some needed more of my attention than others

- Many team members hailed from the South and were used to hot, humid summer weather, but even so without A-C the climate was draining; for me, used to a cooler climate and only occasional high humidity, there were days when I needed to change clothes three times a day because with 90 degrees and 90% humidity, sweat would go right through shirt and pants, besides depriving of seamless sleep

- By the end of our mission, we felt close to each other, bonded by our common experience and love in Christ; when parting time came, it became obvious that many students had become closely bonded to us, and though they were eager to get back home (as were we), they were reluctant to see us go; at the closing ceremony there were speeches (a short one for me):

I stayed in touch with a number of them for some time, one of whom, Pat, remained a longtime friend.

David Bonavio in The Chinese wrote this: "They are admirable, infuriating (yes, that too – they were incorrigible in ignoring directions and proscriptions, like "no talking, no looking at other papers), humorous, priggish, over weaning, mendacious, loyal, mercenary, ethereal, sadistic, and tender. They are not quite like anybody else. They are the Chinese."

We encountered, observed, and sensed a number of these qualities. But at departure time, hearts melted, and there were hugs and tears.

This was, and still is, one of the highlights of my life – thirty Christians on a college campus in a country of a billion people, praying each day for the grace to sincerely and consistently exhibit the love of Jesus to each other and to their 360 non-Christian students. It was a profoundly sanctifying experience. And to observe the impact of that visible witness on the Chinese was a great spiritual blessing.

The privilege of becoming an intimate part of some people's lives and forming close friendships, of showing and leading one to the Father is profoundly moving; to go as Christians who have no veil over their faces, who can be mirrors that brightly reflect something of the being and glory of the Lord – it brings you back to your own part of the world wondering why that isn't more of a natural daily way of living and being of our country's huge Christian community. Wouldn't that have a similar impact, both on the self and the other? I've been wondering that ever since. And I know how easily I/we get sidetracked, untracked by the avalanche of distractions that meets us each day; it takes a strong Spirit-guided intentionality and awareness of daily failures to keep that light shining.

We left our Bibles behind in China, we left many dear friends behind, we left some brand-new brothers and sisters in Christ behind, we left part of ourselves behind.

It was good to head back home, to Ruth, to family, to the college – yes, nearly thirty pounds lighter in body, but grown richer in mind and spirit.

Only four years later Chengdu squares and streets were crowded with hundreds of thousands of protesters in sympathy with the Tiananmen Square student protests in Beijing.

Trouble began when news of the massacre in Beijing trickled into Chengdu. Then crowds swelled and protesters, fully aware of the danger they were putting themselves in, took to the streets holding banners that read: "We are not afraid of death."

I wondered how many of our students and university administrators were among them, and if any of them were among the 300 or so who were shot or beaten to death by police in this place that became known as "Little Tiananmen."

Public Response

My summer in China raised a lot of interest after my return among students, colleagues, and area teachers, which resulted in several from the area committing to future service in China as well as an eventual partnership between CRC and ELIC. There were interviews and writeups and many invitations to speak to church groups. An invitation even came from The Back to God Hour in Palos Heights to be interviewed on its Faith 20 TV broadcast by its director Joel Nederhood. We taped the interview on the morning of January 15, 1986; on March 13 Don Distelberg from Calvin got up at 5:30 in a San Diego hotel where he had been staying; he had to catch an early flight but turned on the TV as he was getting dressed and found to his surprise Joel and me talking about China. All that interest was certainly gratifying.

Music & Drama

How did music and drama become a part of my life?

Through my DNA? Through my environment, like the home?

Quite likely through a bit of both. A musical strain seemed to course through the veins of both the Barons and the Hoekstras. Lots of brass players on the Hoekstra side, and Dad must've somehow learned to be good enough on the trumpet to qualify for the military band. Both parents loved to sing, and so did Hindrik-om, my dad's brother.

Still, I think it's always a bit of a mystery why music means more to one than to another. To me, music seemed early on to call up some soul response, before I even thought about my soul, or even now, not knowing exactly what a soul is. Plato said that "music and rhythm find their way into the secret places of the soul," and that resonates with me. My taste for music started early and even now I have music entering my insides nearly all day, though there are also times when I choose to write or read in almost total silence. I think music feeds me in some way, feeds my longing for beauty, for harmony, for peaceableness.

The music I preferred was classical – symphonic and choral, and as a teenager I began to build my music record library when I had a bit of money to spend, first 45s and then long-play 33s. While still in Lynden I sang second tenor in my church quartet; we sang at programs and even on radio station KPUG. I also joined the Lynden Choral Society, singing in Handel's "Messiah." I took some church organ lessons, and I regret to this day that I didn't have more time and means to pursue that toward becoming an accomplished organ player. I often played on the pump organ in our home and even had a short stint of teaching a young daughter of family friends.

When I started Western in Bellingham, I joined the Glee Club and found it immensely enjoyable.

After moving to Grand Rapids in 1959, Ruth and I soon joined audience membership in the Grand Rapids Symphony and have attended its excellent concerts ever since, most of the time as front row occupants. From that vantage point we have observed and been at times transported and always inspired by many an amazing and world-famous solo guest performer. We don't have much of an idea of heaven, but music can bring you close at special moments that fill with awe and a taste of ecstasy.

Both Ruth and I joined the Neland Church choir soon after we joined that church. It was a serious choir with a number of good soloists, we wore robes, and we often sang for both Sunday services from a challenging choral repertoire.

It wasn't long after joining the South Christian faculty that I birthed the idea of inviting some colleagues and spouses to join us on a Sunday evening for some Psalter Hymnal singing. After that wintry evening beginning on Baxter Ave. in February 1962, we made it a monthly Sing Group event, month after month, year after year after year, till 2020 when Covid-19 kept us apart. (But we resumed in '21 when restrictions were lifted and all of us had been vaccinated.)

Ruth and I also joined the Calvin Oratorio Society and often thrilled to the singing of Handel's "Messiah" for large Christmas crowds, initially in a downtown concert hall and later at Calvin. One can surely be moved sitting in the auditorium and feeling embraced by the music and its message, but I've been more powerfully moved when singing the choruses of the "Messiah" or Brahms' "Requiem" or Haydn's "The Creation" and "Lord Nelson Mass" with another hundred voices or so all around me.

After joining the Calvin faculty, I also joined the Gilbert and Sullivan Alumni Singers.

Their stage productions were very popular and very good. I participated in several of them, satisfying my appetite for both music and drama.

And drama had always been on my to-do list. So, besides G & S, I resurrected my Thespian impulse and tried out for stage opportunities. A musical was one of them (offered by the Calvin Summer Boulevard Theater) – "Irene," a musical comedy from the 20s in which I played (and sang) the part of Madame Lucy, a Paris dress designer.

Later I played Harry in Tom Stoppard's "Enter a Free Man," a debut production put on by Calvin College Thespians Alumni, a debut called "impressive" by the GR Press drama critic. A few years after that I participated in a thoroughly enjoyable dramatic version of Sietze Buning's (Stan Wiersma) book "Purpaleanie," Wiersma's recollection of his early Iowa childhood in poetic form.

It had substance, it had humor, it had emotion, felt by cast members and by the audience, and most of all it had meaning related to faith and the practice of that faith. As cast and director we enjoyed each other, had fun together, and felt embraced by the audience. For me it was even more special because daughter Cindy was in the cast too.

And yes, we acted but we also sang in some scenes, a wonderful and poignant combination of music and drama.

The play ran for three weekends. It really hit home for the audiences, many of them feeling eyes well up at the climactic closing scene.

Then came one more opportunity to be a Thespian, this time after my retirement, when the Calvin Theatre Company presented "Tiger at the Gates" by Jean Giraudoux, translated by Christopher Fry.

The play is about the Trojan war and the failure of preventing it through the foolishness of leaders and intellectuals, carrying an implicit indictment of the flawed diplomacy that led to WWI, followed by WWII. I, (ironically?), was cast as the Mathematician, one of the foolish intellectuals.

224

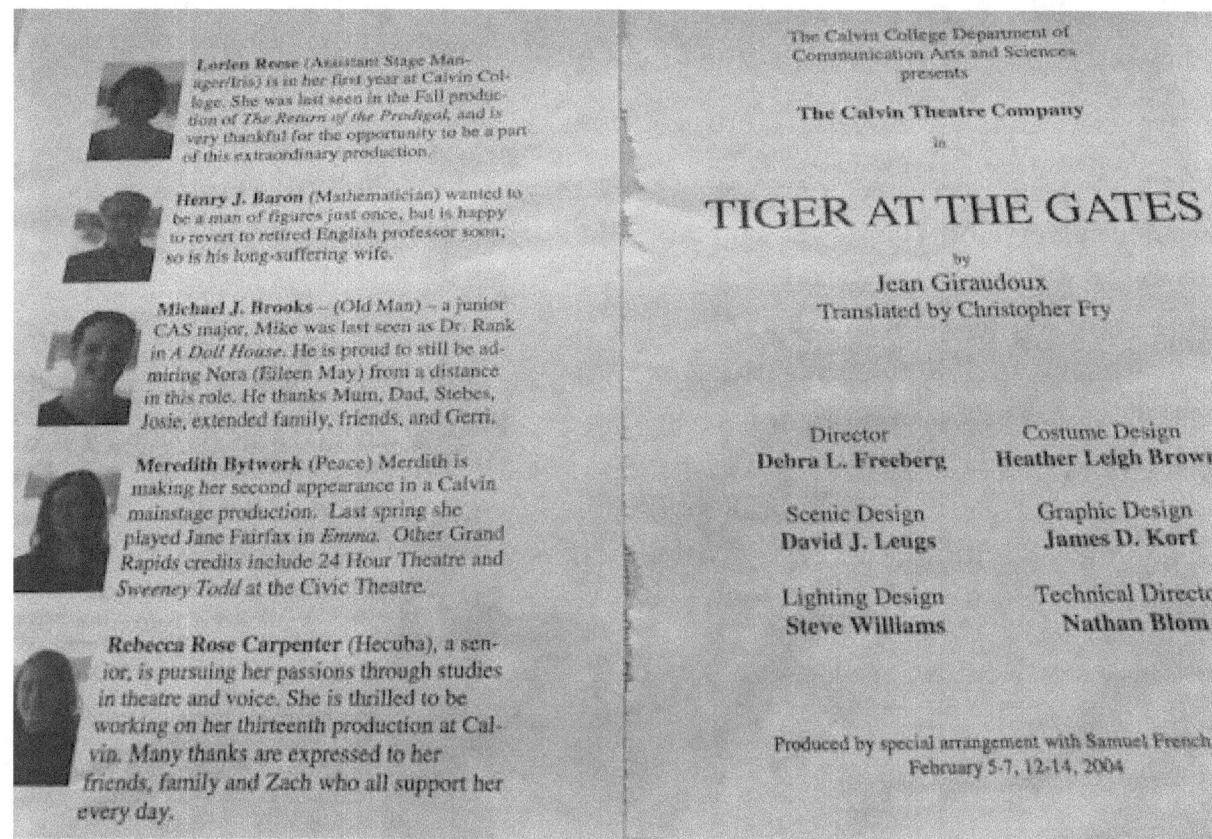

The Calvin College Department of
Communication Arts and Sciences
presents

The Calvin Theatre Company

in

TIGER AT THE GATES

by
Jean Giraudoux
Translated by Christopher Fry

Director	Costume Design
Debra L. Freeberg	**Heather Leigh Brown**
Scenic Design	Graphic Design
David J. Leugs	**James D. Korf**
Lighting Design	Technical Director
Steve Williams	**Nathan Blom**

Produced by special arrangement with Samuel French
February 5-7, 12-14, 2004

Cast bios (left column of program):

Lorien Reese (Assistant Stage Manager/Iris) is in her first year at Calvin College. She was last seen in the Fall production of *The Return of the Prodigal*, and is very thankful for the opportunity to be a part of this extraordinary production.

Henry J. Baron (Mathematician) wanted to be a man of figures just once, but is happy to revert to retired English professor soon; so is his long-suffering wife.

Michael J. Brooks — (Old Man) — a junior CAS major, Mike was last seen as Dr. Rank in *A Doll House*. He is proud to still be admiring Nora (Eileen May) from a distance in this role. He thanks Mum, Dad, Siebes, Josie, extended family, friends, and Gerri.

Meredith Bytwork (Peace) Meredith is making her second appearance in a Calvin mainstage production. Last spring she played Jane Fairfax in *Emma*. Other Grand Rapids credits include 24 Hour Theatre and *Sweeney Todd* at the Civic Theatre.

Rebecca Rose Carpenter (Hecuba), a senior, is pursuing her passions through studies in theatre and voice. She is thrilled to be working on her thirteenth production at Calvin. Many thanks are expressed to her friends, family and Zach who all support her every day.

The rest of the cast were Calvin students and recent alumni except for Michael Page, just retired from the Calvin Communication department, a professional actor, who took the main role of Priam, king of Troy.

At age 70, I discovered that the memory bank seemed to be more cluttered, causing the stage jitters to spike a bit with lessening confidence. I enjoyed getting to know the director, Debra Freeberg, who became a friend, but the age difference with the students made me pretty much a loner. Besides, it didn't feel that the play as a whole connected as strongly with the audiences as the plays I had been in before. And thus, not as satisfying.

So, why did I do it? Why did I do any of those time-consuming workouts in music and drama performances?

I didn't ask myself that at the time, but I need to ask that now.

Was it to gain more visibility? Some of that, maybe.

Was it to exercise the gifts I felt I had, however modest they were? Yes, maybe that comes closer.

There was a time when I indulged in Walter Mitty dreams, being an opera star or a Shakespeare actor. I wished I could be, but I knew I never would.

There was a difference between music and drama, though.

Music at its best was soul food for me; it was what I needed, connecting to the divine mystery and glory of the Creator and Giver of all good gifts.

Drama I wanted to be a means at its best for an actor to move an audience to laughter, tears, reflection, and growth. When younger I might not have articulated my view of it in those terms, but now I think that down deep that's what I hoped for drama and my role in it. Obviously, acting did not become a big part of my life, and I don't regret it. I always had freedom to dream about certain roles I would have liked to have and how unforgettably I would have acted them out, and that always turned out more successfully than it likely would have on stage. Thank God for blessing us with an imagination.

Church

The church has been an inseparable part of my life, almost from birth.

I was baptized in church as a baby (Opende Gereformeerde Kerk).

I was catechized in church as an adolescent (Lynden First Christian Reformed Church with Rev. John Verbrugge).

I made profession of faith in church as a youngish adult (Lynden First CRC with Rev. Louis Voskuil).

Read "De Wachter" at first and then "The Banner" faithfully, later added "Christianity Today" and "Sojourners" and "Christian Courier."

I attended Bible Study, Young People's Society, participated in local mission activities, ushered, led adult ed programs, taught catechism classes, served on numerous committees, served as elder many times including chairman of elders and president of council, served as delegate to synod four times and twice surprisingly elected as first clerk, preached seven times (twice in Frisian in Oudkerk/Aldtsjerk, once in Dutch in Opende, once in Frisian in Grand Rapids and in Woodstock, twice in English near Detroit), served as editor of "Neland News" for many years, and wrote the 75th anniversary book of Neland CRC.

We joined Neland Ave. CRC in 1962 and are members to this day in 2021.

Besides Neland, I was a member of Everson CRC, First Lynden CRC, Sumas CRC (for both Ruth and me), Sherman St. CRC, and temp members of Hessel Park CRC in Champaign.

Now I can look back on all those years of church affiliation and participation and ponder their impact on my life.

What would I have missed without the church? That's almost like asking what I would have missed without the faith. And that's a good question to ask.

For me that's a hard one to even imagine.

I think it was not just my upbringing in a Christian home; even if I hadn't been, it feels like I would have sooner or later responded to an inner sense of the transcendent, of a divine mystery that beckons the soul to reach out and be touched.

In all those years of church life – reading, listening, and membership, I have been touched, often in blessed ways. In my adult years, faith has never been a simple possession of facts and knowledge, or a ready acceptance of doctrines and decisions, or an unquestioned adherence to rules and interpretations. I sometimes envied those whose faith is as steady as a ship anchored in a placid sea, solid and unchanging. As the years rolled by and my sense of the world and its people grew more complex, doubts and questions would often challenge my faith. The church at its worst would add to those perturbations.

Nate Pyle in the "Reformed Journal" of June 25,'21, articulated what I too feel at times, "… longing for the faith of my youth…it's not a faith I can have. Because that faith can't stand up against ectopic pregnancies, friend's marriages falling apart, betrayal, people far too young dying, coming to grips with how little control we have, and systemic injustices. … I need a faith for this world. A faith that has space for every facet of the human experience—right and wrong, laughter and tears, work and rest, friendship and isolation, joy and grief, life and death.'"

The church at its best, and I'm blessed that for me it has been much more "best" than "worst," not only affirmed but enriched my faith.

There were and are troubling times, of course: staying at Neland and Watkins through tensions for neighborhood ministry, women in office, and now same-sex marriage. With each controversy there's division, sometimes acrimonious exchanges, shedding members, and grieving. Usually at its core is disagreement in interpretations of Scripture. Instead of exercising humility in imperfect human understanding of God's will, there is insistence on knowing with certainty what is a right and a wrong faith practice, echoes of what happened in our Opende church in 1944, inflicting the same human relationships with internal pain.

I still have many questions and times of doubt, but I've become more content with seeing through a glass darkly and ready to embrace mystery even gratefully. My lodestar is not an apostle or a prophet or a church leader like Augustine or Calvin or Luther. It is Jesus, simply Jesus, but profound in its meaning. For Jesus was God incarnate and all his teaching and actions were centered on love, love for God and love for each other. Loving God implies loving a neighbor; loving a neighbor is an expression of loving God. Nowhere in Scripture does God forbid either kind of love. And I'm still working on living that out – a life of love. The church and many of its people as well as people outside of church, God's people, at their best have inspired and encouraged me in such a life. John, the apostle close to Jesus, writes in 1 John 4: "Everyone who loves has been born of God and knows God." A truth to live into and to celebrate each day.

Family

We started a family in 1959, 62 years ago as I sit here reflecting and recalling! Thinking back on it now, did we know what we were in for? Of course, we didn't. We knew what it was like to be children, but not parents. Like all parents, we started from scratch, in our case both financially and physically.

Both of us wanted to have a family. I had always loved little tikes and was fascinated watching them explore and experience a world full of wonders and surprises, watching them discover, learn, and respond. To have our own would make it our turn to discover, learn, and respond. It would be a labor of love, sometimes stretched, of course, but love has a long leash and hangs on.

Our first-born became our only Washington baby, born in winter 1959.

I remember taking a day off from school and having Ruth's sister Alice substitute for me. In that day there were no benefits attached to one's teacher contract, so the sub was on me. (But Alice was kind and tore up my check.) I don't think there was health insurance either, but fortunately hospitals and pediatricians were cheaper then.

Cradling a living bundle of flesh from your flesh in your arms for the first time gives a feeling, like few others one experiences in life, that defies accurate description. You touch those little fingers, those little toes, that newborn skin so soft, and watch that tiny mouth so sweet and that round little face try out a gallery of expressions, maybe even a bit of a momentary smile – and you feel in your soul that you are connected to a divine mystery whose beauty floods you with love for that unique new life that you are holding close to you.

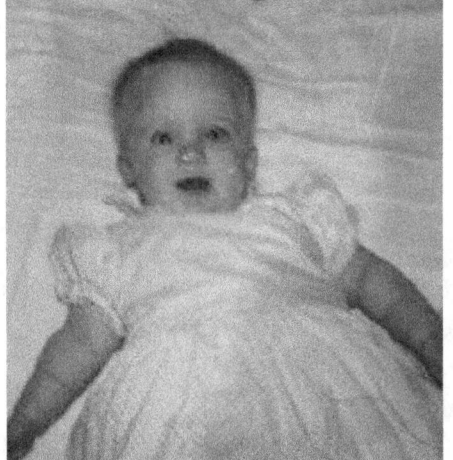

She did not remain an only child for long; Cynthia Rose was joined about a year and a half later by sister Judith Lynne.

The Baxter home became a little "smaller," a little busier, a little noisier. But especially filled with a little more concern, for Judy was born with spina bifida and hydrocephalus. She was born in June with me working part time jobs and finishing my graduation requirements at Calvin, while Ruth was home busy with two little ones now that included learning how to take care of a special-needs infant. It was a stressful time. It preoccupied both of us.

Ruth wrote about that, included in the Supplement (p. 335).

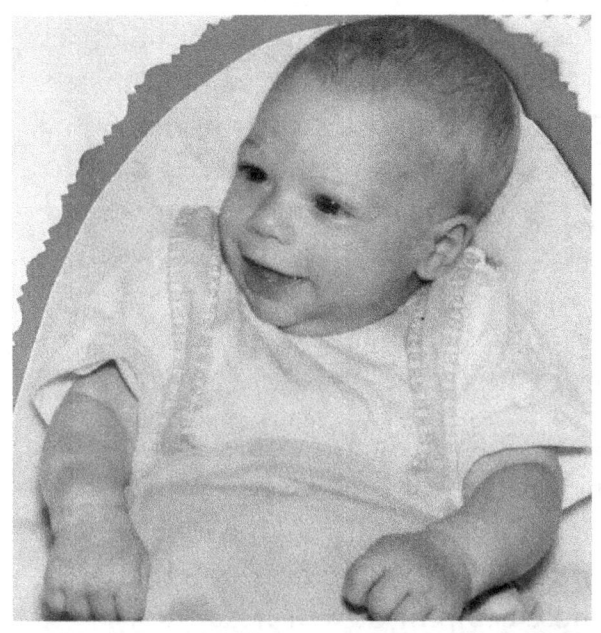

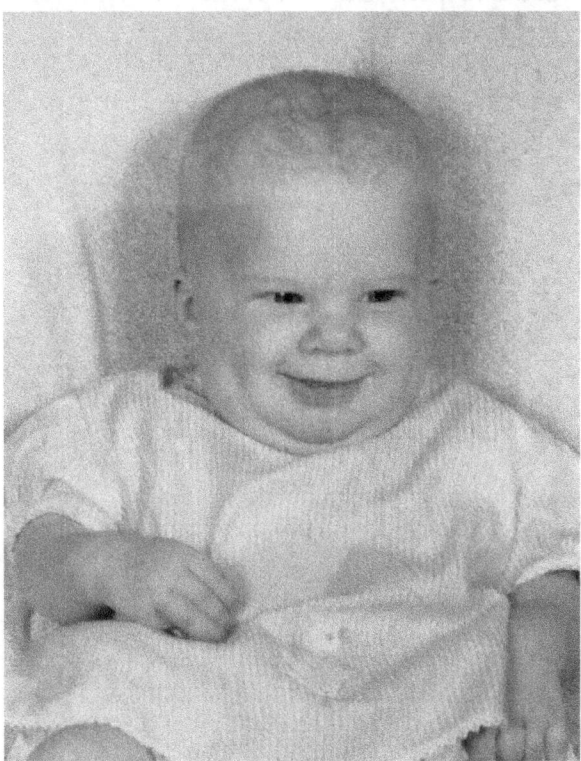

Shortly after our third child, Henry Jr., was born a good year later, we had moved from 1049 Baxter to 1040 Alexander, making us homeowners for the first time. But the family kept expanding. Less than two years later Jayne came to join the little flock, and our modest Alexander home became more crowded.

As time went on, we expanded the kitchen eating area and added a super small half bath and closet bedroom upstairs.

The four little ones formed a kind of self-entertainment company with the oldest gaining valuable experience in leadership, which seemed to come quite naturally to her. Judy, who didn't manage to walk on her own till she was twenty-six months old, was the outgoing show girl whose natural talent was to summon a guest's attention by many a charming smile. Henry was the peaceable middle child who was a willing participant in the company's activities. And Jayne, who often seemed to hear the sounds of a different drummer, added the spice that kept things humming for the others.

As they grew older, they discovered playmates in the neighborhood. It was a good neighborhood to grow up in, with school and church just a block away, a park nearby, and stores one could walk to. I think back on those years now, there on Alexander in the '60s, and my heart feels flooded with gratitude that we had the privilege, the blessing, of watching (and yes, supervising too) the growth of four little ones, each with a unique personality and inclinations, into loveable, harmonious, mature human beings.

We bought a fold-down camper and took many a little trip and some big ones pulling it behind our station wagon. One included Banff on its westward journey. It has always been a thrill, after many long hours of rolling through flat or hilly countryside to see the majestic Rockies begin to appear on the horizon. The pictures in our family albums tell much of those camping adventure stories.

Among the memories is the cross-country trip with the Hekmans, taking the more southern route west. No one will forget the heat beating down relentlessly when driving through Utah and Nevada; at least we had AC, but we felt great pity for the Hekmans whose car was not equipped with air. We arrived in our Las Vegas camping site near midnight, with the temperature still hovering around 100.

And I certainly won't forget the stings of those fierce Canadian horse flies that made us try to put Saskatchewan behind us as rapidly as we could! Nor the time on another Washington-bound marathon when on an all-night drive I started following a gravel truck in the Dakotas into uncharted territory which finally ended when it was discovered that I had been trailing a work crew building the new I-94 freeway. Or the time we woke up to a half-flooded campsite. Or when on another all-nighter my mind went spacey and I became convinced that ominous ghosts and goblins were caught in the headlights, floating in the air, and coming threateningly toward my sleeping family.

Long days after long days of riding together in close quarters can make for some entertaining family time, though. Children will no doubt remember car games played (license plate states, 20 questions, I spy…, hinky pinky, etc.), Dutch ditties learned and sung together ('k Zag twee beren broodjes smeren, o wat was't een wonder….), listening to tapes, and yes, also getting bored of too much sitting and sometimes getting on each other's nerves. But touring and camping makes for a unique family experience that can generate sweet memories for the rest of one's life. I think back on those trips now with some nostalgia and some regret that I probably didn't make it count for more than I did, for the children and for myself.

The favored destination for many of these long rides?

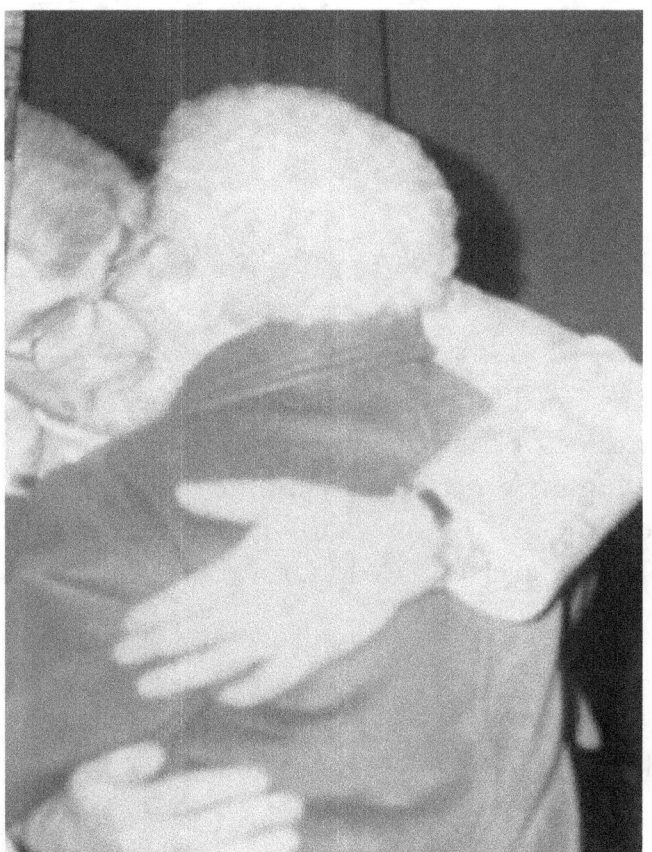

Lynden, the family center we had left behind and always missed, where Mem was waiting for a long-awaited hug and visit with apple juice and tea and almond tarts from the Dutch Bakery.

But also, of course, the Bosman parents/grandparents as well as an ever-expanding extended family.

For me it was also especially brother Sid with whom to enjoy airplane rides in his Cessna 172 enjoying the beauty of the San Juan islands below us, heading for Roche Harbor or Everett's Payne Field for lunch.

And many a flight to other places like Boeing Field and Monroe and Port Townsend.

I loved it when Sid had me take the controls to these various destinations and at times had me practice maneuvers, such as doing a 360 while maintaining the same altitude and speed. I felt proud of myself when I did that perfectly.

But there's also the memory of the flight in which I did the pre-flight checks and take-off and that shortly thereafter almost ended in disaster when oil pressure dropped precipitously and we barely made it back to the airport when on touchdown the engine conked out altogether. And the flight when Mem and cousin Barbara (daughter

of Hindrik-om) joined us on a flight to Roche Harbor, Mem's first ride with her son Sid, which she took with a fatalistic resigned look on her face at the beginning, then gradually changing to a more relaxed look of enjoyment as she looked down at the beauty of the San Juan islands gliding underneath her. And the excitement of the kids riding in the back seat of their uncle's Tri-Pacer landing on a summer twilight evening in Grandpa's pasture on his Haverstick Road farm (in retrospect not wise but both landing and take-off went well).

And the gift from Sid of a flight lesson with an instructor who had me do turns and even a power-off recovery and a stall recovery when pulling the plane into too steep a climb – thrilling, heart-racing, and to me unforgettable. And the airplane ascent over the top of Mt. Baker with the Speerstras in the back and getting a look at its crater that's home to a still active volcano.

The joy of flying with my brother continued well into the new century, my retirement years.

It even included flying in his company's helicopter and turbo jet piloted by the company's pilots.

For the kids, and really for all of us, the great pleasure was going fishing in Grandpa Bosman's boat, often to Silver Lake, having family picnics, sometimes at Silver Lake Park near Glacier, sometimes higher up at Mt. Baker's Artist Point. I think the kids fell in love with Washington through not only its natural beauty but especially all the uncles and aunts and cousins, lots more family than they had in Grand Rapids, and of course they loved being treated special by grandparents and others. It made going there a fond anticipation, and leaving there a sad feeling of separation.

Sometimes we took the train, as we did in August of '83. It did not start out well in Chicago. We were the only passengers in our railcar, the three of us, and we were waiting for the train from New York which had been delayed because of a bridge stuck in the upright position. Its passengers had to detrain and taken by bus to the Union Station. When they finally arrived and had to rush to the waiting train, they were exhausted from tension and fatigue. The older, Hispanic, gentleman who entered our car with luggage certainly was! It took him a while to catch his breath.

When he was somewhat recovered, I started a conversation. He was headed for Seattle, as were we, where his son was waiting for him and had chosen to go by train for safety reasons. His face showed his happiness as he talked about looking forward to the reunion.

I watched him unwrap some crackers which he started to eat.

I went back to reading, but soon something caught my eye. His false teeth were protruding. Something was wrong. He had difficulty breathing, his face became distorted, and his right arm jerked in spasmodic motion.

I rushed over to him. There was fear in my question, "Are you alright?!" But there was no answer, and his eyes were rolling. As I held him, I felt the breath go out of him.

I called to Ruth to get the conductor. He arrived in a matter of seconds, took one look, put out a call for medical help, and advised the engineer to stop the train.

It seemed like an eternity before nurses appeared. All this time I had been holding him and felt immensely relieved to let the nurses take over. They removed his false teeth, cleared his passageway, and after what seemed too long a wait again, laid him in the aisle and began CPR. (Should/could I have done what they did right from the start? Could it have made a difference??) An ambulance eventually arrived, and there had been no sign of life.

We were deeply shocked and concerned how five-year old Lisa would process this traumatic incident.

I was contacted later by his daughter, found out her father was Dr. Bruno Jocson, and was able to tell her about the circumstances of her father's demise, which was deeply appreciated.

The trips out to WA were all special and seldom traumatic, but one stands out especially. We took a car from a local dealer to a buyer in Washington, I would be working that summer for Sid's FM station KLYN as a DJ and announcer, he would provide a car for us to use, and we rented a basement apartment from the Snappers who lived close to Mem on Front St. It was a wonderful summer for all of us.'

Another one was worthy of a written grateful account, dated August 31, '64, and sent to the Lynden family:

Dear Family,

Again we are separated by 2500 long, wearisome miles, the weariness of which we can still feel in our systems. But stronger than that is the memory of some twelve days of wonderful times! We felt the excitement of it when we drove into Washington in eager anticipation, and we keenly felt the sadness when we inevitably had to leave it all again. But with us went the many memories, and for those we want to thank you. We'll long remember the pleasant talks; your good home-cooking and fancy restaurants; the excitement of Shakey's and the serenity of Mt. Baker; the airplane rides and the train we almost missed; Cinerama and the bowling alley we never got to; dinner on top of the Space Needle and the "Music from Holland Party"; the Fair interviews and Sumas Church we couldn't get to in time; the getting-to-know – of nieces and nephews and late-hour World Book demonstrations—-these and many more we'll have with us a long time!

Northern Pacific rates at least as high as the Great Northern in our book. It was less crowded, fairly smooth riding, and had such additional features as a stewardess-nurse, an intercom system, and a lounge-snack car. Traveling was pleasant and enjoyable except for when Jaynie would squirm, fight, run, laugh play, scream, and seldom sleep!

And there was Henry who tumbled down the dome-car stairs, Judy who tried to charm her way into everybody's seats, and Cindy who had to go to the "women's" all the time.

It was almost three o'clock Chicago time when we arrived there. After transferring stations, we went to a small restaurant nearby for something warm. (Incidentally, all the "train-food" we took along supplied us for quite a while and was most welcome!). … On the train to G.R. we all rode together in the lounge car since they were short of seats elsewhere. This was a break for the kids, especially Jaynie who was putting up a fatalistic struggle against sleep; now she had some friends to fight with and some space to walk around in. For most of the trip the coach was stifling hot after a short in the wiring knocked out the air-conditioning. Finally, an hour late, we rolled into G.R. To our relief Wayne and Greta were there to pick us up. What a relief, too, to get all in their beds again for a normal night's sleep.

The next morning I picked up our old faithful VW, and then things really seemed back to normal.

But we miss all of you, and we really hope you allow us to entertain you here someday as you did us there. Thank you again for all your hospitality and generosity, for everything that made our stay there a Wonderful Time!

With our love,

Henk, Ruth, and family

We had our four "lovely bunch of coconuts" – as I'd sometimes called them, but others entered as well and stayed with us for a time.

Terry Forrest joined us in '73 as a foster child and stayed for a year and a half, always longing to be reunited with his mother. Through Bethany we opened our home to Terry, hoping to be a blessing to him and that Henry could be a kind of older brother to him.

Lisa van Essen came to us through Ty and Coby Hofman whose contact in NL led Gerrit van Essen to send daughter Lisa to MI. Lisa was a twin, her mother had committed suicide, and her dad was eager to place her in a solid Christian home to stabilize Lisa's unruly life, exacerbated by the loss of her mother. While with us, Lisa attended Christian High, hung out with a fringe crowd, and played loose and easy, much of it without our direct knowledge. The plan was after her graduation to start Calvin, but a panic attack there sent her back home to NL. A whole chapter could easily be written about Lisa's further colorful self-absorbed journey which eventually brought her back to the U.S. for more adventurous living, but who is now firmly established as Chaya van Essen in Beverly Hills as Estates Director for Hilton & Hyland, a Luxury Properties real estate firm, selling multi-million-dollar properties.

She's married again recently for the third time, but now to an old GRCH friend. She treated us to a fancy lunch when we stopped by her office on a CA vacation and found to our delight that she has become a beautiful, charming, highly successful and esteemed businesswoman who is also a woman of faith. All's well that ends well, and this has.

Her dad had been engaged in WWII resistance forces on many a highly dangerous mission, and when he visited us in GR it was very interesting to bring him together with Calvin President (emeritus) Spoelhof who had been active in Intelligence for the allied forces at the same time. I very much enjoyed getting to know Gerrit and having great conversations with him, visited him in his NL home, and he came to visit us when we were on a home exchange in Drachten. I wish we could've stayed in touch longer.

Ok-Joo came to us through John and Juliana Steensma. She came from Korea to complete her education at Calvin and intended to return to Korea as a super-duper English teacher. She had not grown up in a Christian home, so our home devotions were new to her, as was church and a Christian college. She stayed with us for four months before moving to Calvin dorms. But she spent time with us regularly, almost as a family member, and attended Neland with us most Sundays. To our great joy she eventually made profession of her new faith in Christ there, fell in love with a Korean seminary student, married him, and became a minister's wife, serving a church in Ann Arbor. We became her American Mom and Dad. She strikes me now as a truly saintly person, a blessing to her church, and a wise, loving mother to her two sons.

There were several summers when we hosted German exchange students as well, through the Calvin German department.

But when we said "yes" to Bethany Christian Services seeking a home for a Salvador orphan, our commitment extended over more than a season or two. Milagro Portillo came to us when she turned 15 and knew no English at all. Our home was hers for most of her teenage years, and her story too deserves a chapter or two.

Those were understandably difficult years for her and at times for us too, but it's another story that through periods of stresses and strains ended well: she is married, the mother of three children attending Christian school, active in her church, living in a lovely new home, and calling us affectionately Mom and Dad, with Lisa having been like a sister to her for years now.

Others became more or less regular participants in our family life too, like Judy O, Mary Sullivan/Benedict, and Margriet Dekker. Judy O and Margriet* are both terminally ill now, and Mary B still visits us regularly. (*Margriet passed away in October '21.)

Opening our home to others has both complicated and expanded our lives. There are long and in some cases vexing stories attached to each of them. What motivates it is the inclination to be something needed by and good for others. I think that's God-given. But it requires sensibility and wisdom, and that was at times in short supply. But at its best the giver finds that they too needed to do that and that it was good for them.

But back to our nuclear family.

Number 5

Yes, and then there were five!

We didn't think we needed to add to our offspring quartet, but God knew better: the four, between the ages of 14 and 19, would be joined by a little sister in April 1978. We had thought we were finished and anticipating an empty nest while still in our 40s; instead, we would be keeping company with another amazing, unique creation, entrusted to us by her Creator.

I wrote about that change in our lives:

"To Become a Father Again"

I've never really thought about it much, but I guess if someone asked me if I like little kids, I'd have to admit that I do. Call it fascination, fondness, or love—I've had that for little humans about as far back as I can remember. Understandably, then, when we eventually produced some of our own, I was a proud, pleased-as-punch papa. Of course, they came in somewhat hurried succession, a bit faster than I thought reasonable at the time; as a matter of fact, it seemed to me than that they all came about the same time. That, I admit, made it hard to be always equally fascinated by each, especially when one needed burping, the other tried to pull the third one's few silky strands of hair, and the fourth was trying, without permission, to get a dangerously unsteady bead on the whole scene through Dad's new camera.

Ah, but they grew up, too soon, of course, though more or less in order. Still, the growing up hardly diminished the fascination, fondness, and love. Oh, there was the usual dosage of frustration, fretting, and fear even. It's after all no small matter to see a frolicsome family of four through many changes: changes of diapers, of height and weight, of schools, of preferences, of moods, of voice, of friends and enemies. Not that our family was particularly fickle, I think. As a matter of fact, it's been a fun bunch of young'uns. But as the Dutch say, "time stands not still," and one gets a little winded sometimes trying to keep a firm grip on Time's coattails.

I was beginning to relax a bit, though. Almost finished with an exciting, sometimes exhausting and often difficult task, I'd venture to think to myself. And so far, so good, thank God. Nobody has run away in the last fifteen years, nobody refuses to go to school or church, nobody until this year had even had a cavity (sometimes you almost win them all.). Yes, they had been good years, and the years ahead would be good, too—a little quieter and a little more independent.

Well, that was then; this is now. There came a new development, an unexpected expectation; I'm still flabbergasted. A grandchild some future day maybe. But to start all over again with another of our own? Bibs again, and a crib and a playpen and a highchair and little booties and baby blankies, and toys and teething rings and snow suits, and a trike and—oh my goodness, all this all over again? And what about the population explosion! I've always had a fear of explosions and now I'm causing one of my own? I could feel the accusing eyes of zero populationists smite my conscience. I cringed a little. And I tightened my coattails grip again; we'd be raising a child toward the dawn of the twenty-first century.

The truth is that it does sort of take your breath away; it did for the whole family, in fact, and Mama not least among them. But not just because of the sheer shock of the surprise. Also, and especially because of being in the presence of an unfolding miracle.

And what a miracle it is! The growth of a single cell to an almost fully formed embryo in little more than two months' time! The fluttering development of a soft bulging piece of tissue into a tiny but complete human being. What a wonder of God's creation it really is! And this time the kids are old enough to appreciate the wonder of it all!

They haven't been so excited since they took their first long airplane ride seven years ago. Researching medical books, feeling the baby's lively movements, making cutesy baby things, gathering the necessary baby stuff from everywhere, choosing names, anticipating the actual arrival, praying for a safe delivery and a healthy child—all this and more has been a big part of the family's excitement during the last several months.

As I said, I really do love little kids. It'll be a challenge to raise another one, but also a joy to watch it grow; to elicit the magic of its first smile; to hear the first word, the first phrase, the first original sentence, the first prayer. It'll be a privilege to love another one.

I had always regretted not being allowed to witness the birth of our children, but with our fifth – yes, I could! It became an experience, more than twenty years later, still instantly available for a vivid visual replay in my memory bank: supporting, encouraging the mother struggling with the birth pangs, the rushes of pain that racked the swollen body. I could hold her hand, dictate the deep breaths, but you feel pretty helpless in this drama of extricating/delivering a new life unfolding.

When at last it came, I moved to the rear to take it in, and froze … there was no cry, no motion, just a limp blueish body, quickly wrapped in cloth and handed to the doctor who took the newborn to the wall away from the mother's eyes and gently began to massage its back … but there was no response … only a doctor and a floppy body turning a deeper blue even as the doctor kept massaging and nurses looking on … and no sound … and a dad wholly unprepared for such a scene and shaking and heart racing and fighting the paralyzing fear that he was witnessing the dying of their precious newborn in the silence that hung like a shroud over the delivery room as the seconds and the minutes multiplied into an eternity … until at last a thin sound a sign of LIFE a weak cry BUT a cry … and then a quick handoff to a nurse taking it to the preemie ward … and I not yet recovered walking weakly to face the mother who mercifully had not been aware but now saw my face drained of all color and took my shaky hand and heard my whisper "she's going to be okay."

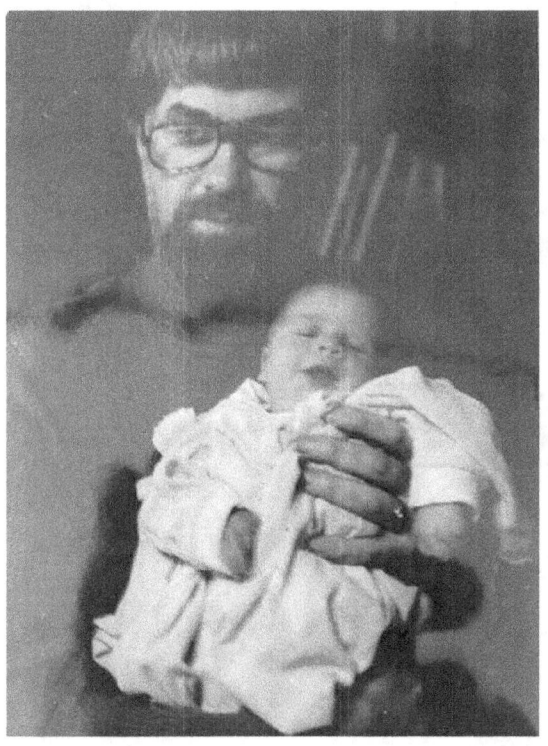

And, thankfully, she was. Mom and baby came home a few days later among mountains of snow from a late winter, early spring snowstorm.

The Accident

Blessed is the family that never encounters a serious, life-threatening accident. We've had a few accidents, but it's the Big One you never forget. And it was the baby in the family whose survival still fills us with awe and profound gratitude. (My account of that searing Sunday is included in the Supplement p. 351).

A Special Birthday

Some birthdays become more special than others. The Lummi Island birthday party in 1980 mentioned earlier was special because of the place and the people that had not been part of our life for some time.

But my 60th held in the Calvin campus manor was made super special through my lovely wife, our children, my siblings, my aging mother, and a host of Frisian and college friends surrounding me. Artist daughter Jayne had created a lasting memory of that occasion in my life which made me nearly speechless when it was unveiled.

There's a DVD of all the special family fun we enjoyed together.

Henry James Raun, Sr.
60 Years

Twenty years later was another special: an 80th birthday party.

Receptions, dinners, friends, and precious family made the day and the time create a bundle of sweet memories to treasure, especially when revisiting those May days in picture albums and video.

One of the special creations the children put together was a poster listing all the jobs and activities that had been part of my life. It made me smile in remembering and a bit tired to look at this list, though it could have included half a dozen more.

A Henry of All Trades!

field work (berry picking and farm labor)
cannery work
door-to-door selling
office supplies store clerk
delivery driver
elementary teacher
junior-high teacher
elementary school principal
school janitor
school bus driver
high school teacher
junior college teacher
GM press operator
warehouse work
carpet store work
shoe salesman
clothing store clerk
house painter
antique clock store work
driver's training instructor
DJ
columnist
journal editor
translator
poet
tutor
published author
Professor of English

Weddings – Beginnings and Endings

The most joyous family times are wedding celebrations. That started with our first daughter, Cindy, when in June 1981 she wed Edwin de Jong.

It was a Calvin campus wedding and a joyful occasion for the two parent families to join in a spirited celebration. As I'm writing this in June 2021, we look forward to the blessing of celebrating Cindy and Ed's 40th anniversary! Sadly, Ed's parents have passed away, and we will miss them for we had meshed well together and genuinely enjoyed the times that brought us together, both in Grand Rapids and in Ontario.

Jayne was next.

Having met Sean Windberg in Bellingham, WA, she found herself falling in love with this brown-eyed good-looking fellow originally from GR too. So, one day Sean flew over to ask a father's approval of his marrying our third daughter, whom we had learned long ago was attracted to marching to her own unique tune. We knew almost nothing of this young man, but he seemed sincerely in love with Jayne, and it was clear that they had decided to marry, regardless of a father's approval. We attended their wedding on the Baron lawn by Wiser Lake in August 1987.

The marriage ended sadly, 1995, in an ugly divorce. But that's Jayne's heartbreaking story to tell. There were, predictably, sleepless nights for the parents too. Jayne was left alone to fend for herself and take care of seven-year-old Amanda and six-month old Lucy. Sean had depleted what little savings they had in the bank; the little family was left in a quite desperate situation. Jayne needed security badly.

She received it when Steve Dobson fell in love with this capable, pretty young woman. He had been divorced for a while and was very eager to establish a home for his own daughter and a good solid marriage with the right woman. He was sure he had found her in Jayne, and they married in December of 1995. Jayne's heart had not healed, however, from the trauma and pain she had been through with Sean, who had been her first love. And Steve, though a good man, had an effusive personality that often irritated Jayne. They built a dream place together in the Laurel fields with a view of Mt. Baker, but the marriage could not live up to the dream. Jayne broke it in 2005, including Steve's heart. That too is Jayne's story to tell. But as her dad, I had to deal with a load of internal dissonance occasioned by this divorce. A father's love for his daughter is unconditional; that is, it will not be destroyed even though a profound disapproval affects the relationship. I could not understand her apparent reasons for divorce, and what little I did understand I could not accept as morally valid.

It didn't help that Jayne had trouble articulating her reasons; in fact, it was hard to get her to talk about it at all. It took a long time for me to get more of a grasp of how Jayne's finely tuned and strong-willed personality endowed with both an idealistic streak and a critical edge clashed with Steve's expansive, extrovert personality that tended to overwhelm and perhaps even negate a more quiescent spirit. The necessary chemistry wasn't there; I think it never had been. But the consequences for Jayne and her children often occupied our thoughts and prayers in those dark years.

Clearly, not all love stories end well. A good marriage is one in which both husband and wife want to bring out the best in each other. I know from experience that we sometimes fail to do just that. But a marriage fails when one continues to bring out the worst in the other or in oneself. And when the decision to end the marriage is not a mutual one, toxic bitterness and psychic scars may not easily fade. Parents who care deeply about the marital happiness of their children grieve even as they reach out to help carry the burden of the breakup.

That, too, became part of our life and prayers.

And then, there was another daughter. And joy when extrovert bubbly Judy attracted the love of introvert Mike Sharp, a gentle, quiet fellow who was not dismayed by her limitations but saw the beauty in her soul and proposed. They sealed their love in a joyful wedding on July 1, 1989.

The father of the brides felt inclined to give each a wedding talk, though I don't have a record of an address to Jayne and groom, perhaps because the wedding was an outdoor, informal affair. (The talks are in Supplement p. 356).

Part Eight: The Retirement Years

I had tentatively decided that I would retire at 62.

Why?

Was it an inner voice that had seemingly so many times in my life led me to a decision that on the surface was rather surprising and maybe not altogether pragmatically considered? Like the decision to start college without adequate preparation and financial support; to leave home (Lynden) and job to attend Calvin; to say "yes" to a PhD track that would test intellectual heft and self-discipline to the limit; to say "yes" to China; and to say "yes" to Fridsma's wish to immerse myself in all things Frisian?

It was an inner voice, yes. Maybe influenced by a vexing long-term hearing problem that had started early after the new TB treatment meds and made it increasingly uncomfortable hearing some classroom voices. Maybe also encouraged by a growing feeling that my quotient of grading tests and evaluating papers was reaching its fulness.

It surely was not that I felt burned out or no longer enjoyed students, colleagues, or committees (well, maybe not committees so much). But I had heard about and known cases of profs who had hung on too long, beyond the time that they were still effectively engaging their students, and finally retired with the awful last memory of a "bad year" staining their retirement.

Whatever it was, I went a year beyond my 62nd, and then, incentivized by a college buy-out program, I, almost literally, took my office home.

And thus, in the fall of '97, I started a very different phase of life – retirement.

Ruth retired a year later, at age 60.

Now, looking back at those years in the late 90s, we sense how unusual that really was – we were still young! Nowadays, Calvin profs often go up to their 70th year or even beyond, and no teacher quits at 60. But we were both ready for less stress and more space for other activities.

And what, then, were the plans for the years to come, should good health bless us?

We did not plot out a series of specific plans on a timeline. Maybe we should have, but we felt alright about being open to options that would present themselves.

We did know we wanted to do some traveling.

Travel

Nederland

Traveling for us didn't start with the retirement years.

The Netherlands had been of course the first draw, and the fact that my land of birth drew me back more than fifteen times indicates that it remained a main draw.

After the first brief visit in '67, the first reunion experience followed in '71, both of which I've included earlier.

Reminiscing on those many visits now fills me with a mixture of feelings: a slender layer of sadness and a thicker layer of gratitude.

Sadness, yes: between 1967 and 2020 so many dear people, who became dearer as our visits multiplied, passed away; uncles and aunts and cousins and friends. Among the people I have missed especially are Tante Marij and Tante Janke, cousin Rein Prins (and wife Pop), cousin Berend Boersma (and, in November '21, Berend's sister Gre Boersma Rog too), and friends Rink van der Velde and Koen Zondag. They were the kind of people you wanted to see first when going back; you feel the absence keenly when they're no longer there to see and interact with again.

But gratitude, oh my, yes – brother Sid and I often talked appreciatively about the likelihood that we became closer to more family after we emigrated than we likely would have, had we stayed. It reinforced the bonds that connect us, enlarged the circle of family and friends, and enriched our understanding and awareness of life lived where our life had begun but would not end. It also gave me needed practice in my first two languages and expanded my bi-cultural identity.

Many crossings followed the first one: '71, '79, '84, '87, '90, '93, '97, '99, 2000, '03, '06, '12 (when all of us siblings made it for the dedication of the Baron Theater, home of Crescendo),

and '13, '16, '19. (Several of these feature descriptions in the separate Travel Section not included here.) They include memorable family reunions and boat excursions on the Frisian canals and lakes, made all the more festive by boisterous group singing of Frisian folksongs and Dutch anthems that brought back my early school days and wartime evenings when we learned and sang the words and tunes that still had power to excite the spirit and touch the heart.

It was so good to be with dearly loved aunts and cousins again as well as meeting many extended family members we had never known.

Many heartwarming and some moving memories press to the surface now, and I can't resist entertaining a few of them:

One unforgettable memory is a poignant one. I was driving the rental through part of Friesland, heading for Opende. With me were Mom, Mary, and Greta in the back seat and Sid next to me in the front. We had had a wonderful reunion the night before with some forty dear relatives. We felt a sweetness inside now from being together and driving in still familiar places from forty years ago. And that feeling launched us into a spontaneous singing of songs from that past and the present – folk songs learned in school and around the pump organ at home; hymns both in Dutch and English learned in church. When we reached the border between the two provinces, we pulled off the roadway and stopped in front of the café where the Boersmas used to live, at the very spot where Omme Marten's small bus had been waiting for us at 3:00 a.m. on that early May morning of our final departure. We got out of the car and looked across the field to the place that had been our home. We looked, we remembered, we felt stirrings. We did not talk. I remember wondering what might be stirring Mom's mind and emotions as she took this long look at her first home with Dad. This place she had come to as a young bride in 1927. This place where husband and wife had made a life together, survived the war together. This place she had left with husband and children twenty-one years later. The husband she had expected to be with her when one day they together would return for a visit. I wondered.

What happened next makes me wonder still. It was as if deep inside our mother a dam burst too long contained by force of will. She exploded into weeping. Her weeping turned into wailing. It wouldn't stop. We held her then. We didn't say anything. The pressure of our arms told her of our understanding and support.

The drive back to our hotel was a quiet one, each of us filled with thoughts and feelings. Sweetness and sadness often move together inside of us when revisiting precious places and people.

Also, I fondly remember what I hadn't expected – the endearing response of the younger offspring when visiting the Baron homeland. With brother Sid and his oldest two sons, Jim and Ger, we visited lots of family in 1979. The boys were often moved when finding themselves among the relatives we left behind. "We're part of this family," they said in wonder. It made them feel like a homecoming. A reaction repeated when other offspring, including our own children, visited that low country by the sea and interacted with parents' cousins, second cousins, and cousins once or twice removed. There was an immediate friendship.

Our last trip back in 2019 was very special too. It brought not only Ruth and me but also three of Sid and Margaret's kids and many grandchildren, as well as two of our children, Cindy and Henry. The occasion was the unveiling of a plaque in the Baron Theater, honoring Sid and Margaret for their generous support of Crescendo.

What made that visit memorable too was my last emotional visit and words with Koen Zondag who lay on his deathbed, and, more celebratory, seeing wonderful friends again like Okke Jansma from Australia, the van der Tempels, the Vriesemas, de Speerstras, the van der Meers, and of course the Tolsmas.

Many of our visits and stays in NL are recorded visually in photo albums and movies (DVDs) and verbally in little notebooks, parts of which are included in the Supplement.

"Never again," I kept saying to myself as we turned our backs to D219 Opende West that had been my home for fourteen years. At that time, I did not expect to return. But I did, many times, and that has been a significant blessing in my life.

United Kingdom

Our first "big trip" that was not family or birthplace related took us to the UK, a 25th wedding anniversary vacation in 1982. Though that travel experience had its nerve-assaulting tensions and mishaps, I will always remember the privileged feeling of walking in Yeats's Dublin, the heart-lifting worship in John Knox's St. Giles Cathedral in magnificent old Edinburgh – a city that excited me the same way the discovery of beautiful Florence had many years before, feeling the literary presence of Sir Walter Scott and Robert Burns as I strolled among their statues and admired the beautifully maintained estates, breathing in the cerebral air of Oxford and Cambridge where for hundreds of years intellectual luminaries had held forth, listening to the glorious singing and organ playing in a Westminster Abby eventide service with holy pomp and circumstance, worshipping in London's St. Paul's and kneeling to receive the holy sacrament of communion with a throng of others from nearly every race.

I kept extensive notes on that celebratory trip Ruth and I shared, which are included in the separate Travel Section.

But there were so many other places to see and explore, and the retirement years offered the opportunity. Some like the adventure of travel and opportunities for learning. Fortunately, both of us did. A reluctant traveler would not make for good company.

So, where to go first?

New Zealand

That turned out to be an easy decision: New Zealand!

It was time to take a personal look at the island Nel Van 't Wout had told us about, so our destination was her home in Dunedin near the tip end of the South Island, nearly 9,000 miles from our home in Grand Rapids. That made for a long sit in too many planes (change in Chicago, LA, Auckland, Christchurch) with too short a stopover in Tahiti.

Nel met us in Christchurch, and with Nel as our driver, guide, and hostess, we saw and did much:

- Admired Christchurch which was indeed impressively true to its descriptive name – the City of Gardens

- Toured Nel's beautiful home city of Dunedin (designated as the best city in NZ to live in) and nearby Portobello and the cliffs with seals, the Pilots Beach with Yellow Eyed and Blue Penguins, and the royal albatross colony at Taiaroa Head, the only mainland albatross breeding site in the world

- Were awed by the majestic mountain ranges like The Remarkables, Mount Cook and the hike to Kean Point with a stunning view of the mountain and Mueller Lake

- Were thrilled by Milford Sound with its towering glaciers and mountains, rainforests and raging waterfalls plunging from as high as 1000 meters, shimmering lakes sunk deep within fiords

- Enjoyed a windy Red Boat cruise into the Tasman Sea

- Saw the bungee jumpers from the high bridge where the "sport" started, and my inner question: would I dare; but my readiness to try parasailing instead, and the disappointment that the long wait would make it impossible

- Were alarmed at the call from Nel's sister Ada that she had been diagnosed with a brain tumor, and the quiet hour we spent absorbing that news in prayer and meditating on Ps. 23

• Driving Nel's car (left side), anxiously watching the gas gauge irreversibly sinking toward zero with many miles to go and without a station along the way, Nel calmly reassuring me that we'd make it; and we did.

Nel was a wonderful hostess, giving back so much of herself in gratitude for what our family had meant to her when at Calvin.

We were reluctant to leave the South Island; in fact, I found it impossible to take in and absorb all its beauty; jaw-dropping vistas, one after another – this relentlessly stunning nature insists on keeping your attention and fill you with awe at the Creator's art.

But it was time to see part of the North Island: sheep shearing (there's an entertaining video clip on DVD of Ruth called to claim her sheep); a rare Kiwi bird; ski lift to steaming volcanic Mt. Ruapeho and hike down; a geyser that erupts daily; bubbling mud and steaming hot water pools; Lake Taupo, the second largest freshwater lake in Australasia, formed by a super-volcanic eruption some 26,000 years ago; Tongariro National Park (a World Heritage Area) that was used as the backdrop for some of the most stunning scenes in the "Lord of the Rings" films.

James Michener said this of the land through which we rode: "New Zealand is probably the most beautiful country on earth."

I felt it as a real privilege to have this chance to see this country! Not only did its beauty impress me, but the pace of life seemed slower, maybe less complicated too with a simpler lifestyle and more nature oriented. And I muse, even now, how life might have been different for our emigrant family had we chosen New Zealand as our destination in '48.

We returned to Auckland, saw its sights, attended the Sunday service at Avondale Reformed Church, met the Maoris, and boarded a plane for the 10-hour flight to Honolulu.

(Ruth put together a beautiful photo album of our NZ and HI explorations; also movies on DVD.)

The last part of our "retirement celebration vacation" (January 4 – February 6) would be Hawaii, a short stay in Honolulu, and then a week in Kauai, the Garden Isle with its endless white sand beaches, lush forests, caves, coffee plantation

(saw a coffee harvester, a converted raspberry picker, manufactured by Lynden Cor-Van!), mission churches, peaceful drives around the island, picnics on forsaken beaches, and even a helicopter tour with a soaring closeup look at its mile-wide Waimea Canyon, a rather scary swooping through narrow mountain alleys and grand views of waterfalls. (I shot a lot of movie footage of this adventure. I was reminded of that flight later when I heard on the news that this tourist helicopter crashed, killing its occupants.)

Hawaii is lush, calming, endowed with a nature diversity that invites exploration and love.

Still, I was surprised, maybe even shocked, with the feeling, contrary to my expectation, that New Zealand had impressed and awed me more profoundly.

Our final flight, a 19-hour endurance experience that included four airports, brought us back to home sweet home, grateful and enriched.

But we had just gotten started! We were blessed with good health and energy and a ready appetite to experience more of God's good earth, this unique, hospitable, and beautiful globe that wondrously speeds us around the sun at 67,000 miles an hour. On many of these explorations we were in the company of friends or family. Sid and Margaret treated us to several cruises to Alaska, but also to a cruise to the Hawaiian Islands, to the Caribbean, to the Panama Canal, as well as a Mexican Riviera and a Mediterranean cruise.

We also enjoyed a New England–Nova Scotia cruise with Don and Kathy and an Alaska Tour-Cruise combination that included two other friend couples. We felt blessed to have the opportunity to join the Bosman sibling couples on short summer get-aways to the Olympic Peninsula, to Vancouver Island, to Whistler, and other interesting Northwest places.

Clare and Jan Walhout and the Huizingas were often our companions on extended excursions, including China, the Russia Volga River cruise, and the Danube tour-cruise. I loved being on the water – the wind and the waves, the peacefulness, and the power when wind and waves would show their force.

The water trips that were combined with land tours or much sightseeing I appreciated especially. The Central Europe tour that preceded the Danube River cruise included a visit to infamous Auschwitz.

It had been on my bucket list for many years, for I earnestly agree with Thomas Hardy: "If a way to the Better there be, it exacts a full look at the Worst." And what happened in that unspeakably awful camp surely belongs to the Worst: more than one million human beings killed in that place between May 1940 and January 1945. I can still feel the chill numbing my soul when I stood motionless before the displays of mounds of victims' hair and shoes and suitcases, some still tagged with the name and address of the owners, young and old, whose lives came to a terrible end here.

The trip exercised my capacity for feeling the pain and the beauty of the world on several levels. There was the still tangible deadly past of Warsaw and Auschwitz-Birkenau, the poverty visible on much of our route through these Central European countries; but also the beauty of Budapest, the soul-inspiring music concert in Vienna; the longing I felt to someday return, as I had felt in Edinburgh and Florence and now Prague, the final destination on our tour and which offered more than we could do justice to in a day and a half.

The Danube cruise was a feast for eyes and soul. When I gazed at the road that hugged the shore of the Danube, dotted with picturesque homes, it struck me as irresistibly inviting for a romantic summer drive.

We joined two Neland couples to experience South Africa and Kenya. Much of what we had heard about before now became eyewitness encounters of awesome beauty and of heart-aching human needs. (The photo album gives visual impressions of both.)

Heartache included visiting a township, Robben Island, and children at orphanages who had lost parents to HIV-aids, as well as drought-stricken villages in the bleak Turkana desert region.

Awe was often felt in the faith, hope, and love of the Kenyan people, but also in God's creatures in nature and creations like majestic Mt. Kilimanjaro we flew close to on our return flight and fortunate enough to have a window seat to be able to snap a photo.

Ruth and I were blessed to have the health and means and opportunity to explore parts of this amazing planet Earth that is our home. And we think with affection of the many occasions we had the pleasure of traveling with brother Sid and wife Margaret, especially the last cruise we enjoyed together when both were still well enough.

Thinking back now on our travels, I feel profoundly grateful for the gift of encountering so many different, beautiful places and people and cultures that enriched my being and my feeling of connectedness as the boundaries of my birthplace and growing-up place and employment place expanded in many different directions. Australia, New Zealand, China, Spain, Italy, Russia, Croatia, Africa, Greece, Costa Rica, Western and Eastern Canada, Guatemala, Israel – each brings back memories now that I treasure and that tell me when a trip is finished it has just begun.

Many of these are remembered in picture albums and notes in a separate Travel Section.

Writing

No, I didn't hole up in a New England cabin where in Thoreau fashion I would let the writing pour out of me that I had fantasized about when I was in my late teens. Had I been enabled to make that happen then, who knows what might have come out. I think now that the reach of my romantic imagination and ambition then exceeded the grasp of my inner resources and my outer skills.

But I did write bits and pieces now and then throughout the years. There was academic writing, of course. And for Neland News as editor, I had written a fairly large assortment of editorials and reflections. Many of these are included in Talking with God, which was one somewhat significant retirement project.

Henry Baron

Talking the walk to God

Retired Calvin professor for 30 years wrote columns to God, now has compiled them in book form

BY ANN BYLE
THE GRAND RAPIDS PRESS

Henry Baron has lots to talk about with God. For years, he held his discussions in the pages of the Neland Avenue Christian Reformed Church newsletter. He wrote a monthly column, often using it to talk with God about his, the church's and others'

Now, his conversations recorded over 30 years are available in Baron's new book, "Talking with God: Prayers, meditations & conversations for God-seekers."

"The columns were my attempt to verbalize, as honestly as I could, the questions a God-seeker has," said Baron, professor of English emeritus at Calvin College. "I tried to go inside the perplexing, exhilarating things that make up life's moments."

Baron, 76, began thinking about creating a book last summer.

He started by finding themes throughout his 30 years of work, then began fitting pieces together within those themes until a logical sequence emerged.

His book is divided into 10 sections, including worship, faith during difficult times, comforting the sick and sorrowing, Holy Week and Christmas.

Most entries are what Baron calls "prose with rhythm," which creates a slower, more thoughtful reading of the text. Questions to ponder are scattered throughout. The Cascade resident speaks to readers on subjects such as fear, doubt, winter, parenting and praying.

"I hope readers will be re-sensitized to their lives of faith in a world which challenges that faith in so many ways," said Baron, who helped found the Calvin College Festival of Faith & Writing.

"Perhaps 'Talking with God' can be a starting point to talk about things of the church, family life, worship, etc. I see the book as a journey into a meaningful, thoughtful, prayerful encounter with the world around us."

"Talking with God" is available at Baker Book House, Schuler Books & Music and the Calvin College Campus Store.

To read Baron's blog, visit henryjbaron.blogspot.com.

E-mail: localnews@grpress.com

THE JACKET

'Talking with God'

Author: Henry Baron
Publisher: Excel
Pages: 242
Price: $12.99

Since I'm not a good marketing or promotion kind of guy, the sales were not off the chart. There are still a couple of boxes left. But the personal responses of readers have been most gratifying. One grateful reader sent me a Word Cloud:

It was a blessing for me as a kind of spiritual discipline to write the prayers and meditations, and reader responses like these tell me that they are also a blessing to the readers:

> *THANK YOU SO MUCH. GOD USED YOU THIS MORNING THIS BOOK WAS JUST WHAT I NEEDED TODAY..*

> *Was privileged this Sunday morning to read again from "Talking," "Letting Go." A poetic marvel. You bless me tous les jours. Merci beaucoup!*

> *This morning I folded the corner on "Forgiveness."*

> *You are contributing mightily to my early morning devotion time. Thanks.*

I had tried my hand at an occasional poem too. But when Frisia entered my domain, the writing began to turn to translation. And after The Trap, more translation opportunities came my way. I also challenged myself to take on Frisian (and occasionally Dutch) poems. Translating theological discourse by John Calvin, Martin Luther, Abraham Kuyper and others from the Dutch for Eerdmans Publishing posed its own challenge. But translation work rarely makes one feel contentedly finished. A feeling nearly always lingers, especially translating literary writing, that further refinement in word choice and meaning is possible though it mostly remains elusive.

I also started a blog which includes a good bit of writing (http://henryjbaron. blogspot.com). Of late I haven't added much. As I often say to my good wife, there are not enough hours in a day to do all I still would like to do.

I often did some book editing too, like for colleague Chris Overvoorde and for friend Peter Buma. And I kept writing reviews of Frisian literature and occasionally of Dutch novels too. The reviews are accessible online: https://www.sirkwy.frl/ index.php/j-page/search-page?searchword=henry%20baron&searchphrase=all It was gratifying to me to learn that these reviews were greatly appreciated by the Frisian literati.

C.A.L.L.

I became involved in the Calvin Academy for Lifelong Learning while I was still teaching when Heni Ten Harmsel, our English Department chair, asked me to lead a book discussion for a CALL class in literature. I accepted gladly, for talking about literature to older, retired adults could make for an interesting variation on teaching young college students. I enjoyed the experience, and that was the beginning of a long affiliation with this organization that led to my participation in more than thirty courses, courses that included a range of literature but also interpretive reading, aspects of WWII, Frisian history and culture, and TED talks viewing and discussion.

CALL grew with the years, and lately attracts more than 2000 members who can choose from more than four dozen courses
each semester.

One day, fairly early on in my retirement, I got a call from Roger Griffioen, who was then CALL president, with the proposition of me chairing the Public Events Committee, a committee responsible for planning and organizing an annual series of travelogues that attracted nearly a thousand subscriptions, and a semi-weekly Noontime Program, free to the public and featuring selected speakers on a wide range of general interest topics. I told him I needed time to think about it, like a year. Surprisingly, he agreed.

And why did I end up saying "yes" to the invitation?

I find now, writing about my life, that it's often not such an easy thing to know why one says "yes" to one thing and "no" to another. To make weighty, consequential decisions had me listening more often than not to that inner self, listening to that voice or feeling that nudged in one direction or another.

I joined the committee, attended the programs, watched Bob Bolt as chair introducing speakers, and concluded to myself after a time that I, with my attraction to the stage, could do that too and maybe was a bit better suited for the introduction part of it than that fine retired history prof whose stage presence was a bit awkward.

I had twice been a presenter on Noontime. Now, in 2005, I took on the responsibility of managing the program itself. And it became a constant mental presence for a 12-year stint. Each semester called for six public presentations. That meant you were constantly thinking about and on the lookout for the next speaker or performance that had the potential for drawing a crowd into the campus chapel on Thursday noons. It was a challenge that exercised my imagination, my social contacts, my verbal creativity, and my stage presence.

In those twelve years we had presentations on a great variety of subjects that included the refugees among us, sex traffic victims, moral injuries of war, escaping Iran, creation and evolution, raising a missionaries' family in China, finding shipwrecks in Lake Michigan, Palestinians in the West Bank, prison conditions, health care, FBI war stories, racism; and presenters and performers who were musicians, actors, preachers, poets, rabbis, imams, athletes, physicians, photographers, artists, philosophers, scientists, politicians, mayors, law enforcers, prison wardens, social workers, professors, military chaplains, and more. Attendance varied but often exceeded a hundred and once was closer to 700.

To make that all happen required a lot of phone calls, emails, research on presenter backgrounds, and crafting appropriate introductions.

For my last Noontime, I put myself on the program when a scheduled speaker dropped out, with a presentation titled *Growing Up in WWII: Memories and Reflections that Don't Fade.* It's included in this memoir and viewable through this link: https://livestream.com/calvin-university/events/4336029/videos/154531131.

Maybe it was the most gratifying part of my Public Events Committee "tenure," for it allowed me to share what shaped me at an early age that should not have been or ever be a shaping force of human life – the dominating and killing of each other for the sake of power. It was good to note that the talk touched people's hearts and moved some to tears. As someone remarked, "you could hear a pin drop." And it ended with a surprising standing ovation, with many people coming up afterward wanting to say "thank you" and sharing their own thoughts. What's so special about such moments is the feeling that for just these moments our lives touched, we shared each other's humanity and felt its precious values.

It was also gratifying to be surprised and honored at an annual CALL Luncheon when I was called to the podium to receive the 2014 Distinguished Service Award.

The accompanying words were sweet too:

"At the annual meeting of CALL, the Board presented Henry with a Distinguished Service Award which recognizes his service to CALL and to the entire community.

Henry has been a member of CALL since 1998 and chair of the Public Events Committee. This committee is responsible for all the Noontime series lectures and the Passport Series (travelogues). In addition, Henry taught at least 16 sessions of CALL courses, e.g., Books and Authors.

The CALL Board unanimously selected Henry not only because of his wonderful participation in CALL, but also for his service to the entire west Michigan community. He graduated from Calvin in 1960 and was a member of Calvin's English Department from 1968 until 1997. He participated in many productions while at Calvin, and authored numerous articles, reviews, translations, and most recently the book Talking with God: Prayers, Meditations and Conversations for God-Seekers. Henry was also instrumental in establishing the Bi-Annual Festival of Faith and Writing held at Calvin College.

Thank you, Henry, for your many years of service. We pray that God will continue to bless you and your wife Ruth."

Church

In my early retirement years, I continued to be quite involved with the Neland Church family, including representing the congregation and classis East at Synod. But when eventually, in leading the council, it became increasingly difficult for me to hear its members, especially the soft-spoken ones, it was clear to me that I should not continue to make myself available for election.

I announced my retirement to the council at the last meeting of my final year in office. No more nettlesome issues to work out when trying to get to sleep, no more agendas to prepare, no more meetings, no more member visits, no more weighty responsibilities – ah, no more.

it was a blessing in many ways to be personally and spiritually involved with the work and mission of the church (except for the many hours away from home and family). But it was also a blessing to lay the work down and leave leadership with the younger men and women gifted with vision and energy. Neland and I had been blessed through the ministry of Seymour Van Dyken, Tymen Hofman, Carl Kammeraad and Duane Kelderman, through the pastoral care of Ruth Boven, through the sermons of Len Kuyvenhoven and Len Vander Zee, followed by the present pastors of Joel De Moor and daughter Cindy de Jong. And it was a joyful blessing to sit each Sunday with the Jousmas, till they made a church switch in 2020. Snuggling close to a grandchild in a church pew somehow makes for a special bonding experience, one big reason I miss them sorely on Sunday mornings.

Maybe here I should come back to what I described earlier as a crisis of faith.

The words of Nate Pyle in a Reformed Journal article (June 25, '21) closely reflect my own experience:

> "Lately, I've found myself longing for the faith of my youth. It was a simpler, more earnest faith. Through the romantic lens of time, I remember it as more vibrant. But while it's a faith I find myself longing for, it's not a faith I can have. Because that faith can't stand up against ectopic pregnancies, friend's marriages falling apart, betrayal, people far too young dying, coming to grips with how little control we have, and systemic injustices.
>
> Perhaps I could have a shiny veneer of faith brought about by experiential emotional highs, but it wouldn't serve me in this life. I need a faith for this world. A faith that has space for every facet of the human experience—right and wrong, laughter and tears, work and

rest, friendship and isolation, joy and grief, life and death. So, I find myself in a place where I can't have the faith of my youth, and my present faith leaves me longing...."

Longing, yes. Longing for what we pray for in the Lord's Prayer: longing for the Father's will to be done on earth as it is in heaven, longing for deliverance from evil, longing for the Kingdom to come. Longing for the Neland faith family to survive the ire and will of many in the denomination for Neland to abandon its welcome to *all* Christ-loving members or be ousted as a CRC church.

My urgent prayer is that Faith, Hope, and Love from above flow through the Church into our hearts and into this suffering world.

Social

I think I've always valued relationships. Maybe my inherent shyness I grew up with hampered making easy relationships. You instinctively hold back part or most of yourself. When, however, you feel free and comfortable with someone, that relationship becomes more than superficial. Maybe shyness and introversion are closely related, and I leaned especially toward introversion. What's interesting to me now, though, is to realize that as the number of meaningful social relationships increased, my introversion decreased. I became far less hesitant to make contact with people and engage interaction. To be sure, I retain both some discomfort with making small talk as well as a degree of social selectivity. Then, too, not untypical for introversion, my sociability remains psychically taxing, though enjoyable.

It's interesting how much the early years at South Christian have figured into our social life. The Sunday night Sing Group stayed intact till the 2020 Covid year when most social in-person interaction came to a temporary standstill. So did the New Year's Eve group. Now, in 2021, we sing again and if the pandemic will really conclude its devastating run, we may celebrate at year's end again (though now in midsummer the Covid Delta variant emerges as as serious an enemy, if not more so, as the initial virus, and now, in early winter, followed by yet another virulent virus, Omicron).

And for many retirement years, our foursome tennis partners (Ed Start, Don Boender, Mel DeStigter, and I) were courtside regularly, enjoying the games, each other, and the Dunkin' Donut rewards after the match. Later, after Mel passed away from cancer and when the cumulative years gradually led to a farewell to tennis (as it had to the racquetball games I kept up for a while with the English department comrades), three of us S. Christian colleagues met for a weekly coffee time; in fact, we're still doing that. Sixty years of knowing each other and having each other's friendship makes it a pretty special part of our 80s. A blessed part.

Other relationships continued or became important to me as well. Some students from both high school and college classes became close too, as well as some students I began to mentor after retirement, one of whom remains in close contact with me more than ten years after graduation.

Ruth and I also enjoyed inviting Lynden Calvin students over for pizza as a reminder that they were in friendly territory though far away from home.

Calvin faculty with Lynden roots joined too, including Spud Snapper, Randy Van Dragt, and Glen Van Andel.

Some members of our Frisian lunch group became good friends, especially Clarence Hogeterp and Pete Buma.

Louis and Jean Tamminga, our Quail Crest neighbors for some 15 years, before they moved to Raybrook, became very dear and close to us. We regularly shared with each other our joys and our sorrows, our hugs and our prayers. Sadly, Jean passed away recently and Lou has beginning Alzheimer's.

Lynden, Wash. students unite '94

It's late. It's freezing out there. You're lonely. You're homesick. The phone rings. Maybe it's that one girl from Sociology 304. Or no, maybe, maybe...could it be? YES, it's professor Henry Baron and he wants to know if you can come over. Now this is college life!

Baron, professor of English at Calvin and himself a Washington native, invited students from the Lynden area into his home for pizza, fellowship and reminiscing about the good old days on the West coast. About 26 students arrived at the festivity, held one day during the these students a little better, and I hope that it will send a

Lynden (Wash.) area students get together to share hometown stories while away at Calvin.

I've mentioned Henk Boersma earlier. Lynden friend Fred Bierlink was important to me too. So was Martin Bakker. And in Friesland, Rink van der Velde and Koen Zondag. Except for Henk Boersma, they have all passed on now, as well as Harmon Hook and Irv Kroese and Jim Lamse and Ken Kuiper and Dale Brown and Stan Wiersma and Harry Boonstra. Each one added value to my life for which I'm grateful and for which reason I will always miss them.

My sociability and interaction expanded through my CALL involvement also. I have become more and more aware that we were created as relational beings. God created us out of love and for love. Love is relational. Our core purpose is to love the Creator and each other. When love begins to flow in our relationships toward genuine friendship, we experience the blessing intended. It deepens, expands, and enriches our life, as it has for me, and for that I'm deeply grateful.

I've also been active in what may be called social outreach activities. For some years it was ESL, tutoring recent immigrants or refugees in learning some rudimentary English. That's included interaction with Hispanic, Korean, Vietnamese, and Chinese. But it also included for a time a seminary student from China who came to earn advanced degrees to equip him for ministry and teaching back in his homeland. He was highly motivated, ambitious, and intelligent. I can't help but wonder how his future will fare in an increasingly hostile China to the Gospel message.

Crossroads Prison Ministries has also been part of my and Ruth's regular involvement (for more than twenty years now) with prisoners who are eager to know more about the Christian life of faith by signing up for Bible courses through CPM. We evaluate their performance on the lessons they mail in and write letters of encouragement and counsel. In the more advanced courses, you may be working with the same prisoner for several years, especially when they continue to enroll for more. I've enjoyed the relationship that may develop and often been impressed by their intelligence and desire to grow in the faith.

And then there's been serving as a mentor. Sometimes that's been a mentor to someone from Neland, but most often the mentees have been Calvin students. Again, it's included mostly international students whose need for spiritual and emotional support far away from home and a familiar culture can be acute. Regular meetings focus especially on spiritual formation but as the relationship develops and the two come to know each other more, the conversation may turn, and often does, to any area of the mentee's life that raises concern and questions.

My last assignment as mentor to a student developed into an ongoing relationship that lasts to this day. He was raised in Michigan and continued to live in this area after graduation. Ruth and I attended his marriage. The marriage sadly turned into a spousal betrayal, and I had the privilege of standing by him through his darkest months of emotional and spiritual collapse. He's now in his early thirties, polishing his giftedness as a writer in the Iowa Writer's Workshop, putting the final touches on his first novel. This relationship reminds me of Fridsma's mentoring me in all things Frisian, but which turned into something much more personal than that. Maybe Fridsma felt a bit like I feel after all these years of relationship with the young man I first met when he was a college freshman. It's a good feeling that fills with gratitude.

Medical

Wouldn't it be nice to have nothing to report here? That would be a blessing few people can claim. At the same time, I don't want to give a stereotypical old-age organ recital.

Actually, my "medical journey" started at a fairly young age. I'm told I did have the usual childhood maladies, some of which I remember but vaguely. Apparently, my caul birth did not protect me from the croup, measles, diphtheria, whooping cough, and what have you.

Nor did it protect me, as described earlier, from hospitalization for viral pneumonia when in my late teens, nor from catching it again less than a year later, double pneumonia this time, with pleurisy, and then segueing to TB; instead of becoming a brawny soldier through basic training, I became a bedridden patient in Army and VA hospitals.

Cancer 1

For the next almost twenty years, I enjoyed the blessing of returning health; in fact, I flourished. But then I got stopped in my tracks again: a lump in my thyroid turned out to be cancer that had grown significantly in the months between diagnosis and surgery and had spread to the parathyroid and a number of lymph nodes.

I will always remember the ride home from Dr. Bratt's office after diagnosis. My mind flooded with thoughts of my mortality. I assume that the invasion and threat of the big C in anyone's life will do that. It's like an icy hand clamp around your heart and shocks it into one solemn feeling: I may die.

But I didn't. The thyroid and more were removed during spring vacation, and I returned to teaching. But a sense of personal mortality had deepened my thinking and response to it. I was not afraid of it, but I think it made me love life more.

Cancer 2

Giving us life (and Life) is the Creator's greatest blessing to us. Especially when that life includes a wife and family you can hug, students you can teach, colleagues you can work and play with, places you can travel to, books you can read, concerts you can attend, movies you can enjoy, and so much more.

My gratitude for that blessing intensified even more in the early years of my retirement when I was diagnosed with prostate cancer and a few years later needed open heart surgery. The life I loved was not necessarily mine to keep. I kept being reminded to "love that well which thou must leave ere long."

I chose radiation treatment for the prostate cancer. I had been scared away from surgery when the biopsy caused profuse bleeding and clotting that landed me in ER. The 42 radiation sessions went smoothly with no noticeable side effects. They would come later, much later, and with a vengeance. But I was blissfully ignorant of the future and was grateful for the treatment.

Heart

A few years later, in 2005, my newly assigned primary care doctor, Mark Beversluis, listened to my heart at our first checkup appointment and promptly made an appointment for me with a cardiologist.

The meeting with Dr. Foster was not short. He was a formal man who had obviously read the stuff on me, including my academic background and practice, and seemed to address me accordingly – that is with an elevated vocabulary and signals of respect. I found it amusing. I favored a more personal and informal style, efficiency and lucidity. (Over the years I grew accustomed to his demeanor and unique interaction and even developed a certain fondness for this gentleman.) But this first meeting was heavy because it confronted me with concerning news: tests and pictures indicated that I needed heart surgery. The supposedly innocuous heart murmur (regularly observed by my previous primary care doctors who never thought it necessary to refer to a cardiologist) had become a seriously leaking mitral valve that reduced the heart's efficiency by nearly 50%. To compensate, the heart had enlarged due to extra strain. Because of its need for complicated and extensive repair, Dr. Foster recommended either Cleveland Clinic or U of M Medical Center.

I don't know how Ruth processed this looming event at the time (though when it came to the actual ordeal, she kept a daily account that expresses plenty of her processing) or our children. I do remember my own anxiety, mentioned earlier, when I as a youngster sat in the waiting room in the Groningen City Hospital while my dad was with the doctor talking about something wrong with him. It made me pray. The hernia surgery went well, and after some days in the hospital (that was common in those days), I went with Mom to pick him up via Opende's horse and carriage service. I remember it was raining, but we were snug and dry inside the carriage, feeling thankful Dad was coming home again.

In periods of crisis or trauma you discover stuff about yourself you might never otherwise. I found out as a young child what terror felt like in the face of pending or potential disaster – it would make me freeze. Later I learned when my body sent alarm signals that I had a bit of a stoic in me who tended to submit to the inevitable and to whatever was medically necessary rather peacefully.

And that felt more like a physical and psychical response than a spiritual one, though I would like to think that God's grace is also in the way we respond to personal crises. It feels like entering an alternative reality. A reality in which you feel closer to the God who wants to be your Father. And that reality intensified when in the ICU, after the surgery of repairing both the mitral and the tricuspid valves, I spent the first night in total misery and discomfort. The Spirit nudged me to keep reciting Psalm 23 and the Lord's Prayer, and each repetition, focusing on each word and phrase, brought me closer to the caring Father at the center of Ps. 23 and to the Lord who taught us to pray that perfect prayer.

The surgery had gone well; the recovery did not. Instead of the three or four days in the University of Michigan Medical Center that had been expected, it became more like a dozen.

Apparently, my body didn't take kindly to the violent invasion. It rebelled in all sorts of ways: against desire and ability to eat (which kept it weak), against desire and ability to get up and try walking (which prolonged the recovery), against the need for bowels to move, against good lung function (a pneumothorax that necessitated emergency action at 3:00 a.m. one very painful night). And the place was like an overtaxed factory – too busy for nurses and assistants to give much more than routine attention and assistance, which didn't accelerate my walking readiness. In one instance, I was abandoned in a wheelchair on a basement floor after x-rays; eventually (more than 30 minutes later) someone must've noticed that I had not returned to my room and went looking. Had I had more oomph, I might've given them a run for the money by setting out on my own, exploring each floor of that place as a mischievous plan to raise general alarm. I had done just that unintentionally when I fainted during a rare walk, this time with son-in-law Matt, and all the lights began to flash and bells and whistles activated a cadre of medics rushing in.

Eventually they let me go. And I was so happy to go home! And so grateful for the concern, the cards, the prayers, the phone calls, the visits through which family, including the church family and Hun and Ok-Joo who lived in Ann Arbor, and friends had passed on the love and grace of God to me.

My own struggle with recovery
had dimmed my awareness of the
devastating news of hurricane Katrina
that caused over 1800 deaths and
$125 billion in damage, particularly
in New Orleans. And, closer to home,
the horrible motorcycle accident that
nearly killed Tom Weaver and Dick
Stob. It left Tom paralyzed from the
waist down and Dick with permanent
injuries. I had been part of the "Neland
Motorcycle Gang" for a few years, and
we had enjoyed some great area and
state-wide outings together.

I knew for them there would be no more such joys.

Those awful national and personal calamities put my ordeal in perspective – a
minor one in comparison. My heart was repaired, it would mend, and I would in
time bike and hike again, though the presence of atrial fibrillation (which neither a
cardioversion nor ablation attempt to correct was successful) would slow me down.
But I would rejoice in the marvelous gift of life and wellbeing and never take those
gifts for granted or forget to thank the Giver.

Aging bodies feature parts that need repair or wear out. Hernia problems seemed
to run in the Baron family: there was Dad, then brother Sid, and yes, me too – all
of us twice. The pain that follows surgery can be nasty, but the body is beautifully
equipped with a medical army designed for self-healing strategies. I relied on that
support force again when I had a cyst removed from my vocal cords. And when
my right shoulder needed replacement in 2014, the many therapy sessions that
followed and the daily exercises restored a usable shoulder.

But there are limits, I discovered.

Bladder

The year 2016 had been a good year.

There had been plenty to keep me busy, looking forward to a two-week winter
vacation in Texas with the Klompeens, had made deposits for travel to Scandinavia,
Cuba, and Galapagos in the year of our 60th anniversary – full of zest for adventure,
keeping in shape, enjoying God's good gifts.

But the year didn't end well.

Within three weeks-time, multiple ERs and hospitalizations, a sharp physical decline, a sense of helplessness and hopelessness – a descent into gloom and doom. And all the while knowing but not feeling that there was still so much to be thankful for.

Around Christmas, the bladder didn't want to empty; there was blood, there was intense pain, and there were ER runs in the middle of the night, and there was hospitalization. Thus began the new year, 2017, as the beginning of a significant life change. I entered a new reality: not only can body parts wear out with aging, but they can also cease to function in the way they were meant and needed to.

The radiation treatment for prostate cancer of more than a dozen years earlier apparently had not terminated nor restricted its intended destruction of cancer cells but slowly and surely reached into the urethra and left scar tissue that eventually spelled the end of its function. The blockage was in a spot where it could not surgically be removed. One urologist soberly told me in the hospital room, "This is as bad as it can get."

Scheduled bucket list trips had to be cancelled, and I had to learn to live with new limitations and procedures.

Eventually a permanent catheter became my new reality, frequently accompanied by recurring and nearly unbearable painful spasms, bleeding, infections, and clogged catheters that sent me often in torture to the ER with a bladder that wanted to empty but couldn't. When my urologist eventually decided to try a different kind of catheter (malecot), hard to get (and sometimes not at all) and very expensive now (though it once had been the forerunner of the newer type and currently used catheter), the present and the future brightened; though periods of acute discomfort persisted, the spasms diminished, there were some very bloody episodes (June '21 was the most severe one with much blood loss that makes you feel like life is flowing out of you; it took me a week of rebuilding and regaining some energy), but there were no more occlusion incidents. Hence, no more traumatic ER runs (except for an occasional infection).

Both Ruth and I kept extensive notes about the initial crisis, but they're not of likely interest to anybody but ourselves. And we may not indulge ourselves either – the notes do not make for pleasant reading and remembering.

What it means for the long haul is not known. I do know, now more than four years later, that this is an unchanging condition with new discomforts and pains continuing to surface now and then, and that the radiation damage may continue to advance, possibly affecting the bowel as well.

So, what has this meant to me.

Besides the pain, discomfort, limitations, embarrassing mishaps, etc., internal dissonance. I've never questioned or indicted God for this yet another national super low percentage type of negative physical affliction. I've always said that anything, even the most terrible and tragic, can happen to anybody at any time. But I have more than once compared myself (enviously?) to others who continue to be able to do so much more than I. And then I feel the loss and a degree of sadness. Yes, I'm well aware that many of my age and much younger, too, suffer from afflictions so much more dire and limiting than mine. I feel more deeply the plight of those whose life-changing disasters that strike them dumb and poison them with the feeling that they can't go on; I more readily think myself inside their skin and psyche than I might have otherwise. My empathy is exercised, and at the same time my gratitude for what I still have and can enjoy is enlarged. And so much is left. Maybe chief among that muchness are relationships. That now segues most naturally to family.

But before going there, I need to get back to daughter Judy. In 2009 Judy's shunt was no longer doing its job. Both mind and body were showing signs of shunt dysfunction – it was no longer draining the fluid properly. She was hospitalized for a month at the new Hauenstein Neuroscience Center in local St. Mary's. Her condition worsened as time went on and specialists failed to come up with a solution. We visited her daily and observed with increasing alarm and distress that her life appeared to be in decline. Her doctor consulted with other neuro specialists in other places. Finally, when the situation became most critical, the decision was made to place a new shunt in her brain that would drain the excess fluid into her abdominal cavity. Simple and pretty standard, but an answer to fervent prayers – Judy began to improve, and the shunt has continued to function well for more than a decade now. Though normal mobility and balance have become more challenging for her, we think Judy's cognitive function has actually improved.

We are so grateful.

As we age, we continue to discover that, yes, body parts do wear out, for some more so and sooner than for others. Ruth's left hip turned out to be the culprit for causing much pain. In 2020 it was replaced, and we discovered that a replacement does not come with instant gratifying painless mobility. It takes a lot of exercises, pain meds, discomfort, persistence, resilience, and patience. (And I had to learn some new housekeeping skills.) But then the other hip began to agitate in the most unwelcome ways with a "Me Too" message that could not be ignored. Thus another hip surgery six months after the first one. And this time it was not a same-day home return. The patient didn't feel very well, low on oxygen, without energy, and unable to pass the test for hospital release. She stayed for the night. She came home at noon the next day and was able to ambulate surprisingly well. The following day was Mother's Day, and the kids came over to celebrate a successful surgery and their mother's special day.

But by mid-afternoon, there was a problem. Ruth's oxygen level dropped alarmingly, and she felt generally lousy. Cindy and I took her to ER. She needed oxygen badly, she had retained too much fluid, her sodium level was much too low, and she needed hospitalization. Only one person from the family could stay with her in the still ongoing pandemic, so Cindy stayed till midnight when they finally secured a room for the patient. She ended up staying for a week while they ran more tests, drained 14 pounds of fluid (due to congestive heart failure?), and waited for the sodium level to rise. I spent time with her every day, and Cindy eventually did visit regularly too in her capacity not as daughter but as minister, per Covid rules.

It was a week of serious concern, and many people were praying for recovery from the surgery and the condition that landed her in
the hospital.

There had been a health alarm some time before that when a CAT scan showed swollen lymph nodes throughout her upper body, a serious telltale sign of lymphoma. But a biopsy was negative. We gave a profound sigh of relief. What, then, caused the nodes to swell? More testing did not give an answer, and the nodes gradually returned to more normal size, though not completely. Monitoring will continue, and so will our prayers.

Such times of stressful anxiety tell us how much family means to us. It's an organism, and anything fearful that comes along and threatens its parts stabs at our inner core, especially when we face the death of a beloved member. Yes, Shakespeare, we must learn to "love that well which thou must leave ere' long."

Family

One thinks about a lot of things when towards life's end they sit down to reflect on all those years that have marked and shaped one's life and to write about that journey and its meaning.

When I think now, staring at the heading of "Family," of a possible life lived without knowing your birth parents, without siblings, without someone to share your life with, without children – I'm overwhelmed with feeling the blessings of having had all of that (even though this family picture may make others wonder.

So, I hasten to straighten the impression.

My parental family was also a dear part of life, one we treasured especially when on special birthdays and weddings and anniversaries we would reunite and surround our widowed mother with our presence.

It reinforces my conviction that a core value, if not *the* core value, of life is being in relationship, being connected, being bonded to others who over time become very dear to you, whose loss would take a part of your heart away.

That's how, and I think why, God created us. That's why I think God grieves with those who never had or lost such relationships and holds out with longing the Father-child relationship that's so movingly depicted in the parable of the Lost Son.

Those who retire, especially when they retire a bit early, often give as a reason when asked "to spend more time with family." Which implies, correctly for many, that there wasn't enough such time spent when work was too often all consuming. As for me it was.

A huge advantage for classroom teachers is their summertime. And we took a slice of our vacation time then, camping, traveling to spend time with family and relatives, but many a summer was spent mostly for more education, research, teaching (house painting in early years), and working for CSI as Language Arts consultant.

Later, the questions come: did I spend enough time with the kids as they grew from toddlers to teenagers? Why didn't I set aside a regular time for one-on-one talks or activities or going out for a snack? That strikes me now as so important. But then? I should've had a close, wise friend to nudge me to do that. Still, I should've been wise enough myself. And maybe I was, but there was always pressure weighing on me to prepare well for the next class or committee or presentation at some church or conference or writing project, etc. And I was not sufficiently gifted to do all things well without much preparation. I had colleagues who could do that or could at least accomplish more in less time than I could, and I had high admiration for them.

It seems to happen to many to be most deeply immersed in one's profession/career/work when the children are too quickly turning from youngsters to adolescents. I have always deeply admired those who seem to be able to do well with both family and demands of work.

That's one blessing of retirement – to spend more time with family, and especially when one gets a chance to once again welcome little ones into the extended family.

Grandparenthood

Maybe there's nothing quite like the emergence of new life that opens the heart so fully and releases buckets of love. Before retirement we had a delicious taste of that with the birth of de Jong grandchildren – Amy and Blake, Sharp grandchildren – Angela and Nicole, and Jayne's two – Amanda and Lucy. Now we reveled in welcoming Matt and Lisa's Lauren, Jackson, and Molly. And it's been such a blessing to have most of them live close by so that we could see them regularly, watch them grow up, and establish a relationship that nurtures and nourishes. We missed that sorely with Amanda and Lucy and now with their children – our great grandchildren: Lucy's Charlotte, and Amanda's Clara and Nolan! To them we're still practically strangers and I'm saddened to think that that may not change much. A bit of FaceTime doesn't go a long way, though we're grateful for the technology that makes such a virtual visit possible. Angela's Cameron and Talia live closer by, and we've enjoyed some affectionate times with them, but we're sorry that we don't often get a chance to see them.

Parent and grandparent relationships flourish through loving contact and frequent prayer.

But there's also a hard truth about relationships – they are fragile in the context of a broken world that can break lives, also the lives that matter most to us. They can unravel through misunderstandings, disagreements, conflicts, angry words, destructive actions.

When they do, there's often pain, bewilderment, regret, distancing, and hurt. Maybe no family is completely exempt from such heartaches, and I grieve that ours hasn't been. But when we go through such valleys, we don't let each other go. And we feel immensely blessed that our relationships are mostly intact, that we enjoy each other, that at the core of our being we love each other.

Weddings

In our twenty-some years of retirement, we've had the blessing of witnessing a few.

Our very youngest, Lisa, was of course the first after our retirement, in '03. Maybe one should never say "of course." Not every child gets married or should be expected to. But it's surely special when your last and youngest does. I know it was pretty special to me when she graduated from Calvin. The joy of that became mixed with some sadness when she decided to take a teaching job in the Seattle area.

As much as we loved the West and the PNW, we were not thrilled when Cindy opted for a teaching job in southern California, when Judy took a job in Washington, when Henry found employment in the Seattle area, when Jayne embraced Washington for adventurous living, nor when Lisa followed the example of her siblings. Fortunately, Ed couldn't turn down an offered position in Grand Rapids after some years in the larger LA area, so we got the de Jongs back. Eventually Judy returned as well. But if it hadn't been for Matt's determined pursuit of Lisa, she might well have made Seattle her home, for she loved living there. We've been more than grateful to Matt for bringing her back by one day flying out to Seattle, surprising her by showing up in her classroom with a proposal and a ring. We couldn't have wished for a better husband for our youngest and the good daddy he would become.

Yes, her wedding was special; emotional too when walking your "baby" down the aisle to "give her away."

Lisa was the fourth and last daughter I was "giving away."

A father can't help but wonder what he's giving his daughter away to – the right man, a promising future, constant love, much bliss? (My Cindy and Lisa's wedding talks are included in the Supplement.)

Dad Bosman must've wondered that too when he "gave" Ruth to this immigrant kid he didn't know all that well and who was still trying to find his way.

And a father knows from experience that a marriage is often and for many the most challenging learning process of all. That's why it gives much joy to parents when they observe their child's good and happy marriage, and much grief when it unravels and leaves wounds in lives of the adults and their offspring, wounds that too often become permanent scars. Parents pray for their children and their children's children, giving thanks for harmony and happiness, pleading for blessings from heaven when such bliss is under threat.

But a wedding is for celebration when two lives join and waves of love embrace the couple and waft over family and friends, leaving their faces aglow when the couple seal their vows at the altar with a kiss.

And we had the blessing of witnessing that again when granddaughter Amanda was next in '15. I felt so honored when Mandikins asked her Pake to walk her through the wooded path in the outdoor wedding to Leo Harrison who was waiting for her at the head of the group that had gathered. I've loved that granddaughter dearly since she was a thoughtful, imaginative, and precocious little tike, and have always felt sad that we live so far apart from each other and see each other but once a year or so, and, as we keep aging, even less and less.

Two years later we were able to travel again to Washington and attend another outdoor wedding. This time it was Jayne's second daughter, Lucy, and the wedding took place on her (adopted) dad's (Steve Dobson) place. Again I felt honored to be asked to participate in another dear granddaughter's wedding by reading a wedding prayer from Talking with God and presenting the newly married couple to the wedding guests.

Some years later there was great joy to see our first grandson, and only one for many years, Blake marrying Elise in Neland Church. It took both of them some time to discover each other as the very right one to spend their life with, but that made the marriage ceremony and reception all the sweeter for us all to witness the couple's obvious happiness and love that united them.

Our prayers are with them as they "learn to be husband and wife, building a relationship and a life which reflect the Lord of Love and Life." (*Talking with God*)

And, added now in 2021, our prayers are with children and grandchildren too when a marriage breaks, as it did for Ami Tse and Lucy, due to Ami's bi-polar condition which in his case made a stable, harmonious union impossible.

Deaths – endings

Weddings are celebratory occasions for family reunions with its greatly appreciated blessings.

Deaths also bring families together, many members of which may not have seen each other for a long time. And though the occasion is a time for grief and mourning (despite the attempt to mitigate those emotions by calling it a Celebration of Life), having siblings, children, nieces, and nephews together is an important and valued source of comfort and support.

Mom Bosman had passed away in 1995, having suffered a stroke four years earlier and needing oxygen toward the end of her life. Both of us were still teaching then. It left Dad alone, and those were difficult years. He missed his beloved Christina dearly, and we, more than 2000 miles away, weren't there to be a presence in his life, other than by phone and summer visits.

My Mem Baron died in 2001. She had been suffering from dementia for some years and toward the end became nearly mute.

It's hard to lose one's parent, regardless of age, I've come to find out. Your life has been bound up with your parent practically from conception. A final parting hurts, as if part of your identity is torn away. I grieved for the loss of both parents, though in Mem's case the grief gave way more easily to gratitude than it did for Heit because of the many years Mem remained a close and loved part of my life. I treasured our hugs.

Due to distance, we couldn't see each other as much as we would've liked, especially during her advancing years. But my concern for her deepened during those years, expressed in a prayer I wrote and included in the Supplement p. 363.

Dad Bosman died in 2003, his last years encumbered not only by loneliness but also increasingly by painful and debilitating arthritis. We were there at his deathbed in Meadow Green, singing hymns for him and saying words of departure. We knew it was time for him to leave and that he was ready for life after death, though shrouded in mystery. He had been a dear dad-in-law to me, and I know we loved each other.

Both sets of parents were gone now. We felt blessed that we were given good parents and that we could remember them in love and gratitude.

When parents are gone, we know that children are next in line. Brother-in-law Harvey Spoelstra died suddenly in 2004 from a heart attack. A painful shock to all of us and especially to Alice and family. Harvey was a gentle soul, easy to love and appreciate. Ruth and I will always remember the two of them visiting us when we had exchanged homes and cars with a family in Friesland. We lived on a hobby farm just outside of Drachten, and Harvey enjoyed taking bike rides on the friendly bike paths that the Netherlands is famous for.

My oldest sister Betty and husband Bernie both died in 2013. Their last years had been difficult and unhappy because of arthritis, other ailments, and some dementia. Betty was not easily figured out; she lived a conflicted life. At times love and tenderness flowed out of her heart; at other times there was darkness and anger in her looks and words. She did not readily disclose the issues that disturbed her soul, some of which may have gone back to the church split in '44 and a broken relationship. She always gave me the feeling that she admired and loved me in a way, and she opened up to me a few times when we had lunch together on summer visits, but the distance between Grand Rapids and Lynden did not help to wholly overcome a personal distance between us. The enigma remained for all her siblings: who was our real sister?

Closer to home, sister Greta's husband Wayne died also in 2013. He had suffered from Parkinson's for sixteen years. The strong, sturdy builder, farmer, baseball player was gradually but increasingly sapped and diminished by that debilitating disease. It was hard to see, but by God's amazing grace, though the body weakened steadily, his inner strength did not: he accepted his affliction with fortitude and grit. I think of him with much appreciation; he had always been generous in sharing their cottage and boat and water skiing and motorhome rides with us when the kids were small and eager for such vacation times. And I will always remember riding in his pickup with him shortly after Judy's birth and hear him offer to help us with whatever we would need for Judy's special care. That moved me and showed that lovable part of him that was always ready to help others. Judy's first Wayne-made "walker" was one of his contributions.

The loss of Sid and Margaret is more recent and still touches a raw nerve. Margaret developed dementia and passed in 2018. Brother Sid's MS, which for more than forty years had allowed him to live a fairly normal life with only periodic attacks, began to take its toll more tellingly in his upper 80s. When he began to be hit by early Alzheimer's while also deeply grieving the loss of Margaret who had been his faithful wife and closest friend for nearly seventy years, normal communication took a steep dive.

His pending demise was deeply painful for me. Their Wiser Lake home had been our home away from home for so many years, and now it would be no longer.

Ruth and I flew out shortly before he breathed his last on March 24, 2019, and that night we joined the family gathering by Sid's bedside. It was a time for tears and long hugs. Sid was no longer conscious of us, so far as we could tell. I knelt by his bed, my cheek against his, kissed him, and whispered last words in his ear. A few hours later he died.

We stayed for the funeral, which was streamed so family in Michigan and even in Opende could be with us virtually too. Ruth, Mary, and I sang "Abide with me," and I did a eulogy, included in the Supplement. I had sometimes thought that I would die before Sid, not prepare a eulogy for his funeral. But it turned out differently, and it felt right to do the last loving thing I could for him.

Now, the only brother I had was no more. The only one who could help me remember things from our youth, things we could laugh about (sometimes hilariously), things we could share that made us wistful – we would no longer talk by telephone, fly together in the Cessna 172 to his favorite airport lunch place, lunch together at Bellingham's Denny's or Lynden's Dutch Mothers. We no longer had each other. And as gaining grandchildren and friends enlarge our lives and hearts, so the loss of loved ones diminishes us. Yes, the good memories that remain bless us, but they cannot replace the blessing of good living and loving relationships.

We spent time with Sid and Margaret's children, including spouses and some grandchildren. It was a time for talking, remembering, and grieving together. It was a time when love for each other was palpable, though each person experiences and expresses grief – induced love differently.

I've always had a special warm place in my heart for the Baron nephews and nieces, maybe because I knew them almost from birth and had frequent interaction with them and good long talks with all of them. My deepest hope was and is that the Sid Baron children always remain tightly bound together by family ties and thus honor their parents' love for all of them.

Anniversaries — Celebrations

I was but a little boy, but I remember vividly the golden wedding anniversary of pake and beppe.

I remember it for a number of reasons, but especially for that whole great company of descendants, happy being together, gathered around one pair of aging human beings without whose wedded life there would have been no celebration.

Celebrations accent our relatedness, express the joy of our unity, and renew the strength that comes from belonging. Celebrations are communal expressions of gratitude. Maybe that's why they're so important. For what's a nation without its Independence Day? What's the Christian Church without its Christmas Day and Easter? And what's a family without its birthday, anniversary, and holiday celebrations? Taking celebration out of life is like leaving the yeast out of your bread or taking the yolk out of your egg: you don't have much left.

Golden and even silver wedding anniversaries are extra special. It's a time for pausing, looking back, and remembering the day when a young bride and groom looked each other in the eyes and promised to love and honor each other. It's a time, in a circle of family and friends, to joyously celebrate the goodness of God for all those years of life and love and togetherness.

A wedding celebration is, of course, especially a celebration of human love. And even after 25 or 50 years, such love remains largely a mystery. Maybe it is better so. Maybe the best celebrations always honor what is at its core a mystery, like God's love for a sinner, or a citizen's love for his country, or a woman's love for a man. Still, one learns something of human love: it is not always passionate nor is it ever perfect. When Shakespeare wrote Sonnet 116, it is doubtful that he had just been gazing at Ann Hathaway or reminiscing his many years of married life.

Still, an anniversary deserves something like a sonnet. Maybe even a sonnet like Shakespeare's, sort of, for I've modified it some:

Sonnet 116—RV

Let me not on the marriage of two lives

Impose perfection. But love is love still,

Though shaken by alterations in the wife's

Appearance, or the husband's stubborn will.

Oh, yes! True, love is frail, a flick'ring light,

Trembling through tempests, swayed by many fears;

It is no star which, in solitary height,

Remains unmoved by human pain and tears.

Love is not constant like the love of God,

But through God's love and grace it does' mature:

In ten or fifty years it's been well taught

To give and to forgive and thus endure.

If this be false, then I would say on oath

We never loved, nor pledged each other' troth.

Anniversaries didn't begin during our retirement.

In fact, looking back, it looks like we didn't miss a chance to honor lots of anniversary dates.

Ruth and I had our 20th celebration on a Caribbean Cruise in 1977, Sid and Margaret's gift and who also celebrated it with us as they had on our honeymoon trip to Disneyland. That cruise became memorable especially for the Big Surprise – the conception of our Lisa Joy!

The addition of another family member didn't cause us to bypass our 25th wedding anniversary – we spent two wonderful weeks in the UK, including

Ireland, Scotland, and England. It began with a stressful, shaky start, detailed in one of my travel notebooks, but we've always hoped we would someday get a chance for a return to the treasures of that history and culture-loaded isle.

Did we skip the 30th? No, no – our whole family celebrated that date with family in our beloved state of Washington.

And the 35th? 1992 was also the year of Mem Baron's 80th birthday, worth a double celebration, so we were there for that too.

Our 40th merited uniting the whole family, including grandchildren, for a stay in a Holland hotel, Lake Michigan beach time, and a family dinner at the Hoffman House. (Ed made a great DVD of and for the occasion that will always be a delight to watch for the family.) I will always remember the unpardonable of leaving little Blake behind in a Holland Park, and my growing anxiety and panic on Ottawa Beach when I saw Amanda struggling in the Lake Michigan waters against riptides that were pulling her away from shore.

Then, now in our retirement years, we reached the 45th anniversary, this time having the family clan with us in rustic (very!) cabins up north, by a lake and near the dunes.

The biggie of course was our 50th when we pulled out all the stops. We rented a splendid large home on a lake near Pinckney, not far from Ann Arbor. All the children and grandchildren came, and we spent a week making full use of water and land toys that came with this place. Our celebration included an Open House for family and friends in the Woodlawn Ministry Center. Picture albums tell much more than my hundred words.

We had enjoyed our stay at Pinckney so much that we wanted to do something like that again for our 55th. This time we rented a large home on Hemlock Lake in the south-central part of the state. Album pictures testify to the fun we enjoyed together that week.

Gratefully, we made it to our 60th. Again, all our children and grandchildren were able to make it, staying in three cabins in Saugatuck. Opportunities for recreation were all around, and we ended by enjoying a celebrity dinner at Saugatuck's popular waterside restaurant.

I had intended to have a family talk during that gathering, a very personal talk focused especially on my faith journey, the kind of talk that likely too seldom becomes a part of a parent's oral history. As it did on this occasion too, and despite intentions. The setting has to be intimate and conducive to serious listening. A family picnic on a front porch with small children vying for attention is not such a place and time. So, my talk was short and only lightly touched what I really wanted to leave with them. But it left me with an occasion to think about it more later and to expand it in a written version.

That too is included in the Supplement p. 369.

Will there be more anniversary celebrations to come? Now in our eighties, we take nothing for granted. We count each new day as a day of grace. But as I look back on all the anniversaries, all the family gatherings and celebrations we have been blessed with, the heart overflows. And then I think – in a less broken world, all human lives would know the joy of family celebrations, of long-lasting committed relationships, of love that flows between and among parents and children and offspring; how sweet and right would that be! Isn't that what the Creator intended? It hurts to see so much brokenness.

By disposition I tend to dwell on that dark side of the human experience, the source for weeping and lament. I need to balance that more with eyes wide open to the beauty and wholeness that is left in so much of nature and human living. We were and are blessed with heart-filling slices of that, and we pray that they may be passed on to children and grandchildren, and that they in turn will "pass it forward."

Friends

Not only am I grateful for family, but also for friends.

The joy of friendships had a small beginning when Henk Boersma and I from first grade on grew our connection. One friend, but it seemed enough. Not untypical for introverts, I think. And that friendship continues to this day.

We met again when I discovered that he lived in nearby Ontario. With the help of one of his daughters, I made a surprise appearance at his 60th birthday party. And we have visited each other since and never miss a Happy Birthday phone call.

It wasn't until my life began in Lynden, WA that my circle of friends gradually expanded. First through fellow immigrant kids, like Bert Tjoelker and Fred Boonstra. Somewhat later through church activities Fred Bierlink and to a somewhat lesser extent Arnie Veldkamp and Peter Mans were added. And when Michigan became our home, the circle continued to expand. With some there were deeper connections than with others. Some were rather temporary while others are still ongoing. And when I became seriously involved with Frisian, many friends and acquaintances were added, both in N America, NL, and even Australia, who have given me a rich measure of satisfaction and appreciation. Sometimes those friendships led to home exchanges in NL (Drachten, Osdorp, Jorwert), sometimes to extended stays (in Hylke and Roelie Speerstra's Heerenveen home when they went on vacation, and Rink van der Velde's "arkje" on a petgat in de Veenhoop).

One index of which friends count is to answer the question, "whom do you want notified of your death when that occurs?" My list today would include, besides the Baron and Bosman siblings and extended families, Nel van't Wout in NZ; Okke Jansma in Australia; Henk Boersma and Allan Romkema in Ontario; the remaining cousins families in NL and the Tolsma family; but also there the van der Meers, Speerstras, Vriesemas, van der Temples, Oppewals; and closer by of course the Neland Church friends, the Sing Group, but also Sid Post, Clarence Hogeterp, and Pete Buma, and the Calvin English Department.

Every meaningful friendship left its mark on me, enriched my insights, widened my understanding of human formation and experience, and enlarged my love for fellow human beings whose real "Mensch" issues from their heart and not just their brain.

End Reflections

I was 21 when I wrote in my journal:

"of itself – whereto?"

Now 66 years later, this old man, finding himself in a placid stream that hardly features a ripple, gazes back over a lifetime and, maybe not unlike Garrison Keillor's Guy Noir, finds himself still "searching for answers to life's most urgent questions."

Partly true, yes.

The political and ecclesiastical divides disturb me deeply. The responses of millions to the Covid and climate and refugee crises make me sick at heart. The emergence of a leader who turned a respected party into a cult that threatens the future of democracy in our country confounds me. At times I feel profound sadness when I think what the challenges and crises my grandchildren and great grands will have to face. And then I wonder, how far will the God who holds the whole world in his hand let it go? This world of such great beauty and wonder, inhabited by so many who in awe-inspiring ways seek to serve and save it and each other, will it flourish?

But this reawakening of many memories has been more a searching for ikigai, for personal meaning, for an answer to "whereto?"

It's been an interesting return journey – to travel in your memory and imagination all the way back to your beginnings. "We write to taste life twice: in the moment, and in retrospect," said Anais Nin. The Danish existentialist Søren Kierkegaard, in a journal entry, noted that we can only understand life backwards — we analyze the course of our journeys with the benefit of hindsight.

I've discovered some truth in that; and I hope it shows in spots.

I've also discovered some truth in what the writer Tobias Wolff said: "We're in an unceasing flow of time and events and people, and to make sense of what goes past … we leave things out and we heighten other things, and in that way … we can give it significance."

Indeed, a great many things have been left out (some of which have been relegated to the Supplement), but I hope I have included something of what has mattered most to me.

The process of selecting entails a reflection on what one regards of having had meaning in one's life.

God has created us with a need for personal significance. I have tried to find it in the gifts God blessed me with: teaching, family, church, prized relationships, music, love, writing – often in flawed ways, but not meaninglessly, as the Teacher in Ecclesiastes intones.

Tom Boogaard in a recent essay in "Reformed Perspective" spoke to that beautifully: "We reflect on the meaning of our lives not because we believe we are so important; we reflect on our lives to discover that we are not alone.

"We need to know whether or not our lives are taken up into something larger than themselves, whether or not God is working all things together for good as Scripture claims.

"Meaning does not lie on the surface but deeper down. We discover it by self-examination, by tearing apart our experiences and hoping to find the elusive presence of God."

Yes, and that process of discovery is not finished with the writing of one's life story. I know it will continue, if my mind stays more or less clear, till my breath returns to its Giver.

At age 87 I'm well aware that my time is running out.

And I often think of those who've gone before me and spent their last years suffering the progressive loss of memory, of names and words and independence and identity, and so much more.

Besides many friends, those include Mem Baron, and to a lesser degree sister Betty, brother Sidney, as well as several other extended family members.

Though I have trouble remembering names of people and often find my hippocampus reluctant to issue names of things on demand, as well as finding it harder to focus and block the mental distractions, I'm grateful for the mental functions that are still in place. I pray that this part of my humanity and personality may prevail.

But should the time come that the infirmities of body and mind and spirit render me nonfunctional, I trust that the Father will continue to know me and love me and renew me for the New Heaven and the New Earth.

Memoir Supplement

Contents

Mom's Song in the Night 308

Sinterklaas 311

WWII 313

    Details 314

    Memories 318

    Aerial fights 318

    Plight of the Jews 319

The Crossing 321

Family Letter Excerpts 333

Judy's Birth 335

English Department Writeup 337

Frisian Sermon Translation 342

The Immigrant Adventure: The Quest to Belong 348

The Accident 351

Wedding Talks 356

Prayer for a Parent 363

Sid Eulogy 365

A Family Talk 369

Closing Quotes 376

Mom's Song in the Night

Note: one night, April 21, 1987, Mom couldn't sleep. In her tossing and turning, words from a song she had memorized 76 years before as a young girl in Surhuizum Chr. School came into her mind. She wrote it down that night, as best as she could remember it and as best as she could render it in the language she had learned it, though she had never written in Frisian before; but it expressed the truth of the life she'd lived. This is a corrected version of the page I found in her own handwriting. The author is A.M. Wybenga, in it "Fryske Sangboekje" of 1911. There are two other stanzas, and the tune is "Come ye sinners, poor and needy...."

Faak dan suchtsje wy by 't skreppen	*We often sigh while we slave away*
Wy bedije suver neat!	*that we seem to get nowhere!*
't Liket, smyt wy 't sied yn d' ierde	*And fear that the seeds we sow*
Dat it nea wer ta ús keart.	*will never yield us anything*
Mar wy moatte op hope ploegje,	*But in hope we plow the land,*
En op hope siedzje wy,	*and in hope we sow our seeds*
Dat wy yetris swiere stûken	*that one day we will surely load*
En in folle skuorre krij	*an empty barn with heavy sheaves.*
As yn 't libben lijen parset,	*When our life turns into groans,*
It jin drôvich is en near	*When we feel oppressed and sad*
Trillet d'opstân faak yn't kleiyen:	*and there's anger as we moan:*
't Krús my oplein docht sa sear!	*"The cross I bear gives so much pain."*
Bliuw o Kristen dôchs yet hoopjen	*Then, oh Christian, do keep hoping,*
Polske wédom yn dyn hert,	*even when your heart is filled with woe,*
Wat God jout is jimmer 't goede	*what God gives is always goodness*
Ek al fetsje wy dat net.	*though we may fail to understand.*

Sinterklaas

The boy lived in a land that was sometimes visited by saints. At least one saint, anyway. His name was St. Claus, or better known in that small northern country as Sinterklaas.

On December 5 each year he'd come riding on his beautiful Arabian horse, his long white beard flowing down to his waist, his red robe a bright symbol of cheer in the pale winter sun.

In the daytime he would be everywhere—in parades waving at all the little children clutching their mama's hands; in children's hospital wards, bringing presents and telling Zwarte Piet (Black Peter), his helper, to throw an extra handful of pepernoten (gingernuts) on their beds; walking slowly on city streets, his tall staff tapping the cobblestones, his eyes always searching for children who needed a kind word.

But the young boy knew that the busiest time for Sinterklaas came after the sun went down. Then he would visit every home, at least the homes where children lived, where he would surprise and delight everyone with presents. But he couldn't get to every home before the children's bedtime.

So, before going to bed, the young boy would fold his clothes carefully and leave them neatly at the foot of the bed. Then, under the warm wool blankets, he would think of Sinterklaas coming in the night, stealing softly up to his bed, pick up the pile of clothes, stuff them full of presents from his bottomless bag, and hide the clothes throughout the house. Soon, his eyelids grew heavy, and thoughts of good things to come turned into sweet dreams of a kind old saint who didn't rest till he had made all the children happy.

For some reason he would wake up earlier than usual the next morning. He would look down to the floor for his clothes pile.

Nothing.

His heart jumped, for now he knew that Sinterklaas had indeed come. He'd be out of bed in a flash, shivering in his underwear in the unheated bedroom. But he didn't mind much because the most exciting adventure was ahead: finding his clothes and the surprises hidden inside.

He'd look in the kitchen first where the stove was hot and beginning to melt the frost off the windows. Maybe Sinterklaas had been extra kind and hidden most of his clothes in a warm place. Yes! He found his short pants (for young boys don't wear long pants there) under his own chair by the kitchen table. His hands quickly examined its contours. There was something inside, wrapped, for it crinkled when he touched it. He eagerly reached for it, unwrapped it before taking time to put his pants on, and hauled out a warm winter cap that would cover his ears as well as his head.

Now he was most eager to find his stockings, not only because his bare feet were getting cold, but because he knew that Sinterklaas liked to put candy treats inside the long wool stockings that young children wore in wintertime. After a bit of looking, he found one stocking on the kitchen shelf behind the stove. It felt toasty warm to his fingers, but the bag of sweet licorice and piece of nougat inside made him even happier. He quickly stepped into his stocking and continued the search for his shirt and other stocking. He could find nothing more in the warm kitchen, so with one bare leg and no shirt he ventured back into the unheated living room. He couldn't find anything until at last he spotted his blue shirt wedged behind the family pump organ. This time he took the wrapped present out and first pulled his shirt on. Then he hurried back into the warm kitchen to open it. He beamed when he unwrapped a tall gingerbread man. He broke off a little piece and stuck it in his mouth, though he knew he should eat his breakfast first. But wait, there was more! His very own checkers set! Wow! Maybe he could take it over to his friend's house to play a game.

Now there was only the one stocking left. His toes were really cold by now, and he had to go badly.

He searched more frantically now in the unheated living room and bedroom, looking into corners, on shelves, in drawers, in the closet, but nowhere did he find his warm stocking.

He decided he couldn't hold it anymore—he'd have to go wee-wee first. He slipped into his wooden shoes in the hallway, opened the door to the cow stalls, and awkwardly clomped along the gutter behind the cows that led to the inside outhouse. He hurried in, closed the door, and then he saw the lost stocking hanging right above the toilet seat. He stopped and stared a moment, wondering: did Sinterklaas himself have to use the toilet during his visit? Did saints really have to go to the bathroom too? And had he forgotten to take his stocking back inside the house? Strange. But then eagerness to know what was inside took over again, and for the moment he forgot why he had come here. He snatched the stocking down, reached inside, and hauled out a small box with an H on the outside and a dark chocolate letter on the inside. Immediately he forgave Sinterklaas for hanging the stocking in the family outhouse. Maybe he'd done it to be funny. But he'd been good, for the young boy liked his presents very much—every one of them!

WWII

People were not free anymore. The Germans had quickly defeated a small, unprepared country, had killed many of its soldiers and citizens, had destroyed the city of Rotterdam and badly damaged many other places. Now they were in control. Their hated uniforms and military vehicles were everywhere. All the Dutch people had to do what they were told to. Their own queen had escaped to England. Germany was now running the government.

Young men were picked up and forced to work in German war factories. If they didn't want to, they had to go into hiding, afraid every day and every night of being caught. Many were and ended up in slave labor camps where they knew they might never come home again.

Pamphlets from the German authorities would often be posted on utility poles. Everybody would stop and read the notices. Often they would announce new rules, like:

- Everybody had to turn in their radios

- All gold jewelry and other gold articles had to be turned in

- All guns had to be turned in

- There came a day when bikes and wagons and horses had to be turned in

- All persons of Jewish blood had to register and wear a yellow star

- No groups larger than three would be allowed to gather outside in a public place

- No one was allowed outside after 9 p.m.

- Every adult had to get an ID card and carry it with them at all times

- All males 19 and above had to register

Tante Marij was crying about her son, Reinder: in a few days he would have to leave for Germany. Her heart ached with the fact that she might never see him again.

She almost didn't.

But she prayed each day that the Lord would take care of her son. And I did too when I found out about this cousin. For Reinder had always been my hero.

Details

- One group of German troops that was part of the invasion action traveled through Opende on May 11, 1940, into Surhuisterveen; moved on to Franeker and then to Afsluitdijk

- Blackouts in effect in fall of 1940 already

- July '41: had to turn in precious metals; that summer many items became scarcer; tobacco unavailable by October

- From 1941 to first half of 1943, 59 downed planes; for Surhuisterveen 38 and 142 bomb impacts

- 1942: butchering cattle was strictly forbidden, though it was done often at our place

- 1942: many societies forbidden to meet, funds confiscated; transportation of meat illegal; Dad would use meat for barter for feed (for the cows) and cover it with burlap sacks on the wagon to pick up feed

- 30 April 1943: milk strike by many farmers, in Opende too, and attempts at train derailment; also arson, including in Surh'veen; many area men arrested

- June 1943: radios had to be turned in; later bikes were also confiscated; many kept unregistered, older radios and listened to Radio Oranje and the BBC, which was strictly forbidden; the penalty for non-compliance was deportation to Germany; many who were caught were never heard from again; we turned in our beautiful new Blaupunkt and kept an older one hidden in the hay where it would be listened to regularly

- 700-750 onderduikers were aided in the nearby Achtkarspelen; many among them were Jews, especially Jewish children who had to pass as non-Jews in schools, etc.; Mr A Tjoelker, the principal of the Surh'veen school and well known by us was very active in their protection

- Dutch sympathizers with Hitler: NSB – National Socialist Move't; underground resistance: NBS= Netherlands Interior Forces

- Resistance forces: raids, sabotage, strikes, espionage

- 107,000 Jews were deported (75% killed by Nazis); 30,000 hiding

- 30 October 1943: attempt to assassinate Pier Nobach while milking, but it was his son instead; Pier blamed the resistance in Surh'veen and went berserk;

on Nov. 4 in the early morning two in civilian clothes arrested, among many others, Teake Schuilinga (a highly respected leader and businessman in Surhuisterveen and a relative on the Hoekstra side and the bakery owner I would always include in my Saturday shopping for Mom), took him in a car to Oosterwolde area, and dumped his mutilated body by the side of the road

· In 1943 bomb damage in Surhuizem, etc.

· Need for food stamps for the 300,000 in hiding by '44

· March 1944: near Harkema-Opeinde, some 5 km from our place, about 500 firebombs were dropped

· June 1944: many men forced to dig holes (foxholes) near important roads or railways, also along the main street in Opende; in October males from age 16-50 called up to work for Germans in various places (included the town of Surh'veen next to us)

· September 1944: Sietse Gjaltema, living a way behind us along the same road (De Skieding), was caught by the Germans and executed in October at Westerbork

· October 1944: horses had to be yielded to the Germans

· 20 December 1944: a razzia in Surh'veen; one who tried to flee was shot down by Germans; this was likely the razzia that spilled over the provincial border to our place, recounted elsewhere (we had a resistance member in hiding wanted dead or alive)

· Hunger winter of '44 that took 30,000 lives (18,000 starvation)

· 1944: the underground Chr. paper "Trouw" became widely circulated and was stenciled initially in nearby Stroobos and circulated in the area, including Opende where Mom became its prime delivery lady; it's still in circulation

· November & December 1944: major weapon drops and its transportation in Achtkarspelen; extremely dangerous; probably the time when our guest in hiding had to go under

· April 1945: sabotage – removed the traffic signs; had a hard time of it in Surh'veen—they blackened the signs

· 13 April 1945: reports that the Canadians were in Marum (some 5 km east from Opende) and would enter Surh'veen during the night of 13-14 (Friday-Saturday), but instead they came through Drachten, at about 3 PM, and continued on to Dokkum

- 15 April 1945: report that a group of retreating Germans in civilian clothes in direction Surh'veen were on the move; along the street from Opende to Surh'veen reinforcements were stationed; NBS (resistance force) men also circled the Willeminahoeve on De Skieding where the Germans gave themselves up without a fight

- 15 April 1945: Pier Nobach was caught in Achtkarspelen; he tried to get away by jumping in a canal but was quickly fished out by two NBS'rs; he was sentenced to death but inexplicably was freed; some time later a son of Schuilinga discovered him in The Hague; the reason for his release has never become known

- Cost of war – deaths: total> 62-78 million; civilians: 40-52 million (incl. disease, famine); military: 20-25 million; Netherlands: 284,000 civilians, 17,000 military; Germany: 5.3 million

There was a conference in 1995 at Dordt College in Iowa to commemorate the liberation of Holland in 1945.

Our former neighbor Rev. Louis Tamminga was there, and this is the story he tells:

> Above all expectations, some 500 people came with their war stories. In one small group was an old lady who kept quiet. But at last, the group leader gently prodded her to tell her story too. And then she did.

Her son was 18 when he was picked up by the German SS. She agonized over what they might do to him. Then she received the news that her son along with others would be executed in the dunes near Scheveningen.

That morning she and others found a hiding place in the dunes from which they would have a view of the site where the cruel drama would take place.

The military trucks came. The young men were pushed out. In a single row they were led to a low spot in the dunes. But before they reached that last place on earth, the son spotted his mother. She waved at him, carefully. He waved back, just as carefully. Then his arm went up and he pointed to the sky. His mother did too. And then the others did too. Till at last all the young men raised their hand and pointed to heaven. And the old folk began to sing, Ps. 43:4: My soul, why art thou sad and grieving?/ Why so oppressed with anxious care? Hope thou in God! His Word believing,/Thou shalt behold His face, receiving/ The blessings of His countenance fair—/ What bliss beyond compare!

The story was finished, a story she had never told before to anyone. Some of the people around the table began to weep. They went over to the old mother and wrapped their arms around her. Then she too began to weep. She felt herself connected to others who their whole life long had also carried a great sorrow in their hearts and who were now here to carry each other's burden.

***

Some 374 Dutch resistance fighters are buried in the Field of Honor in the Dunes around Bloemendaal.

While the south was liberated, Amsterdam and the rest of the north remained under Nazi control until their official surrender on May 6, 1945. For these eight months Allied forces held off, fearing huge civilian losses, and hoping for a rapid collapse of the German government. When the Dutch government-in-exile asked for a national railway strike as a resistance measure, the Nazis stopped food transports to the western Netherlands, and this set the stage for the "Hunger winter," the Dutch famine of 1944.

Memories

- Close to war's end when any transportation on roads or rails would be shot at by allied planes, a Spitfire came right over our home, so low I could see the pilot's face as he unloaded his machine guns on a moving target on the nearby road, the shells clattering on the tin roof of the milk house

- Sneaking out after curfew in the semi-dark on back paths to get our goat "serviced" at a distant neighbor's place

- Playing war games with big brother as darkness fell, hiding behind and attacking from the potato mounds in the field

[see also Sid's *The Way It Was* for more]

Aerial fights

- 1942, during the night of 15 and 16 January, there was an aerial fight above Rottevalle; a Zeppelin opened fire on a Lockheed and downed it; 255 windows in Surh'veen area were broken; two parachutes were observed; Dr Folkerts, our sometime house doctor, was able to locate one of the downed pilots and took him in; that same day the German Wehrmacht caught one of the airmen in Opende, likely the one Dr Folkerts had initially rescued; three of the crew were buried in Rottevalle; the German plane was shot down that same night above the North Sea; later in June a Wellington bomber was shot down near Surhuizem, about 4 km from Opende; three crewmembers were seriously injured and transported on a hay wagon to the security post in Kortwoude, right next to our grandparents' place, and from there to an A'dam hospital and later to Germany

- With increased allied air missions to Germany, the number of casualties increased too; a number of planes crashed in the area of Opende and Surh'veen; on 28 July in 1943 an American bomber was downed east of Kortwoude, about a mile from our place; it was the Sky Queen out of Northamtonshire in England on a mission to Kassel; but the mission was canceled and on its way back the Sky Queen was hit by a German fighter plane; it exploded in the air; only two crewmembers survived (Sid had contact with one, Sgt. Adams); the others were initially buried in the Opende church cemetery; a German fighter plane was also downed and made a perfect emergency belly landing a couple of miles farther north

At the time of Holland's capitulation, approximately 140,000 Jews resided in the Netherlands. By the time of the war's end, the Nazis had deported 107,000 of them. Of these, only 5000 survived to return home following the war and 30,000 managed to survive in hiding or by other means. Thus, over 75% of Holland's Jews perished at the hands of the Nazis.

60,000 Jews were deported to Auschwitz; only 972 survived. 34,000 Jews were deported to Sorbibor; only two – two out of 34,000, lived to return to the Netherlands.

This represents the largest percentage of Jews to die from a particular country except for Poland.

Why was loss of life so high in the Netherlands? Were the Dutch particularly anti-Semitic or callous? The answer to both is "no." More Dutch have been honored by Yad Vashem, the Holocaust Martyrs' and Heroes' Remembrance Authority in Israel as "righteous gentiles" than from any other country. However, several factors, some of which made escape during those five years impossible, are responsible for this tragic loss of life, one of them being the Netherland's unique geographic and cultural features.

Culturally, Dutch society was stratified largely on the basis of religion. Thus, close friendships between Jews and Christians were uncommon in war-time Holland. For those Jews with Christian friends, to accept shelter carried with it the knowledge that discovery placed their friend's lives into jeopardy. Additionally, most Jews who went into hiding did so as individuals. Rarely were entire families hidden, as in the case of the Franks. Thus, to go into hiding not only endangered the well-being of one's benefactors but often meant abandoning other family members, including elder parents, spouses, siblings, or children. (internet info.)

***

In Friesland, 500 people who took Jews in have received the Yad Vashem distinction from the state of Israel. That is a distinction for the help of non-Jewish people to Jews. But of the 800 Frisian Jews, more than 600 did not survive the war. Shame and guilt about not hiding and saving more Jews has surfaced. Recently, the Protestant churches acknowledged that they left the Jews to their fate during World War II. The PKN churches in the Netherlands read a statement of repentance in a Sunday service, joined a bit later by the conservative churches.

A few passages from the statement:

> "We were negligent when serious anti-Jewish measures were taken at the time of the occupation, and we remained silent. We were negligent when Jewish citizens around us were picked up and taken away and we allowed that to happen. We were negligent when the reality of the extermination camps began to become known to us and we closed our homes to them, and we did not denounce that injustice. We acknowledge our negligence. It is our prayer that God will forgive our shortcomings."

The Crossing

[tr. From the Dutch diary I kept just before, during, and right after the journey of the Baron family when it emigrated from Opende, Gr. to Lynden, Washington in 1948]

Note: I tried my imperfect, elementary school English a bit now and again, such as in the "preface," indicated by quote marks:

> *"In this book is written the travel to the USA made through the fam. Baron. This travel is written through Henry Baron."*

Also, I've tried hard to retain the style of the original writing of an adolescent in Dutch.

May 24, 1948; Monday evening, 11:30 PM.

I'm sitting by the table that's loaded with stuff. Tante Janke is sitting behind a mountain of buns that she's buttering. I have no idea where we're going to put all that.

Sietze and I just went to pick up Jan Westra. It's been a terribly busy day. Handshaking all day long.

Bouke and Lies are snuggled next to each other on the sofa: one would almost get jealous.

Dad and Mom are getting ready.

Folkert and Griet are sleeping on a bed in the barn.

We're staying up, except Griet and Marijke.

I'll be glad when it's 3 o'clock and the bus stands waiting for us.

Well, I've made a start: the rest will simply follow, we hope.

For now this is enough.

May 25. Tuesday morning.

We did not go to bed. At twenty-to-three the bus stood by Boonstra's. At 3 we took off.

The bus was not full. Let me tell who all went along:

-the fam. Baron (7); – the chauffeur (1); – Oom Roel (1); – Tante Anke (1); Oom Andries (1); Tante Luts (1); – A. Kuperus (1); – Tante Janke (1); – Tollie (1); – Albert Baron (1); – Henk Boersma (1); – Jan Westra (1); – Bouke Steiger (1); – altogether 19 people.

The first consternation was Marijke's vomiting. The swaying of the bus must have made her sick.

At 3:35 we were in Leeuwarden. It was almost light enough by then for the lights to be turned off.

Every now and again Jan Westra would liven up the trip with a little harmonica music. At 4:20 we were on the Afsluitdijk. There's not much else to tell about the trip.

At 5:40 we were in Alkmaar, so we made pretty good time—a good 60 km. on the average, which is pretty good speed for a bus.

In Velsen by the ferry we discovered that the people from Stroobos who were returning to America stood behind us.

At 7:30 we were on the outskirts of Den Haag. There we dropped off A. Kuperus because he had some business to do there. At 8:15 we were in Rotterdam at the Wilhelminakade.

Note added now: What followed were several hours of meeting, greeting, hugging, handshaking friends and family, often with tear-stained faces, thinking at the time that these would be the final farewells. The emotions must have been felt much more deeply by the parents than they did for us, the children, who were eager to embark on that beautiful big boat anchored in the harbor.

***

As I am quietly writing all this down, the VEENDAM peacefully continues its journey.

We are now at sea. Dad and Mom and the others are downstairs in their cabins. I'm quietly writing in the tearoom, and Sietze is sleeping on a sofa not far from me.

Not much news right now, and it's gradually getting time to start thinking about dinner. It's 6:15 now, and at 6:30 it's dinner time, so I'll quit for now.

May 26, Wednesday, 4 o'clock.

This morning I had a slight case of seasickness. This is what happened: I had had a great sleep. When we sat in the dining room and we were served our meal, I suddenly felt sick. I couldn't eat a bite, but I ran as fast as I could to the cabin and threw everything I had in me up into the toilet. Not a nice start, I thought to myself. But it didn't turn out too badly, fortunately. I went to bed for a while, and then got up again, and I was OK. I still did feel a bit nauseous, but I sure had improved a lot.

Mom felt worse at first, though. But when at 10:00 we sighted England and when at 11 or so the boat lay still (to allow the mail to leave and people to board), Mom struggled out of bed. We went up to the deck, where Mom lay down on a deck chair. From our 1st – class deck, we had a beautiful view of the English coast. At 1:30 we got underway again. We were enjoying dinner at the time.

Now we see nothing but water. And it's going to be quite a while before we see land again. Sietze and I spent some time in the smoking room where they were showing a sound film. But we didn't get much out of it because it was all in English.

Now I'm sitting at a writing table. Outside it's blowing a storm. The boat is going 14 mph. A fairly good speed. Sietze is going down to get the camera because there's still a piece of the English coastline visible. I'm going to quit now because I'd like to see it, too.

We admired the last view of England's chalk mountains. Took a picture of it, too. That's fun to do. Well, I'm going to drink my tea. Till next time.

May 27, Thursday morning. 8:30 A.M.

All of us had a great night and now are almost ready to go for breakfast. Oh yes, I should tell of my adventures of last night. First what came before:

We had met an old Scottish lady. She talked English, of course. But we were able to talk together a bit, though it wasn't easy. We had had something to drink in the smoking room (where Sietze earned a $1 from her) and took her at about 10:30 to her cabin. Then we went to our own cabin. And then it happened:

I had to go to the lavatory. At the conclusion of that ceremony, I was going to wash my hands. First I turned on the cold faucet. Then the hot faucet. And then it happened. First everything worked normal. But then all of a sudden, the water began to spout out of the side of the faucet. That scared the dickens out of me. I adjusted the faucet so that the flow lessened a bit. For a while I held it like that, but I realized I couldn't stay standing there like that. Then I discovered a bell button.

I thought to myself, let me press that once, maybe somebody will show up. But to do that, I had to let go of the faucet and the boiling hot water would spout in full force, and the stream was directed right at the spot where the button was. Still, I took a chance at it. But nobody came.

Then I could think of nothing else to do but to start screaming for Sietze with all my might. The first to appear was a steward and right after him came Sietze. The steward said I should take it easy. "Yes, but sir, take a look at this," I stuttered. The steward saw it all too well. He abandoned us in a hurry to fetch an expert who set things right again.

But that isn't all. When after all this we were tanding in the hallway, a man emerged from the lavatory dripping wet. He had been on the toilet and then got the full shot from the piping hot water right on his brand-new suit. What an experience: "What kind of an outfit is this here," he said.

We had ourselves quite a laugh then.

Now it's 11:00 o'clock. I'm writing this in bed. We've had a wonderful fun day since I started feeling sick again. But I quickly headed for the deck and lay in Coopman's chair (he's really a good fellow) and didn't go down again for the rest of the morning. But it didn't get any better. At about 10 I fell asleep and had a good nap for a couple of hours. I threw up just a bit. Griet had a worse case and Mom was bad off too. I didn't go for dinner at noon. I just stayed in my deck chair. But around 3 I tried again and fortunately it went well. I walked around a bit and gradually started feeling better. Tonight, I enjoyed eating in the dining room again. Griet didn't.

We're really enjoying the boat. The days fly past. Lies seems to be enjoying herself, too. Nothing bothers her—not seasickness nor homesickness. You see, that's how it should be. Bouke has nothing to worry about.

Tonight we watched boxing a while with Chris Kooistra. His brother Jelle was sick in bed too. All in all the evening passed quickly, and now it's 11 already.

Readers, listeners (in case someone should be reading this to you), I'm going to end this again for now and will try to catch myself a nice snooze. "Good-night!"

May 29, Saturday evening, 10:30.

I better begin with the beginning again, and that's of course this morning. This morning all of us, except Mom, were present in the dining room. We took Mom upstairs, so that's a sign that she felt a little better. But then the sea wasn't nearly as tumultuous either.

I find the time racing along, so it's clear that we're not bored. We've been playing games, such as ring throwing, table tennis, etc.

And now it's night already again. Pretty soon when I go to bed I'll have to set back my watch another hour. That'll be the third time. In Holland now it's quarter-to-one.

I'm sitting in a very quiet spot here. Everybody is sleeping peacefully while I'm writing at a writing desk. Yes, we have a desk in our cabin. Rather nice, eh? I can hear the ocean roar below me. Very interesting! Well, people, tomorrow is another day, so "Cheerio!"

May 30, Sunday evening, Dutch time about 2 o'clock.

So, there they're in deep rest. My watch says 10 o'clock. I've turned it back an hour for the fourth time.

This morning all of us except Mom made it to the dining room again. They brought Mom some food in our cabin. After that I played some table tennis and to the church service at 10 in the tourist class lounge. Well, it wasn't a very good preacher, to be sure. First, we sang some hymns, then some scripture readings. Then a short meditation, and after that the people could request some more numbers for us to sing together. At 11:30 it was all done.

We didn't do much in the afternoon. This is a very strange Sunday, one we'll not likely experience again for some time. By next Sunday we'll be a long ways from here. The weather was beautiful today.

Two were missing at our table tonight, namely Mom and Marijke. The little tyke was in need of sleep. After mealtime we spent most of the night on the lower deck visiting Kooistra's. We did some singing, etc. At 9:15 there was another service, but we didn't go. Dad and Mom did, though.

I'm the last one again tonight, so I better end this. People, goodnight, and people in the fatherland, sleep well!

May 31, Monday evening, 10 o'clock.

I just moved my watch back half an hour, so not an hour this time.

Well, I'll make it short this time. There's not much news to tell.

It was a beautiful day today. This noon there were nine of us gathered around the dinner table, namely our own whole family and Beverly and Elizabeth Commager. Both of those are girls who talk English and don't understand us, but still, they're always with us.

Marijke raises a fuss every night. Last night was another really bad one. There's an old man in the cabin next to ours. He's bothered by all the racket and then he knocks with all his might on the wall. And once awake, he told us, he can't get back to sleep again. Well, he turned in a complaint on us, and now we're going to try something else. Dad is going to sleep in our cabin and Griet is moving to 109.

June 1. Tuesday morning. 11:00 o'clock.

I'm sitting at a table here in the smoking room with Sietze. A steward just brought us bouillon.

It went well with Marijke last night. She never gave a peep. But at 6:30 she started calling for Mom. But Dad had her quiet in a hurry.

When I woke up this morning, I heard the foghorn. A thick fog hung over the ocean. But at around 10 the sun broke through and by now the mist has cleared up to such a point that the foghorn is now silent. Otherwise, it sounded every minute.

The trip is coming along nicely. We're far past the halfway point.

Every night they deliver a paper to our cabin— "The Oceanpost." It includes the news of the whole world.

Well, I've told most of the news now. Oh, yes, I forgot to tell that there's a kind of a theater on ship. They show movies there every day.

In the evenings at 9:15 there's entertainment in the dining room of the tourist class. Till 10:30 there wasn't much fun. They played with cards with numbers on them. Somebody called off certain numbers all the time, and when the number appeared on your card, you'd have to put a red tag on the number. Whoever had the completed card would get 50 cents. But at 10:30 things got a lot better. A magician was going to demonstrate his tricks. The magician was a waiter from the first class. All of his tricks were really worth seeing. I'll describe a couple of them.

He took two small balls in his hand—in the right hand a red one and in the other a white. Then he made some motions, blew some air over them, and both balls disappeared. Then again, a white ball in his right hand and in the other a red one. I couldn't follow so quickly how he did that. And so, there were all sorts of tricks that made you watch with amazement.

It's really interesting to see something like that. It was 11:30 before we got to bed sound and safe.

June 2. Wednesday morning.

It's 11 o'clock, and therefore 4 o'clock in Holland. Right now I'm peacefully scribbling in the library or non-smoking room. I just enjoyed a cup of bouillon with a cookie. The service is fine here, to be sure.

It's getting warmer, let me tell you. Time for the jacket to come off. The boat makes a lot more motion now, too, which means that Mom is getting worse again.

The voyage will soon come to an end now. I believe we're supposed to arrive in New York at 4:00 on Friday.

This afternoon at 5 we took a bath. That was nicely refreshing. Sietze didn't feel like taking a bath.

I had a scare this afternoon. I came to the discovery that my watch cover was gone and that only one hand was left. What a pain! And I couldn't figure out for the life of me how that ever happened. Anyway, nothing I can do about it now. I put the watch away; it's no good like this. And the funny thing is that the watch was still running.

People, it's a late night again. So, it's high time for this "little boy" to get to bed!

June 3. Thursday evening. 10:30.

I'm alone in the cabin. Sietze and Lies are still in the tourist class where they're enjoying a jolly party. They have singing and readings, etc. Really fun. Griet and Marijke are asleep.

I have the chance now to catch up on this diary a bit.

The dining room was beautiful tonight. They had the whole place decorated. And there were all kinds of goodies on the long table and a decorative centerpiece with the words "Au Revoir!" Well, I thought to myself, that might be a long time before you see me again. But let's hope for the best.

Griet and Marijke are lucky. I picked up 6 balloons for them from the dining room.

In the meantime the boat just keeps on steaming along. The foghorn blasts continually because it's very foggy again.

LIST OF PASSENGERS
FIRST CLASS

Mr. L. G. P. Aalbersberg
Mr. J. F. L. Akkermans
Mrs. M. Aldrich
Mr. W. H. André de la Porte

*Mr. W. Baines
*Mrs. W. Baines
*Mr. D. Barling
*Mrs. D. Barling
*Miss Barling
*Miss Barling
Mr. J. Baron
Mrs. J. Baron
Miss E. Baron
Miss G. Baron
Miss M. J. Baron
Mr. S. Baron
Mr. H. Baron
*Mr. Johan van Beusekom
*Mr. L. A. Block
Mr. Carl. Blocker
Mr. Martin Blocker
Mr. A. C. Blokland
Mrs. A. C. Blokland
Mr. H. A. Bok
Miss Elia Bolanz
Mr. K. Bolk
*Mrs. L. R. Bollard
Mr. R. R. Bonthorn
Mrs. R. R. Bonthorn
Mr. L. M. Boot
Mrs. L. M. Boot
Mrs. E. van den Bos

*Miss J. A. Bowman
*Mr. Joan Brunner
Mr. Rolf E. Büchler
Mrs. Rolf E. Büchler
Dr. O. Burgauer
*Miss B. Burrell
Miss Phoebe Buzard

Mr. Henry Coehler
*Miss J. M. Cole
*Prof. H. Commager
*Mrs. H. Commager
*Miss N. Commager
*Miss E. Commager
Rev. Maurice Coopman
Mr. E. Cramer

*Miss M. E. Danvers
*Mr. Davies
Rev. Father G. J. Dean

Mr. Th. Ehrlich
Mr. B. Th. Elias
Mrs. B. Th. Elias

Mrs. Liesel Froehlich
Mr. K. L. Fueter
Mr. F. P. Puykschot

Mr. H. J. Gans
Mr. G. J. Gast
Mrs. G. J. Gast

A lady stopped me a moment ago to ask me if she could use my mouth harmonica. Well, I didn't understand her too well because she said it in English, but I did figure out what she meant. I told her that Lies had it in her pocket and I didn't know where she was. Well, if I then would be so kind to find her? And she dropped an American quarter in my pocket. Well, at that point I couldn't very well refuse her, right? So I went to the lounge, and sure enough, there they were! I got the thing and went back upstairs. But they sure had a lot of fun in that lounge. The lady was still waiting, so I gave it to her. Tomorrow morning, she is going to return it.

I must have sent at least 10 picture postcards of this boat to the Netherlands today. Really!

Now I've never said anything yet about my best friend. His name is Casperd Coopman (though he's listed as Maurice). He is 55. He is Belgian by birth. Lives in Hawaii, I think. I believe he is a priest. Blue eyes and always jolly. There you have him—my friend. He's an awful lot of fun. I often play table billiards with him—for the championship.

Dear folks, I'm just about talked out. Dad and Mom better not know that I'm still here, because I was supposed to go to bed early tonight, and now it did get late again.

So, till tomorrow! Dididididadida!

TRAIN TRIP: NEW YORK – CHICAGO – SEATTLE

June 6, Sunday evening, 9:15.

I'm in the smoking car again. Not far from me lies Sietze because we are going to try to sleep here tonight. We're now on the way to Seattle. But first I have to catch up.

When we stepped off the boat, we walked to a large area where all the First-Class passengers gathered with their baggage. A lady from the Seaman's Home took us there. We must have waited there at least two hours before they inspected our baggage. It was then that we experienced the inconvenience of not being able to speak the language. When our turn came up, though, things went very quickly. Fortunately, we didn't get a real tough customs inspector. We saw the Kooistras again too.

A brother of Oom Gilbert took us to the Seaman's Home. He was going to take the Nieuw Amsterdam to Holland the next day. He also in part arranged the train trip for us. The Kosters had already left.

We spent about an hour in the Seaman's Home. We bought a few things there, such as candy and bread, etc. Then on to the station. We left New York around 7:45. It got dark before long, and then we had to try to get to sleep. That wasn't easy, but eventually you get used to everything. Of course, you don't sleep nearly as well as in bed.

We woke up early the next morning. It gets dark early at night and light early in the morning here.

At first there wasn't too much to see but when we got closer to Chicago the landscape improved. I won't say much about it because then I'll never finish. It's better to experience and see it for yourself than to describe it. We haven't seen any mountains yet.

On Saturday, June 5, at around 5 o'clock we arrived in Chicago. We had to transfer to another station, and there they told us that we could depart at 11:15. So, a wait of 6 hours. That's a long wait. How to spend all this time? Well, we ate first. It was almost 7:30 already when we finished. We still had to take care of some things then, like tickets and information. We also bought some candy, drinks, timetables, etc. (Yuk, it's miserably hard to write on the train.) We did some window shopping and looked at a tape recorder and went into one of those booths where you can take a picture of yourself. That works like this: you deposit a quarter in a slot. Then you see a bright light. When you'd hear the quarter drop, they snap the picture. Then you'd hear all sorts of sounds inside the machine and within 5 minutes you'd have the photo inside a neat frame in hand. Unfortunately, I didn't have a quarter left.

Mom and Marijke slept. At 10:30 a lady came to bring us to the train. First, we bought some apples, and then to the train. That was quite strenuous because we had quite a load to carry. All of us were relieved when at last we sat safe and sound in the train. This then would be our "home" for a few days. By now we really began to look forward to the end, but there would still be lots to see before getting there.

What a strange Sunday we had, like one I never experienced before and maybe never again. Sunday on the train. We stopped often. I don't like that. But we knew the time of our arrival, and that is Tuesday morning at 7:30. We took food along out of Chicago and in the train we bought our drinks. In Milwaukee we bought some candy.

We didn't get bored because there was a lot to see. Beautiful scenery. And you won't believe the number of cars we saw—thousands of them. We're not used to that.

Sietze and I decided to sleep in the smoking car at night. It's quiet there and we're able to stretch out. But it took quite a while before we could settle down. People kept coming in and then it's hard to go to sleep. But at last we went ahead anyway. The people just kept sitting around and we got sleepy. This is the first night that we slept well.

June 7. Monday, 2:00 o'clock.

We can't stop looking. The world is beautiful here. High mountains with eternal snow. It's simply indescribable.

Now and again it gets completely dark. That's when we go under a mountain. Sometimes fairly long, sometimes short. Or we twist our way up a mountain. I'm looking right at the mountains now, covered with evergreens. A beautiful sight.

It's very warm outside here. That's not for me. It makes you sleepy. I better quit for a while now.

Till the next time.

OK, here we are again. It's evening now, 8:30. The clock's set back another hour.

This afternoon we enjoyed the beautiful scenery around us. Mountains and more mountains. High ones with snowy peaks, and smaller ones too. And the train just kept twisting through it all—now climbing a mountain and then again going through it for a ways. We had a great time!

Gradually we're getting closer to our goal. The three days which at first we dreaded haven't been bad at all and have gone rather quickly, it seems to me.

The train is way late; I hope it'll do some catching up tonight or else we won't get there by 7:30 in the morning.

We did some singing a little while ago. A couple of ladies liked that, so we roared ourselves hoarse to the accompaniment of the mouth harmonica. I'll put down my pen again for now. Till tomorrow. "Good night!"

June 9. Wednesday. 9:30 PM.

I'm sitting here in the front room by Oom Gilbert and Tante Jeanette. We've just finished eating. Late, right? But it isn't like this all the time.

Let me start by telling about yesterday's experiences.

At 7:05 on Tuesday morning we arrived in Seattle. First we saw a huge airport with all kinds of airplanes, large and small. A lady was waiting for us at the train station to help us. Oom G and Tante J were not there. I'll tell you why pretty soon. The lady took us to the waiting room. Then she called Oom G and Tante J.

Let me tell you now why they weren't there. There were other reasons, too, but they are of lesser importance. They had gotten confused by the three brothers Koster who came here for three weeks of vacation. They left New York before us and therefore arrived before us too. And the agreement was that all of us were going to get picked up together from Seattle. So that's how things got tangled up.

In spite of all that, we got here OK. Dad and Mom talked with Tante J a while on the telephone. They were going to pick us up in Bellingham. So, we bought tickets, etc., and then on to another station. At 8:30 we were on the train. The last lap is always the toughest. I think that's true. I got a headache and lost all my pep. I tried to sleep and succeeded for a little while. We thought we'd arrive at 11, but it turned out to be 11:45. That was a long time. We all were glad to be here.

It was unbearably hot on the train besides. We did get to see some nice scenery again. But all of us were very happy to finally get there.

When we got off the train, we spotted familiar faces at once. Oom G and Tante J as well as M. Tjoelker with his wife. Then in the cars and off. We drove through Lynden. It looks like a nice place to me. Nice surroundings, too. At 12:30 we arrived at Oom G and Tante J. There we were treated to a wonderful dinner. Tjoelker and wife also stayed for dinner. It tasted terrific after such a long trip. Since Friday we had not had a warm meal. We really received a very warm welcome here. It couldn't have been better.

And now I will record the experiences ahead of us in the other journal. Thus, I have reached the end of my story. The handwriting wasn't always the best, but the boat and the train share the blame for that.

Readers, I hope you've enjoyed this: then the effort of the writer is rewarded. So, this is then the conclusion of this diary.

"End of this little daybook."

***

This should have been added to the diary:

After our arrival in Hoboken, NJ, we took the train from one end of the land to the other. I had had one year of ULO (academic middle school) English, and I thought I knew something about the pronunciation system of the language. So, I asked a fellow passenger: "We stop in Chai-cai-go?" I soon discovered there was no such place, but we definitely would stop in Shee-kah-go.

We transferred to another train there that would take us all the way to the state of Washington. When passengers asked us how far we were going, I announced confidently, "To Seetle." There wasn't a soul that had ever heard of "Seetle." Fortunately, we did make it to See-eah-tul eventually, but my confidence in what I knew of English plummeted dramatically. We were very much strangers in a foreign land, objects of curiosity and even entertainment.

Family Letter Excerpts

What follows are some translated fragments of parental letters to relatives in the NL:

- "We'd like to start on our own, if we can hold out here for three years and get some equity in the cattle. Not many farms for rent here. Hard to get on your feet this way.

- Hard to get a place when you have nothing and go in debt for everything and start at the bottom; hard to save enough to work your way up

- We had 500 eggs today, which cost 70c per dozen

- Everybody has a gun here and goes hunting in open season; then you hear gunshots all around

- The men get up at 5, eat at 8 and at 12 and 5; they work a lot with tractors

- We have a large house now: 5 rooms on the ground floor, a bathroom, and 3 bedrooms

Thompson place:

- "We live close to the high hills now; that often makes for a beautiful scene; this huge country is so different from Holland; it's all hills and dales here; the "drukte" from moving is fortunately behind us again; as far as land and work are concerned, we have improved ourselves; it's good river bottom here; the house is not as big and the old beppe [Margaret's Beppe Zwaanstra] came along with us; at this moment she's in a conversation with Jeen about doubt and faith; I have to make coffee now. and then take the old lady to bed, just like a baby.

- The boss (Thompson) doesn't curse and rave like LeCocq, but he's terribly tight; is eager to take in his half but doesn't like the expenses that have to be deducted, like gas for tractors, etc. If something needs fixing in the barn, it's really tough to get his approval to have it fixed; he's in the clutches of the money-devil"

(Dad adds a part to the letter)

- We now have our third place. We have a contract for 3 years, but we can leave earlier if we want to. We have 100 acres here (40 hectare), no chickens, 87 head of cattle with half of those heifers and calves. We have to buy half of the cattle and of the machines, etc. We get half the income too. Lots of work, as you can imagine. Most of the land is in pasture. The owner is an American and seems a lot better than the last one we had. The cows suffer from neglect and it was a terrible mess in the barn, but we've cleaned it up pretty well by now. We had to borrow all the money for this and have to pay 6% interest. It's hard to get on your feet at first, but we are of good cheer. The Lord will provide and therefore his is all the glory.

- Nobody goes out for a walk here, just flying around in cars.

- We have to wait and see how adequate the income will be; the owner expects his cows to be fed royally; they can't eat my potato peels; a lot of medals hang in the barn; we have to invest $5,000 into this, all on credit; we hope it will go well, for too many changes is no fun

- We are surrounded from three sides by mountains that are already snow-covered; behind us is the ocean, not so far away; we live close to the Canadian border too [*now on their last farm*]

- I remember, Martin (Mom's brother), that you when you were young were so interested in going to America, and Mom would tell you to throw the propaganda in the stove for you couldn't go there anyway; strange how things turn out; what if she had known that her youngest would one day go there; I wish the whole family was here too, for it's likely better here than in Holland; we should have gone sooner" (*my added note here: sadly the time would come when she said "we should never have come...."*)

Mom's impression of an American lunch program:

- "Piano music and dramatic readings, reading of the Bible, everything very orderly w/o applause

- Those who wanted to smoke just left for awhile

- After the program everyone in the audience got a paper plate with something very American: cold potatoes with raw onions mixed through, etc., and a leaf of lettuce ... and salad dressing; a fork and a napkin too, a raisin bun, a double slice of white bread cut in triangles with butter, ham, a sausage and a cookie. After that a piece of pie which the Americans get practically every day with their meal. They bake two dry crumbly cakes in a round form, fill them with everything tasty in between with apple crisp or bananas, etc., then a big piece of ice-cream with the pie, which is here also a typical American treat. What do you think of that? We gave that pile of cold potatoes a funny look. Jeen passed it up; he doesn't care for onion taste. I picked away at it slowly and pretended that it was something we'd always been used to. Except for that cold pile, everything tasted very good. Coffee with it, of course."

334

Judy's Birth

Personal Crisis

Grand Rapids looked beautiful in mid-June as we drove along tree-lined Plymouth Ave. to Blodgett Hospital for the arrival of our second child. We were young and optimistic. Yes, this pregnancy had interrupted my second year of teaching, but Cindy's birth had delayed my teaching eighteen months earlier, and we were doing fine. Maybe this would be a boy, and then we'd have our perfect family! Oh, well, as everyone said, "just as long as it's healthy." I had no doubt about that!

She came quickly, surprising our doctor, who barely made it in time to deliver her. It was very quiet in the delivery room after her birth. I only remember a nurse saying, "She has all her fingers and all her toes." Judy was swaddled tightly in a blanket before they handed her to me, and then called my husband in to see her. We admired her strawberry blond wisps of hair, such a contrast with Cindy's dark mop of hair at birth. So now we had two girls, a blond and a brunette!

When Judy was two days old, the pediatrician came to see her and reported to me, "She's doing ok—you know she has this spot on her back." No, I did not know about that. "Well, fortunately it's a mild case. She has spina bifida—a partially open spine. This means she may have difficulty with bowel and bladder control. Maybe she'll walk funny. (He demonstrated to me—I can still visualize it, because later Judy did walk that way!) But since the spot is already healing over, she may be fine. Just to be sure, let's make an appointment for me to check her at two weeks."

"How does this type of thing happen?" I asked. He didn't know. He said he was just amazed that there were so many babies born with miraculously perfect bodies.

We resumed our lives as a happy little family, thankful that things weren't worse. We carefully replaced the gauze dressing on her opening each day. Judy slept a lot, but she seemed to be growing nicely. As I wrote home, "Even her face seems to be filling out." So, when I brought her to the pediatrician at two weeks, I was surprised to see the concern on his face as he measured her head. He said, "It's growing too fast—I'm afraid she has hydrocephalus." My head was swimming with the enormity of that term. Suddenly this carefree young mom turned into a concerned parent preoccupied with the uncertain future of a disabled child. The memory of those vacant-looking babies I'd seen a few years back at Pine Rest haunted me. They lay neglected with huge heads and tiny bodies. The future looked bleak.

Sharing the news with my husband brought a shadow of gloom to our home, as we became very concerned parents. The reality of a child who hurts preoccupies a parent's mind from waking moments until the end of the day when sleep comes slowly.

We hadn't worried the family back home with the news about "mild spina bifida." Now it was time to ask everyone to be in prayer for our child's head as it filled with spinal fluid. Cards and notes of congratulations were soon followed by cards of consolation. Many ended their notes with Romans 8:28: "All things work together for good to those who love God."

At that time I wondered how any good could come out of this.

Judy's baptism at Sherman St. CRC was an emotional one – we didn't know at that time how tenuous her life would be, and Rev. Mulder's prayer reflected that, but we knew God loved her, and so did we. That summer was a busy one not only because our new baby needed special attention and time, but also because my husband had some courses left to take and had to get as many hours in on part-time jobs as possible to pay the bills. And then there was the new teaching job waiting which would need a good deal of his preparation.

So what about that question I asked when this became a personal crisis for me? How did this work together for good ? I'm not going to try to answer that question because I know so many people have had much more difficult crises to deal with than mine. But it did change my outlook immediately in so many ways. Never again will I take for granted that a newborn child will be healthy. Life has become more precious for me. I have been sensitized to the feelings other parents have when they feel that God reached down and struck them for no reason. And I've learned, although God does not prevent all birth defects, he does give us grace to deal with it, and He sends people to encourage us.

English Department Writeup

(Bill VandeKopple took it on himself to feature a writeup of a colleague with each issue of the departmental newsletter. This one has me on the hotseat.)

Our Colleague: Henry Baron

Personal

Not everyone knows this, but the idea for the Festival of Faith and Writing originated back around 1988 or 1989 in a conviction that grew strong within Henry. He had become convinced that people in the Christian community struggling to become writers needed to be encouraged and needed to find a way to be connected to one another. He thought that a conference for such people would be a good idea. When he discussed this idea with Ed Ericson, who was then the department chair, Ed told him to "run with it." Part of that involved recruiting Susan Van Zanten and Dale Brown to help define and describe such a conference and then to take the definition and description of the overall event to Peter De Vos, who was Vice President for Academic Affairs. After Peter gave the go-ahead, they formed a committee and began to work in earnest. Henry stressed to me that they had nothing in place for advertising, for fund-raising, and for identifying participants, but they assigned one another tasks, they raised as much money as they could, they extended their personal and professional networks, and they succeeded in holding the first conference, in 1990. That conference attracted about one hundred people, and Henry described it as a "sweet experience." Participants said that the conference was exactly what they had been waiting for, and after the last event most of them agreed that they had to find ways to keep in touch with each other and with what would be going on with writing and literary study at Calvin College in the future.

Henry described some of his favorite moments from festivals over the years. For him, Katherine Patterson's talks have always been a highlight. He remembers a wonderful talk by Donald Hall. He reminded me of the special evening when Frederick Buechner packed the Fine Arts Center Auditorium and left all of us in the audience mindful of how we should be "paying attention." And Henry said some things similar to things that Shelly told me: He really enjoyed Yann Martel when he was here. Martel was a delightful person, he impressed Henry with his description of how he came to write Pi, and he was open and honest about his journey from a lack of faith to the point of embracing faith. Plus, he was so interested in the people of and places in West Michigan. He came early to the festival and stayed late. He wanted to ride out to Grand Haven to see what a lakeshore community was like. And he stayed around Grand Rapids long enough to hear Rev. Rob Bell preach.

When I asked Henry about potential evaluative comments on how the festival has developed through the years, he gave me some interesting material to think about. He is thrilled that it has grown into a national, if not international, event. And he is open to inviting writers from outside the Christian faith and from non-faith communities. But he wonders a little about the festival's focus and identity. In this regard, he cites Lionel Basney, who was also in on the early planning stage, and often used to remind everyone about keeping a clear identity for the festival. Do we run any risk, Henry asks, of presenting more of a national conference on literature and less of an event that will foster connections among and encouragement for Christian writers?

I made a transition and asked Henry about some of his favorite memories of teaching. The first class he mentioned was The Teaching of Writing. It was a challenge, he acknowledged, but it was very fulfilling. He still has memories of wonderful "Philosophy of Life" papers that his students produced. He went on to call the teaching of Young Adult Literature "lovely." And he regrets that Canadian literature, which he introduced, fell by the wayside after he retired and after Chip, who had picked the course up, "had the gall to leave Calvin." In that course he always loved teaching the Margarets—Avison, Atwood, and Laurence— among others, and he wonders to what extent they are represented in our curriculum now.

Henry said that he never has had hobbies in his life, and he viewed that as "a great defect in my character." Having no hobbies, he added, must mark him as "very dull." But then I asked him about music. "Well," he responded, "music is more than a hobby; it's a big part of my life." His dad and mom loved to sing, and their family often would gather around the pump organ to sing hymns and folk songs. His dad was a band director, and he insisted that Henry learn how to play the organ and piano, instruments that Henry still plays. He very much enjoys classical music (he started his collection of classical music as a teen, even before "he had much money at all"). He has been a part of a male quartet. He sang in his first Messiah when he was still in his teens. Some of you may remember the Gilbert and Sullivan productions that used to be put on at Calvin, and Henry sang in the chorus of many of these (was he ever a modern major general or a pirate king?). And the Grand Rapids Symphony, as well as theater, has been a large part of his life for years.

In addition to music and the stage, Henry enjoys "playing around" with creating photo albums and family videos on his computer. And for exercise he likes to play tennis, ride bike, and hike. Some of us could think back and tell some interesting stories about the days when Henry played racquetball. The only Frisian words (ah, the guttural sounds!) I know came from Henry—with force—during tense moments on the court, such as just after he was drilled in a hamstring by a shot off Jim's racquet.

Henry's wife, Ruth, might not be happy about this connection, but she was my fourth-grade teacher. According to Henry, she has the same hair color now that she had when she was twelve years old. Ruth loves to travel (you may recall notes from Clare about how the Walhouts and Barons have taken several extensive trips together). She does a lot of tutoring and volunteering (for example, at Global Gifts). And she is a member of more than one book club; to prepare for the meetings of these clubs, she does a "ton of reading."

Henry and Ruth have five children. Cindy is the oldest. I am certain that you know her since she is the Chapel Coordinator at Calvin College.

Judy is the next in line. Judy was born with spina bifada and hydrocephalus, so she has had many exceedingly rough times in her life, including some brushes with death. And with each medical crisis comes the potential for some loss of cognitive skill. Yet she has married and has two children.

The third child is Henry Jr., who is an electrical engineer living in Seattle. He loves the Pacific Northwest because it affords him so many opportunities for outdoor activities such as skiing, hiking, and outdoor photography.

Next is Jayne, who like Henry lives in the Pacific Northwest. She and her two daughters reside close to Bellingham, Washington.

The fifth is Lisa, who works part-time as the mentoring coordinator at Calvin. Henry says about Cindy and Lisa that it is very gratifying to see them doing important things at the college they have come to love.

Professional Development

Henry mentioned several projects and activities that he uses to keep himself alert, engaged, and professionally active:

1. He stressed that China has been extremely important in his life. In 1985 he was the team leader for a group of teachers visiting China in order to train Chinese teachers how to teach English (the country had switched its main language-teaching focus from Russian to English). On that trip something happened to Henry that has happened to many others over the years. As he put it, "the people get inside you." Since that first trip, he has gone back to lecture to

graduate students about the influence of the Bible on Western literature. And he and Ruth often have friends from China as well as children of friends from China visit them here in the states. One of these children actually calls Henry and Ruth "Dad" and "Mom." Also, Henry said that it has been wonderful to be able to meet with Ling at least once a week while she is visiting us.

2. Friesland also remains a big part of Henry's life. He carries on considerable e-mail correspondence in Frisian and has translated three books from Frisian into English. He is a regular reviewer of Frisian fiction and poetry for World Literature Today. He also translates Dutch material for publication. And he says he very much enjoyed the opportunity to teach a semester of Dutch at Calvin, when Herman De Vries was on sabbatical. That means he's taught four Germanic languages: German (in high school), Dutch, Frisian, and English. He's been trying to add Spanish to his repertoire of languages but complains of lazy memory cells.

3. Henry and Ruth are dedicated movie buffs. He described for me the last film they had seen, Ikiru, and talked about how he found it "profound in many ways."

4. Many people within the department have an iPod. Henry has an iPod touch but that is inscribed with the word Ipake (pake is "grandpa" in Frisian; Henry and Ruth's ninth grandchild is on the way). This was a surprise gift from his son, and Henry delighted in showing me some of what he could do with the device. He carries favorite passages and poems from the literature he used to teach on it and downloads for re-reading such classics as The Brothers Karamazov. I resonated most to his description of using the digital dictionary, because it was in Henry's English 200 course that I was led to begin a vocabulary list, and I am still adding to this list today (although I have left off all the Frisian words Henry has taught me).

Publications

- directed and edited many English curriculum projects for Christian secondary schools through CSI

- directed the writing of and edited two series of literature texts for Christian junior and senior high school readers through CSI

- co-authored a column for Christian Educators Journal for more than 20 years

- Wrote Neland CRC's 75th anniversary book This Far by Faith

- translated a novel, The Trap, and a collection of short stories, Lowland Tales, from Frisian to English, published in 1997 and 2000, respectively

- translated book on Dutch emigrants: Cruel Paradise in 2005; and a book, The Comfort Bird in 2017, on two families whose descendants ended up fighting on opposite sides in WWII

- translated a book from Dutch, Ecclesiastes for Managers, published in 2018

- published Talking with God: prayers, meditations and conversations for God-seekers in 2011

- many book reviews for various publications; continues to be a regular reviewer of Dutch and Frisian literature for World Literature Today

- many articles in a variety of publications

- many academic essays for Salem Press, published in their various academic Reference publications

a complete listing is in the Vita, a separate document

Frisian Sermon Translation

WANDERERS SEARCHING FOR THE TRUE COUNTRY

(tr. of sermon preached by hjbaron in Oudkerk on July 9, 2000; text: Hebr. 11:14)

Once there was a place, according to the Bible, where Beauty and Truth, in the words of the English poet John Keats, where Beauty and Truth were one. A place where everything was right, where not one bad or untrue word was heard, where peace and harmony dwelled together, where one could feel forever content, safe, and at home.

But that didn't last, as you know. There was a "snake in the grass," as we say when a fiend is present who makes everything that was straight crooked, who turns everything upside down.

Adam and Eve lost their home; they were driven out and became wanderers.

Wanderers in a world that had changed completely: a world where one brother murdered the other; where finally all the affairs of men turned to evil.

In that world Abram received the call: "Go from your land, from your family and your home to a land that I shall show you."

Thus Abram became a wanderer; and Jacob who had to flee from his brother and then from his uncle; and Moses who had to wander for years in the wilderness, always searching for the promised land; a world where David had to go into hiding and where his life often hung by a thread; where even the Lord Jesus didn't have a pillow on which to put his head.

The Bible is full of stories of wanderers, "in deserts and on mountains and in caves and holes in the ground" (verse 38)—all of them people in motion, searching for a country of their own.

But we also know wanderers from our own history, from our own world and time.

A world where Menno Simons could expect his own neighbors to hang him because his faith conflicted with the teachings of the church; where his followers were driven from one land to the next and from one century to the next.

Wanderers of our own world—because of persecution; hunger; injustice; and war.

Wanderers searching for freedom; but also for a little more space; for a chance to make something of their life; and especially for a better future for their children.

The thousands of Frisians who left as emigrants to America, to Canada, to Australia, New Zealand, South Africa belong with those wanderers, searching for a fatherland.

But to live as strangers in a strange land—that's not easy.

Abraham discovered that, and Moses, and Gideon. And most of the emigrants did too. The country of their own they were looking for often turned out to be a cruel paradise.

That's why the faith in which they had been raised became for so many wandering immigrants the center of their life. It offered an anchor in a place and a time of too much change and confusion. A place and a time where they often experienced betrayal, and loss and doubt and privation. That's often the case with wanderers.

In China too.

When I spent some time teaching there, I listened to stories from students who during the Cultural Revolution were sent away from home far into the countryside. And there they had to slave hard for strangers from early in the morning to late at night. They were often sickly, often mistreated, often hungry, always homesick, with never a word from back home.

They said to me, in the English of a Chinese: "Dr. Baron, we became empty inside." They said: "We were brought up to believe in Mao Tse Tung. He was our god. But that turned into a great betrayal. Now we believe in nothing; our hearts are empty."

It was different for many Frisian wanderers.

Hebr. 11 gives us a review of the difference that faith can make in the life of a person.

In the life of Abraham and Joseph and Moses; in the life of Rahab and Jefta and David; in the life of Samuel and, later, also in the life of Peter and Paul.

We would be able to give a similar recital of the Frisian immigrants who, through faith in the cruel paradise of 1847, in a place that they called Vriesland, built a church, who through faith endured the suffering of poverty and loss and grief and privation and held fast to the God of Abraham, Isaac, and Jacob.

The faith of the immigrants wasn't a mere custom, a ritual that really had nothing to do with their daily life. It had everything to do with their daily living, and that didn't pass unnoticed by their children.

Their faith as trust in God; faith that through the tears of loss and grief is able to confess: "The Lord is my shepherd, I shall not want."

Faith that floods your heart with the love of God through the Lord Jesus Christ.

Such faith changes a person; it changed that whole assembly of heroes of faith in Hebr. 11.

"Through faith," says the writer of our chapter, "they conquered kingdoms, established justice, closed the mouths of lions, and endured scorn and floggings."

But it also changes the people who witness such faith in action:

The witnesses of the faith of Abraham, and of Joseph, and of Moses, and so on. That's always been true.

That was also the case in China.

I had students there who said: "We know that you are a Christian. But we don't understand it, because we were taught that faith in God is childish superstition that educated people reject.

You are a professor and yet you are a Christian.

And we can tell that you have something in your heart that we don't have. Our hearts are empty. We would like to know more about your faith."

That made a deep impression on me.

I've often had struggles with faith in my own life; I'm afraid that will always be that way.

But I'm also a witness, as to my students in China.

And it's been a tremendous blessing for me that I was able to find my spiritual and intellectual home in a church and a college where I could find the heroes of faith that I needed.

A church where the people relate to each other as friends and as siblings who can have fun together, who can cry together, who bear each other's burdens, who love each other through the love of God in the Lord Jesus, who always stand ready to help others in a world of need.

And I've been able to do my life's work in a place, really in a community of students and teachers where faith and science do not face each other as enemies, but where faith runs smack through all the courses of study; where one has the freedom to ask profound questions which sometimes are not easily accommodated by faith. There I learned what it means to love God not only with one's whole heart but also with one's whole intellect.

What a witness observes and experiences in the life of those around him must affect his/her own faith, to be sure. And that doesn't begin in church and neither in the workplace, but at home. In the home of Abraham and Sara. In your home; in my home.

I said a moment ago that the steadfast faith of an immigrant leaves an impact on their children. Most of the children of immigrants whom I know have retained the faith of father and mother.

In my own case I was the witness of a faith which still gives me aid and support each day.

In Hebr. 11 we read that Isaac, through faith, pronounced a blessing on Jacob and Esau, "also with an eye to the future. Through faith, Jacob, when he was on his deathbed, blessed both of Joseph's sons."

And through faith, my Dad called me to his bedside when he was consumed by pain, which had suddenly taken him from his labor and struck him down.

He must've sensed that this would turn into his deathbed.

Dad wanted me to come close to him, a Dad who otherwise never showed his affection openly.

He took my hand into his. There was pain in his eyes but at the same time such tenderness that I had never seen before. He pulled me close to him as if I were a small child, though I was 21 then. I could tell that the pain of the bowel obstruction (for that's what it turned out to be) penetrated his whole being, but he tried to say something.

"You're such a dear boy," he said, and then he put his arms around my neck and said: "I've wronged you sometimes; will you forgive me?"

Then he kissed me.

And at that moment I was a witness of my father's faith that I shall never forget. That day, his last day on earth, he gave me the blessing of his love, of his regrets, and of the grace of God that made all this possible.

The 11th chapter of Hebr. is about wanderers.

We read: "All these people were still living by faith when they died. They did not receive the things promised. …They admitted that they were aliens and strangers on earth. People who say such things show that they are looking for a country of their own."

Dad was one of the wanderers. He lived in his new country for seven years. Then he was called to a better country; and through faith, he was ready.

We're now celebrating Simmer 2000 in Friesland.

Wanderers from all parts of the world are back again for a short time in the old fatherland. Frisians who stayed here welcome us with open arms. And that gives us a wonderfully warm feeling and is greatly appreciated.

Soon we will leave again, back to our new fatherland.

Still, we remain wanderers.

And you do too, though you stay behind. Because what Hebr. 11 teaches us is that all of us are wanderers.

O yes, I know, there are times when, if we made something of our lives, we feel right at home, here or in America, or wherever.

For the truth may be that we live in a nice house, the children are doing well, we have plenty of friends, and enough money to enjoy life.

And yet there's still always that snake in the grass.

The comfortable world of our personal life can turn upside down in an instant. An accident, a heart attack, cancer, trouble with the children, alienation between husband and wife…

No, disasters, betrayal, loss—there's no one here this morning who's exempt from any of these things. And there's no one here who doesn't know that we live in a world that for many people is a cruel paradise, from the day of one's birth to the day of one's death.

Who then can really feel right at home—in a world where sin so often gets the upper hand; where the light of day and goodness can so quickly darken into the blackness of night and the evil of hate, jealousy, pride, greed, and all the other human vices which make it so clear that we have not yet found our way back to the true homeland.

Long ago there was a place that God declared very good.

God lived there with his children whom he had made in his own image. But something came between God and his children.

And the children became wanderers, searching for the true homeland that they had lost.

And the wanderers who didn't know what they were looking for had despair in their empty hearts.

But the wanderers with faith in their true homeland had hope; hope in the God of all the heroes of faith in Hebr.11; hope in Jesus Christ as shepherd and savior, who for them is the way, the truth, and the life.

And that hope changed their life and gave them love.

In Cor.13 we read: "… these three remain—from Adam and Abraham in Genesis to the Revelations of John—[three things]: faith, hope, and love."

In the land of faith and hope and love God dwells, and where God is, there must also be the true homeland.

May your life, as wanderers, clearly show that you are searching for the true homeland.

Amen.

The Immigrant Adventure: The Quest to Belong

Speech given at a Symposium on Emigration, held in Ljouwert (Leeuwarden) in October 1999, featuring talks by Dr. Henry J. Baron and Dr. Annemieke Galema, and an interview with the author Hylke Speerstra.

---

http://www.nwlink.com/~hbaron/baronfam/nlspeech.htm

Excerpts from that speech:

I've had my nose in the books practically all my life. The "School with the Bible" in Opende couldn't boast of a large library in the 40s; I must've read through the whole collection at least twice. The reading and teaching of literature eventually became my profession; literature that reveals all the ways in which humankind practices its humanity and inhumanity. And in literature one soon discovers that a person, in order to remain human, has certain basic needs. One of the most important is a sense of belonging. A feeling that one is part of things. We need it for security. It gives us a feeling of satisfaction. It gives a sense of significance, the conviction that our life has value and meaning, for we cannot live without that.

Not really. But the immigrant experience jeopardizes that sense of belonging. Now it's true, that sometimes, when people feel they don't belong, they don't count, they have no standing or they've lost it, they flee, they emigrate, to pursue that quest in another place. But more often, I think, the decision to emigrate is made without much thought of that basic need to belong.

However, it quickly raises its insistent cry when the immigrants wake up in a strange place where they don't know anybody, don't understand anybody, and feel estranged from the culture.

***

Language is the glue that connects us together.

But when language fails as the language of the land where you live, the connection is jeopardized or broken. And that was often the case with immigrants.

I remember what a struggle my dad had with the new language at age 52. How frustrated he would get when he had to communicate with the farmer with whom he was in partnership and didn't have the words. And Dad was a man who never had to search for a word, because he was a reader and facile with his pen. Now he had to depend on his children to find the right words for him. It's not hard to imagine how frustrating that must've been for him. How could the immigrants feel at home without the language of the new land!

When you finally gain some mastery over the new language and you can handle it well, but still it's not altogether right and there's still a thick, foreign accent, your tongue is a constant reminder that you don't quite belong, that you're different.

It's a struggle, self-conscious or not, that plagues nearly every immigrant who came to their new country too old to fully master the new language. It's the reason that typically immigrant children at a certain age would feel embarrassed by their parents and tried to distance themselves from their parental roots. It's one of the reasons that I, because I don't have native fluency in Frisian and Dutch anymore, don't and can't feel as much at home here as I do in the States. It's an important reason that most immigrants never quite come to feel at home in their adopted land.

But if language jeopardizes their necessary sense of belonging, what then takes its place?

For many immigrants, that's been the church... the church where they could listen to sermons in their own language... where everything was familiar. Where everything could and should stay as it had always been for them: the doctrines and interpretations, the points of view and practices, the liturgy and the music. Where they could meet and talk with fellow immigrants in their own tongue. Where they could feel at home; where they could belong. Church: the safe haven in a sea of change that sometimes threatened to swallow them; the point of stability when everything else was in flux.

Not every immigrant belonged to the church, of course. Those that didn't often had an even more difficult time with loneliness. They tried to establish Frisian societies, but that succeeded only in those large cities where many immigrants had settled.

My leitmotif in this talk is "the quest to belong." The language, I said, had much to do with that quest.

***

I could, of course, go on to talk in detail about a lot of other things. About what happens when the church changes too. About the years of hard work for most immigrants before the future began to look a little brighter. About the ambitions of immigrant children and the remarkable success achieved by so many of the first and second generation. But we have Galema's book and Speerstra's book, and we're

349

still going to have a discussion period.

Let me end on a personal note; and I wish that my dad and mom could've heard me say this, especially right here in the capitol of Fryslân, for I think it would've warmed their hearts.

I don't know why my parents emigrated. I regret that for them, for the most part, it turned into "it wrede paradys," especially because dad died before he had the chance to enjoy the heavy labor of his hands. But my brother and sisters will always be grateful that they did, for it has enriched our lives immeasurably. [I must add something here too, at my wife's request. She said on the way to the airport where she was dropping me off, "Tell them that your wife is happy too." Wasn't that sweet of her?] Emigration opened up a New World of experience and opportunity in a land we have come to love. But it also intensified our connections to the Old World, our fatherland with its unique beauty and identity; the place of our roots, of the family we left behind: uncles and aunts and many cousins. We've kept coming back to all of it because it still fulfills for us our own "quest to belong."

The Accident

I felt at once that something was wrong. It's that feeling that steals inside your blood and chills it. It comes unbidden, not because something is badly out of place and even before there's a sudden telephone call or someone isn't there when she should be. It comes when an internal signal calls the alert, before you know why.

I let my eyes wander over the crowd that was mostly seated already. We stood at the back of the chapel auditorium on the Christian Reformed Conference grounds right on Lake Michigan. Ruth and I had come from Grand Rapids, met our friends at their nearby cottage, came with them to take in the service, after which we planned to spend a leisurely evening together back at the cottage and the beach. Now I looked hard. Someone should have been here by now. But she wasn't.

Earlier that afternoon, still at home. It was a warm, lazy Sunday afternoon in August, when young blood and old feels sand and surf beckoning, away from the hot, crowded city to the vast waters and the cool breezes of Lake Michigan.

"Dad, Tasha and I would like to go the lake too. We can meet you at the chapel, spend some time at the beach, and then drive back to GR. Can I take the car?"

Lisa was sixteen, had just received her driver's license, and had not yet driven the freeways on her own.

"Honey, I'm not comfortable with that; you've never driven there, you may even have a hard time finding it, and the freeways are busy because of the holiday weekend."

"Trust me, Dad. I'm a good driver, I know how to find it, and we'll be careful."

"Yes, Mr. Baron, Lisa'll do fine, and I know the way too. Please, can we go?"

I look at my wife, but I know she's leaving it up to me.

I swallow hard, and I give in.

It's what parents do, because they love their kids.

And sometimes they don't, and shouldn't, because they love their kids.

The service started with a short song service. My mind was more on the two missing girls than on the songs. Still, when we sang "What a Friend we have in Jesus," the uneasy feeling of something pending, something not good, intensified.

When the minister took his place by the pulpit, I had already expected the messenger who now made his way to the podium to whisper something in the minister's ear. And I expected the minister to ask next if there were a Henry and Ruth Baron in the audience. But, when it came, a piece of cold steel dropped around the heart to keep it immobile. We were asked to leave through the side door to meet a party waiting for us. Outside, we saw a police car and two officers. That's when blood freezes, before, much later, it explodes through all the veins and arteries into turbulent waves of emotion.

"Do you have a daughter Lisa?"

"Yes."

"She's been in an accident."

All thinking stops as you wait for what comes next.

Heading west, the two friends soon left the humidity of the city behind. Ah, the exhilaration of freedom! The freedom of driving somewhere on the open roads, just the two of them, Lisa and Natasha. Cool breezes and sand between their toes just an hour away. They felt exuberant by the independence of their adventure and the limitless powers of their youth. They felt hungry for life, for experience, and yes, for food.

Near Zeeland, they stopped at a Dairy Queen.

They enjoyed an early supper, and then took dessert to go. Lisa had a Reese's Pieces Blizzard between her legs and kept getting spoonfuls while driving. They were listening to a tape of Wally Pleasant, a local humorous musician they liked. Life felt free and vital, with windows partway down, music turned up, and the two friends [teens] boisterously laughing and singing along with Wally, having the time of their life.

Traffic was busy on US 31, particularly on southbound, with many returning from a weekend up north and from a day at nearby beaches. The Mazda 323, on cruise control, hummed along smoothly at between 60-65 mph., though the speed limit on that stretch is 55. Lisa was driving in the northbound left lane. Up ahead she would need to make a left turn toward Lake Michigan and the Conference Grounds.

Getting to the bottom of her Blizzard, Lisa looked down to find a last spoonful. At that moment, the left front wheel edged off the pavement. None of her training and experience had prepared her for this. She looked up when the steering wheel began to shake and jerked it hard to the right to get back on the road.

Then a scream.

As she lost control and consciousness, the Mazda hit the median, the tire blew, the axle broke, the car flipped and slid upside down across the median strip and the southbound lane of traffic, finally coming to a stop, tilted on the driver's side.

Tasha, practically unhurt, looked at Lisa, hanging unconscious by her seatbelt, blood dripping from a cut on her head. She thought Lisa might be dead, but she had to get her out of the car in case it should explode. She tried to unbuckle her friend and get her out of the car. It was too hard. She managed to crawl out to get help. Then the police came.

You wait for the words you never want to hear: "I'm sorry; your daughter didn't make it."

Instead we heard: "Your daughter was hurt and taken by ambulance to the Grand Haven hospital. Her friend is O.K." And instantly the heart lurches into action. They're alive, yes! Then moves to concern: but how serious is Lisa?

"Is she hurt badly?"

"We think she'll be all right. She was coming to when the ambulance took her away."

"Thank you."

We go back to tell our friends. They want to come with us to the hospital. We don't talk. Thoughts and emotions tumble and churn together: what happened where is she hurt is it her face is she going to be ok oh God please not her brain....

In the chapel at the Conference Grounds, the minister tells the audience about the awful day when he lost a teenage child in a fatal car crash. Then he leads in prayer for the parents and their child who was in an accident.

 A policeman meets us at the entrance to Emergency. He tells us: "They were going too fast. Other drivers told us that they had the windows rolled down and music turned up high. Not sure whether she was buckled in."

We're not sure why he's telling us this now. We want to see Lisa.

We enter Emergency. We see Natasha and hug her. They lead us to a room. We stop at the door. We're not allowed to come in or talk to her, but we can see her. Our hearts fill up. She's alive! Thank God we still have her!

They tell us she just had a slight seizure. They need to x-ray her. As she's wheeled out on the stretcher, Lisa sees us. Tears well up in her eyes as she squeezes out the words: "I'm so sorry." We give her a tight smile and tell her it's all right. Oh yes, it's all right!

We wait.

When the doctor comes back, he says that there's some swelling of the brain, a sign of closed-head injury, and that Lisa needs to be taken to Butterworth in Grand Rapids by ambulance.

Our car is still at our friends' cottage, so we take our friends' car and head back to Grand Rapids. We take Tasha with us. We feel so grateful that Tasha's only injury is a sprained finger, but we're tight with worry about Lisa's brain injury. We talk very little.

In Grand Rapids we drop Tasha off at her home, explaining briefly what happened; we feel the need to apologize for our daughter's accident. They understand.

Then we hurry on to the hospital.

We enter Butterworth Emergency. We're told that Lisa's been admitted to the ICU. A Social Worker comes to meet us and offers her services. It increases our anxiety: do we really need this?

Finally, we're led to Lisa's room. In the shadows we see her form on the bed. There are tubes and monitors, but she's there and getting the care she needs. And there's relief in that.

This is not a time to talk. She's heavily medicated and obviously in discomfort. But it's enough now just to touch her, to hold her hand, to kiss her cheek, and to whisper our love.

When we leave, she's alone with her pain, her intense discomfort, her thoughts, and the nightmares to come.

Fragments of Lisa's Journal

"what really happened...oh...yes...

I feel sick and I'm scared...how could this happen...

"so much noise...so much noise...are they cutting me out? I'm floating away from my body ...away...away...

but they're loading me into the ambulance now...

and somebody is asking me questions...my name...what year...where I'm from...

but I can't think...I can't remember...who's president...I say Jefferson...

the man in the ambulance says to just rest in the arms of Jesus...

"I feel so guilty...I've caused so much trouble...I see my parents looking at me... tears welling up in their eyes...but aren't they angry?...thinking that I deserved this...for letting them down...for making them take time off from work...for wrecking that wonderful car...for all those bills they now have to face...

"I can hardly move...I feel so rotten inside...and I'm so hot...

will I ever feel better again?...will I ever get better again?...

but I'm still alive...thank you, Jesus...

but why...why did God spare my life...is there a reason?...is my life really important?"

Wedding Talks

When a Daughter Marries (Written when Cindy married.)

Summer is a time when for many young lovers wedding bells ring.

It's been a few years since our youngest daughter's wedding feast.

And the weddings of her three older sisters are an even more distant memory.

But this is what I remember, now dedicated to all the parents who will be "giving their daughters away" this summer.

(An awful phraseology, really, but that's a topic for another time.)

When a daughter marries, you smile and laugh a lot.

Partly from tension, of course.

But mostly from relief.

For all the hurly-burly of the preceding months (Adam and Even never knew what they were missing) is at last culminating in a peaceful ceremony of beauty.

The families are there.

Friends have come.

The dresses all fit, and the colors complement.

The music is melodious and joyful.

Bride and groom are radiant.

The vows are spoken, and no spurned lover appears at the last moment to object.

You smile with relief: it's going well (though much too quickly) now.

And you smile and laugh because this is a festive occasion – this is a wedding feast!

Though the wine doesn't flow like it did in Cana, the spirits are high, the talk is animated, and currents of warm affection float everywhere.

The Creator's gracious gift of love is celebrated!

But there's another reason you smile and laugh a lot: you try to cover up.

For when a daughter marries, what you really want to do is cry a little.

You try not to, of course, for fathers don't cry.

So they smile and laugh a lot.

But she's flesh of your flesh, after all, and after all these years rather firmly attached.

And it hurts to part with what is part of you, to let go, to let your flesh unite with other flesh.

But it is the way of love: for man and woman to leave father and mother and to cleave unto each other.

God made it so, and it is right and it is beautiful.

And therefore parents say Amen to it; in fact, they would have it no other way.

Still, even the most beautiful things can hurt a little.

Maybe it's especially the beautiful things that make you cry.

There's something else you do when a daughter marries: through your smile and through your tears you breathe a prayer.

Up to this moment, bride and groom have experienced the delights and frustrations of romance: tomorrow their history of husband and wife will begin.

You breathe a prayer of thanks that it will begin in the Lord.

For in our time, marriage is a fragile institution.

The strains and tensions of this age wreak their havoc all too often.

God's children are subject to that too, for they too are vulnerable.

Life can get messy; and marriage is part of that life.

That's why you pray for a union that will be steadily sustained by the grace of God.

And in George Eliot's words, you pray that this young couple may be joined for life:

"to strengthen each other in all labor,

to rest on each other in all sorrow,

to minister to each other in all pain,

to be one with each other in the silent, unspeakable memories now of last parting."

Judy's Wedding

Hello everybody:

We're glad all of you are here sharing in this celebration of marriage. That means a lot to Mike and Judy as it does to us, the Sharps and the Barons, their parents.

I understand it's an old Dutch tradition for the parents to give a little speech at such occasions. I don't know what Ruth is going to do; and I don't know what Jim and Lois are going to do; I'm not even sure what I am going to do. I do know that I'm not good at giving Little speeches. You see, I'm a college teacher, so my speeches are usually about 45 minutes.

But I don't want to give a speech really—I just want to say a few things to Mike and Judy while I have their attention; who knows how often that might happen again.

Let me start out with a little story.

Once upon a time there was a girl named Judy. She was tall with long brown hair and blue eyes. And when she smiled, you knew she meant it just for you. And when she talked, her heart opened to let you
come inside.

She headed the working staff at a Christian summer camp. I was there too, with a lot of other young folk from churches all over the state
of Washington.

I thought Judy was special.

One warm summer evening she and I took a walk into the woods.

I don't remember exactly what we talked about, but I know it was about the challenge of being Christian in the world.

It was a good walk, and it was a good talk. We felt comfortable with each other. Judy and Mike, maybe you remember the first time you felt comfortable with each other—that was a good feeling, wasn't it.

Well, before the walk ended that evening, we stopped at a tree and for no reason at all that we could've mentioned, we carved our initials onto that tree; and in my memory.

That's where the story ends. I didn't marry Judy; in fact, I never saw her again.

As you. know, I married another girl— a girl named Ruthie, another girl with a lovely smile, and one who had studied Dutch in college. Besides, besides— gentlemen prefer blondes, don't they?

But, when you were born, our second daughter, you became Judy in honor of that special memory.

Judy, you did not grow up to be tall with long straight brown hair.

But you quickly became special to us as you struggled to overcome a difficult start in life; as you opened your heart wide open with affection and for affection; and as you grew up and demonstrated that in the face of obstacles and difficulties, you had determination, you had pluck, and you had a strong faith. That makes you special. And Judith—the name that means PRAISE—we praise you here and now for always having been a good and loving daughter. And we praise God for you.

I said a while ago that that was the end of the story; but a good story never really ends, you know—it just starts another. And that's what happened here.

Judy, you grew up in GR, and so did Mike. Eventually you met, once and many times again, in a Bible Study group. But you hardly noticed each other. And then, for some time, you lost track of each other. But you hardly noticed that, either. In fact, when eventually your ways crossed again, both of you had tried to make your peace with singleness. And that, in your case, turned out to be the right time to begin to take notice of each other. Mike never knew the Judy I met long ago on the Olympic Peninsula in Washington. But he got to know this Judy, and he began to discover that she was special. Between them, love grew, slowly initially, but ever more strongly. We discovered that one night when we heard Mike and Judy sing, "You are my sunshine" to each other. Now Ruth and I rarely sing together, other than in church and for devotions, but there's one song we have sung on several occasions on this continent and even in Asia—though always by request, you understand. And so tonight. Mike and Judy asked us to sing their favorite love song. (sing You are My Sunshine!)

I don't know if you ever carved your initials on a tree. You didn't have to. What grew between you became far more than a memory. All of us here witnessed that today when you spoke your vows and we saw the happiness flow out of your eyes and your smiles. You put your signature not on a piece of bark today but on a document that says to the world and to God that you chose each other to be husband and wife. Ant that's the end of another story. We praise God with you for that story, for when you stop to think about it, it's really His story, isn't it.

But again, the ending of one story is the beginning of another. Except that we don't yet know what this "other one" will be. But you will be the main characters. And as interested bystanders, we have some advice.

Let me tell you what I did. I went around to a number of people whose advice I thought both of you would appreciate and take to heart. (I went around mostly to Judy's side of the family and friends, because at this point I still know them a little better.)

I started out with Dan Vander Haar and asked him what he thought marriage was good for. Dan said he thought it was a great institution, but for himself he didn't feel ready for an institution yet. Then I asked Barb Newman, newly married and former housemate of Judy: Barb said that in her considered opinion marriage was still the best method for getting acquainted.

I turned from Barb to one of your cousins, Lori Voorhees. I asked Lori what to her made a good husband. She said a husband is one who stands by you in troubles you wouldn't have had if you hadn't married him. I thought that would be helpful. Then I turned to your new sister-in-law, Mary, and asked her what advice she might have for her brother. Mary said that Mike should be careful not to question his wife's judgment, because after all she married him.

But the big question of course—what makes for a successful marriage. I paid a visit to your wise Uncle Wayne, Judy, and his answer truly reveals him as an original thinker. He said that success in marriage is not so much marrying the one who can make you happy as it is escaping the many who could have made you miserable.

Since I knew you would also appreciate the advice of your Uncle Harvey, your only farming relative, I asked him the same question. Uncle Harvey put it this way, "making marriage work is like running a farm—you have to start all over again each morning, whether you like it or not."

And then I asked Beppe, and since she is your oldest relative, her wisdom ought to be taken very seriously. Beppe said that the greatest secret of a successful marriage is to treat all disasters as incidents and all incidents as disasters...no, no, no,—that doesn't sound right; let me try that again: to treat all disasters as incidents and none of the incidents as disasters.

I forgot to ask your sister, Cindy, and she kindly reminded me that I had. I think you'll be glad that she did, because I think she, too has good advice: she said that in a successful marriage the partners don't so much try to make each other a good husband and a good wife as they try to BE a good husband and a good wife.

But for me, friend John Meindertsma who's given a couple of daughters away in marriage summed it up best; he said marriage is oceans of emotions surrounded by expanses of expenses.

Judy and Mike, your lives today have officially become a part of the lives of two families—the Barons and the Sharps. We welcome you. We pray such joining will enrich your lives and ours too. And as Judy's family now, we would like to express the prayer of all of God's family, and we would like to do that in song.

"The Lord Bless You and Keep You!"

Lisa's Wedding

More than 25 years ago, Lisa was only an idea—an "unexpected expectation."

When her mother and I thought we were almost finished raising our family (the youngest was almost 15, after all), surprise! We thought a four-leaf clover was pretty special, but now we would have the extraordinary privilege of a five-leaf one.

Shortly before her birth, her Dad wrote his reflections in the church's monthly publication. I wrote: "…it sort of takes your breath away…not just because of the sheer shock of the surprise…but especially because of being in the presence of an unfolding miracle… It'll be a challenge to raise another one, but also a joy to watch it grow; to elicit the magic of its first smile; to hear the first word, the first phrase, the first prayer. It'll be a privilege to love another one.

And her Mother wrote shortly after her birth: "Our little girl has arrived—she's complete, she's healthy, she's alert, and—in the eyes of her family—she's beautiful! …It's even more wonderful to see, hold, and talk to this little miracle of life than we imagined."

Well, Lisa, that little miracle of life is all grown up now—and you're still beautiful, to your parents, to your family, to Matt, to your friends, and to God who made you and gave you to us, as he has now given you to your brand-new husband.

It's been a joy to watch you grow; it's been indeed a privilege to love you as our child. We now look forward to loving you as our married daughter and to loving

Matt as the new son that has joined the family.

Finally, these words by George Eliot: "What greater thing is there for two human souls than to feel that they are joined for life—to strengthen each other in all labor, to rest on each other in all sorrow, to minister to each other in all pain," and, I add, to walk with each other in the joy of mutual love.

God bless you as you begin that life together today.

Prayer for a Parent

Lord, I hope you have a large department of ministering angels specializing in care for the aged.

I'm thinking of my mother today. I regret those more than two thousand miles between us for nearly four decades now. Yes, that's made those annual visits pretty special. All those parting times, too, with warm hugs and teary eyes. I'm grateful for all the hugs and tears that told me more convincingly that I was loved, that I was missed. And I'm glad she always knew my feelings for her were the same. But a visit once or twice a year and long-distance calls hardly equaled a presence in her life.

I know of your presence in her life, though. I know of those sleepless hours that would plague her now and again, and how you would give her a song in the night, a song from her Girls Choir days she thought she had forgotten long ago, or a beloved Psalm from church days in the Netherlands, or a poem she had memorized for her favorite teacher. Thank you for visiting this widow, Lord. I know how much that meant to her.

I'm grateful, too, for my visit two years ago, when she still had her own apartment. I remember fondly the day I fixed her lunch; then we sat on the sofa together. I began to read her a poignant Frisian story about an older lady who's struggling with the first symptoms of Alzheimers and whose children settled her in a Rest Home. I left the book with her, and when I came the next day, I discovered she had stayed up 'til 2:00 that morning to finish the book. I was astonished, for I hadn't seen her read much for a long time. We talked about it then. We laughed together about the funny parts of the story and shared the quietness of thinking about its sadness. Were you even then preparing her for the difficult journey ahead, Lord?

When I visited her six months later, her spacious two-bedroom apartment had been reduced to a 12x12 room in the Christian Rest Home. She needed care now. I don't know, Lord, how much she prayed her way through those very difficult days and weeks and months of transition. You know that her children did. And you answered our prayer for her peace of mind. She did not improve in mind, but you blessed her with an extra – ordinary spirit of gentleness and acceptance and affection. We're very grateful, Lord.

So I pray now for your ministering angels to bless what's left of Mother's life. You know that sometimes past and present blur for her. So many memories we can share no more. And one who loved to talk about friends and family and world tensions has become nearly mute. I wonder if she's praying now for self and all those dear to her. I'm not sure she still can. But Lord, you can understand even the unarticulated losses and longings of her heart. May she hear your voice in the silences. Your voice of promise, of comfort, of hope.

I know that you do keep your ministering angels busy, Lord. I've seen them in the nurses and aids that take care of my mother.

I've seen their love in action—their thoughtfulness, their words of kindness and encouragement. Lord, thank you for that; it means more than I can say! Please keep them mobilized, Lord—as a blessing to my mother, and to all those aged and ailing children of yours who need a light in their darkening world of human mortality.

Sid Eulogy

Saying goodbye to one whom you will not see again for a long time, has always been hard for me.

It may be a favorite cousin or nephew or niece or aunt or friend or uncle – you feel the hard edge of a long absence shake your emotions.

Saying a final goodbye to my brother who's been such a huge part of most of my life bites into my soul.

Sometimes we need to weep about all the losses in our life.

A Memorial Service is often called a Celebration of Life. And it should be that too.

But it's also an occasion to grieve.

If death grieved the Son of God, why should it not grieve us?

Death separates, irrevocably and irreversibly. It is painful. It is ugly in a way that no amount of floral arrangements can fully disguise.

Even if we have unshakeable hope in the Resurrection, death shakes us to the core.

Even when someone is very old or very sick or suffering decreasing mobility and communication ability, and death ends their suffering, death is no friend.

St. Paul calls it an enemy.

We grieve today our separation from Sid, as his children, grandchildren, great grandchildren, as his siblings; as his friends; as so many others who knew him and loved him.

An older brother can be a hero and a model to a younger one.

Sid was that when I grew up.

His life, even as a youngster, was full of dreams, ambitions, creations, possibilities, and stories.

I looked up to him as my big buddy, who was daring, smart, and inventive.

One favorite memory, I was maybe 7 or 8, going out in the fields with him early in the morning, before breakfast. The dew would still lie heavy on the grass. Our footsteps left a trail across the silent fields, footsteps searching for the silver strips tossed from allied planes to jam enemy radar. Sometimes we would be able to gather a big bundle of these strips and pass it on to underground resistance, for silver paper was much in demand.

Yes, the world was at war, The enemy ruled the land, and danger was never far away.

But those occasional forays in the mist-shrouded hours of early morning with my big brother and the silence of the still slumbering world all around would make me feel at peace.

Sometimes, closer to the end of the war, I would sit close to my brother on the hay wagon in the backyard, looking out over the fields that were slowly fading in the descending dusk. We would talk about war, the war that was raging in nearby lands where the German enemy was pursued by soldiers from England and Canada and America. Even then we would hear the steady drone of planes overhead on their way to bomb Germany. I listened intently when my brother began to talk about his dreams.

"I'm going to tell you a secret," he said. "I know you're good at keeping secrets. And this will be our secret, nobody else's. I'm building an airplane with my friend, Steffen. Someday I'm going to fly it, just like the pilots are in the planes above us. And I want you to fly with me. I want you to be my navigator. That means you will sit next to me in the co-pilot seat. We will fly all over the country, maybe all over the world. And if the war is still on, we will drop baskets of food for the hungry people."

My eyes grew wide, and my imagination nearly exploded: flying a plane, sitting up front beside my brother, becoming heroes for feeding the hungry from the air. Suddenly, in the chill of early evening, I felt warm and good all over. The future had lost some of its mystery. My big brother and I would be part of the future and part of an exciting adventure that then became my dream, too.

That night I dreamed about floating through the air, dropping food to the hungry people, and watching the children race to find white loaves of bread and oranges and candy bars—all the things they had not eaten during the hard years of war.

I was blessed to have this brother, my only brother, in my life.

It's not so common, I think, for a teenage boy to include his kid brother, four years younger, in more grownup activities. He took me along when he played Sinterklaas at his friends' homes. I tagged along when he went door-to-door selling garden seed. He even invited me to tag along when he went for an evening walk with what may have been his first girlfriend. I learned a lot.

I watched him punish a kid who had destroyed a bird's nest with young birds in it. I watched him lead a motley group of boys marching off to the nearby woods where he would train them in enemy warfare.

He always treated me as an equal, and he expected me to be a part of his life, and I was honored.

When he for the first time climbed behind the steering wheel of a salesman's car parked on our yard, managed to start it, he wanted me next to him in the driver's seat. Somehow he got it in gear and it became an unforgettable hair-raising ride around fruit trees and manure pile and wagons. Fortunately, he found a way to finally come to a stop, but not without picking up some dents and scratches.

After the war I became part of his beekeeping, amateur radio, driving lessons.

And much later, in this country, when the shack that was to be our home proved too small to accommodate the whole family, I joined him in the house trailer parked on the yard; every Saturday night we would drive to Hinotes Corner to stock up on candy for the week ahead; sometime later he had me riding with him in his car with big loudspeakers fastened to the roof, playing hymns on summer Sunday afternoons to the Birch Bay crowds working on their tans; he had me join him selling Raleigh products, glow-in-the-dark ornaments, delivering TVs, putting antennas on roofs, working at KLYN, and yes – flying with him in the navigator's seat.

He wanted to be part of my life too. And he was.

When I spent some time in Denver's Fitzsimmons Army Hospital, he would write nearly every day letters and poems, often composed while doing chores on his little Custer farm, for he was a very busy man with both a business and a farm to tend to. He even shipped a tape recorder so I could gather stories from fellow patients. I still have that tape recorder. It weighs 25 pounds.

I think of it now as the weight of his love. Which I felt also when I was in bad shape after open heart surgery in Ann Arbor and he would call in emotional calls to encourage me. It meant so very much to me.

I remember when I was a Calvin student and a part-time school bus driver, he wanted to join the students as a passenger on my school bus.

He joined me on the long flight to Australia when I was invited to speak there at a Christian Educators Conference. He managed to steal the spotlight there with his crazy stories and hilarious jokes.

And we would often go back together to the land of our birth, to see the places of our childhood that were still lodged securely in our memory, and to see uncles and aunts and cousins again.

One time Sid and I were staying at one beloved aunt's place. That night we slept together in a double with a mattress that would roll the bodies irresistibly toward the middle, maybe an ideal bed for honeymooners, which we were not. The bed induced a mood of hilarious memories, stories, and jokes that kept us laughing till our stomachs ached. When I woke up in the morning, I found my brother still fast asleep, his arm around me, and probably dreaming of his beloved Margaret, whom I was not. But the affection between us was palpable.

Sid was a model of generosity. I think it was part of his DNA. But especially a part of his Christian formation, his character. Giving blessed him, as it did the receivers.

It wasn't just being generous by picking up the tab in restaurants and hotels, not even by treating family and friends to splendiferous cruises that were hugely enjoyable and appreciated.

But what activated his generous spirit especially was sensing an important need in someone, a struggle that a gift of money or counsel or both might alleviate. His heart was blessed when he was able to help.

All of us are complicated beings. We have more than one side.

Today I'm grateful for that big part of Sid as my brother that blessed me most.

The loss of those we love diminishes our life. We feel that today as siblings. Sid and Margaret's children and their children surely feel that too.

For Ruth and me the Sid and Margaret home on Wiser Lake was our home away from home for many years. Our lives were so closely connected.

We mourn the loss, even as we thank our heavenly Father for all the good years we had each other.

But what I take with me as a parting, permanent gift, and what those of you have visited him in recent months take with you, is the smile on his face as you said goodbye and the whisper of his words, "I love you."

We loved you too, Sietze.

A Family Talk

Henry J & Ruth Baron's 60th Wedding Anniversary Celebration,
August 13-16 2017

> (I, understandably, used only some fragments of this "talk," which became an occasion for me to try to articulate components of my spiritual biography.)

First of all, let me tell you what a joy it is to see you here to help us celebrate this tremendous blessing in our life.

It took us 60 years to get here, and those 60 years comprise quite a story, but to still be together and have each other, and have all of you – why that's worth some celebration!

This is an occasion when one might reminisce about that 60-year journey.

But that's not what I have planned to do, though that might carry some interest.

What I've been thinking about is something else.

I heard the Calvin College chaplain say recently to a group of grandparents: "What students tell me is that one of the most important things you can do is to tell your children (and grandchildren) your faith story."

I took that home with me. And I realized that I grew up in a faith tradition where one was shy to talk about one's personal faith; that was private territory and much harder to talk about than who's going to be saved.

So I started thinking – what would be my story. And how would I tell it. And I knew the right words would be hard to come by, because it is so difficult to render the experiences of the heart and the turmoils of the mind absolutely truthfully, and even then they may so easily be misunderstood.

I found that out when I wrote some of those meditations in *Talking with God*.

(In that book you find a lot of rather personal writing about faith, some of which are included here.)

What I am going to share with you here is of course not all of the story, but important parts of it.

Three parts: Faith and Doubt, Faith and Fears, and Faith as Act.

So first of all, my Faith and Doubt have been in close companionship for most of my life.

My faith got hammered a few times. Or you might call it "exercised" or put to the test.

I'm sure that's true for lots of people.

It got exercised for me at a young age when WWII became and remained a part of my life.

It got hammered when a high school education became impossible.

It got exercised when I was diagnosed as a fresh draftee with TB at age 20, eliminating the chance to spend military service time in Germany and have the GI Bill make a college education possible.

It got exercised when Dad died suddenly at age 59; I was 21 and I felt devastated.

It got hammered when I enrolled at Western WA University and humanism and rationalism and empiricism brought faith into question to such a degree that I sank into depression and despair.

It got put to the test when daughter Judy was born with spina bifida and hydrocephalus.

It got challenged when I was diagnosed with cancer at age 40.

And later with another cancer, and then with serious heart problems.

And this past year with permanent radiation damage problems that sucked the starch right out of me.

And throughout my life, the problem of evil has gnawed away at my faith.

     I. So, first of all, my faith journey has not been without doubts and questions and searching. Maybe few faith journeys have. And maybe that's the time when real faith is born.

We are told in Sunday School, maybe even in the pew, that God loves you; you never need to be afraid. He is always in control; he won't let evil bring you harm.

I learned at age 6 that it's not that simple; and as I grew older, I learned to doubt the truth of it.

For in our congregation,

> one member was shot dead when she was still a teen

> another teen was burned like trash when she was searching for Home

> a beloved son drowned when life glowed bright with promise

> a daughter lost her legs when trying to help others

> a thirteen-year old's brilliant smile suddenly froze into the mask of death when the snowmobile crashed into a tree

> a colleague was killed by cancer at age 39 when so many good years were still supposed to come

> a friend was struck down by debilitating MS when he wasn't finished playing and wrestling with his kids

> the refugee in our midst lost both her father and mother to violent death when she was hardly old enough to remember them

> and there were more, so many more....

Often sooner than later, when we discover or especially experience that bad things happen to all kinds of people all the time, all the well-meaning lessons of our youth explode in our face.

Often our faith does too.

I listened to many a student going through a faith crisis.

Their struggles had been mine too, and sometimes still were.

And I reminded them and myself that the Bible stories don't lie:

God didn't kill the Garden's snake.

He didn't prevent floods, or war, or droughts and famine.

He didn't cure Saul's paranoia, nor prevent David's sin.

He didn't save Christians from persecution and torture.

He didn't even save his own Son from suffering and execution.

No, God doesn't knock the gun from the killer's hand.

He doesn't disable the child abuser or the rapist.

He doesn't grant immunity to cancer or to fatal accidents.

He doesn't wrest away the cockpit controls from a terrorist.

So, who's in control?

Was God, when millions were murdered in gas chambers?

Or slain in the Gulag?

Or vaporized {and maimed) one sunny day in Hiroshima?

Is God, when we let millions starve or be aborted?

Or when a lover, in a fit of jealous rage, kills your only daughter?

For there's still always the question, WHY?

Why so much rampant evil and unmitigated suffering?

Why are there so many singles looking for marriage partners, but never find one?

Why do so many marriages fail?

Why do some couples pray for children but never get them, while others get more than is good for them?

WHY?

Students, and I, want no blind, unthinking faith,

no more pat answers to these WHY questions.

In my study I often have occasion to look up to a polished wood plank on the top of a bookcase; it's what Stan Wiersma left with me when he departed on his sabbatical from which he would never return. It has an inscription burned into it that says in Frisian, "Sjuch, God is great en wy begripe him net." Indeed: we encounter so much that makes us confess, "Behold, God is great and we don't understand him." In that inscription we acknowledge God's greatness and in humility (and often confounded perplexity) our own vast ignorance.

Sjuch, God is great en wy biqripe Him net.

Yes, there's a hunger for Truth and for faith too, but it will be a faith that will always have more questions than answers.

II. A second part.

Faith does not necessarily eliminate natural human fears; at least my faith didn't.

I've known the fears of a parent:

the fear of losing life's most precious possession.

I feared when the new-born baby's back was not closed and too much fluid pressed upon the brain.

I feared when I sat with my six-year old in a hospital room one long, dark night, his illness undiagnosed.

I feared when curfew struck and I hadn't heard a car come home.

I feared when the police came to church to tell us there had been a roll-over and a closed head injury.

I feared when cold distance broke down communication and no arms were long enough to reach across.

I feared when my daughter's husband betrayed her trust and abused her love until it died—to be a parent is often a fearful thing.

I am grateful that I had someone who shared my fears; I'm grateful for faith that welcomed my fears. For faith that reassures me that ultimately God, the Creator of the universe wants to be my Father and has my back. For faith that reminds me, "Fear not, I am with you."

III. A third and last part.

I've come to see faith not so much as a private possession than as an action:

an act of *seeing* the impenetrable mystery of God in the people and world a round me –

of seeing God in the awesome beauty of nature –

of seeing God in the lives of those who have suffered injustice and bear no burden of bitterness –

of seeing God among those who really do love their neighbor as themselves.

But also seeing God in the anguished faces of those who have lost a home, a job, a spouse, a child.

In the desperate eyes of those who are dying the slow death of starvation.

In the loneliness of those who feel like aliens in a foreign land.

For in my faith God inhabits the wind-swept hollows of the human hearts,

>he scuttles around the edges of desperation and despair,

>he creeps inside the cracks of failure,

>he enters the places of poverty and pain.

Yes, faith as an action – an act of seeing God at work, but also as act of being the people he made in his image to fill this sadly broken but beautiful world

>with compassion for the suffering,

>with holy anger for all that's unjust, inhuman, evil,

>with the will to make a holy difference in this world,

even if it's only in our own home, our own church, and in the voting booth.

And faith as an act of being that finds delight and joy in all that is good and beautiful, that cultivates relationships that intensify our love for God, for his world, and for each other.

I'm still learning how to do that better.

But I'm a slow learner.

For I'm also still learning to feel more fully embraced by the incomprehensible love of this God who searched among the sharp-edged, slippery rocks and along the treacherous, deep ditches for that lost black sheep. And when he found it, according to the story, he didn't beat it with words or with the shepherd's rod, but he joyfully put it on his shoulder and carried that (light?) burden all the way home.

Who, in another story, came for that wild, wayward son weeping among the pigs, longing for what had been and was no more, and who nudged him in the direction of home, where the Father was waiting, waiting with open arms.

Who came for greedy little Zacchaeus, hiding in a tree, went home with him, and changed his life forever.

Who came for Paul when he was hell-bent on killing every Christian, and turned him into a fearless missionary.

Who came for me, and gave his life for me.

The mystery and magnitude of that, "no tongue or pen can ever tell."

[A children's story about two hares captures something of that magnitude, and is one of my favorites: LOVE — p 65 in *Talking with God*]

Closing Quotes

-From Louise Erdrich's *The Painted Drum*:

"Life will break you. Nobody can protect you from that, and living alone won't either, for solitude will also break you with its yearning. You have to love. You have to feel. It is the reason you are here on earth. You are here to risk your heart. You are here to be swallowed up. And when it happens that you are broken, or betrayed, or left, or hurt, or death brushes near, let yourself sit by an apple tree and listen to the apples falling all around you in heaps, wasting their sweetness. Tell yourself you tasted as many as you could." (Faye Travers in *The Painted Drum*)

-From Heidi De Jonge in "The Twelve"

"There is something incomplete about the span of your life – no matter how young or how old you are when you die. This incompletion is painful, but it can also be hopeful. C.S. Lewis envisions the gospel promise of what is to come in *The Last Battle*:

As [Aslan] spoke, He no longer looked to them like a lion; but the things that began to happen after that were so great and beautiful that I cannot write them. And for us this is the end of all the stories, and we can most truly say that they all lived happily ever after. But for them it was only the beginning of the real story. All their life in this world and all their adventures in Narnia had only been the cover and the title page: now at last they were beginning Chapter One of the Great Story which no one on earth has read: which goes on forever: in which every chapter is better than the one before.

Jean Tamminga, along with her husband Louis, was for many years our much-loved neighbor and friend. She spoke also for me in the words with which she ended her memoir:

'And what remains to be said? Our life was a gift from God's hand. To Him I give thanks.'"